DATE DUE

DEC 2 3 1991	
JUL 7 1992	
MAR 22 1993	
JUN 3 1993	
APR 1 6 1994	
NOV 2 8 1994	
ILL 12-8-95	

Steel Valley Klan

STEEL VALLEY KLAN

The
Ku Klux Klan
in
Ohio's
Mahoning
Valley

WILLIAM D. JENKINS

THE KENT STATE UNIVERSITY PRESS
Kent, Ohio, and London, England

© 1990 by The Kent State University Press, Kent, Ohio 44242
All rights reserved
Library of Congress Catalog Card Number 90–34701
ISBN 0–87338–415–6
Manufactured in the United States of America

Library of Congress Cataloging-in-Publication Data

Jenkins, William D., 1941–
    Steel valley klan : the Ku Klux Klan in Ohio's Mahoning Valley /
William D. Jenkins.
        p.   cm.
    Includes bibliographical references (p.).
    ISBN 0–87338–415–6 (alk. paper) ∞
    1. Ku Klux Klan (1915–)–Mahoning River Valley (Ohio and Pa.)—
History.   2. Mahoning River Valley (Ohio and Pa.)—History.
I. Title.
HS2330.K63J44   1990   90–34701
322.4′2′0977139—dc20   CIP

British Library Cataloging-in-Publication data are available.

Contents

To the memory of my father, WILLIAM, a Welsh Methodist;
to my mother, DOROTHY, an Irish Catholic;
to my wife, PATRICIA, an Italian Catholic;
and to my children, MICHAEL and CARRIE,
where all these cultures blend.

Preface

Secrecy has often clouded our knowledge of the operations of the Ku Klux Klan during the 1920s. Because meeting records and membership rosters disappeared once the Klan began to decline, historians interested in the Klan have had to rely on insider's accounts, court records, congressional hearings, contemporary observations of journalists and students, and, of course, newspaper accounts. Although the credibility of these sources varies, as well as the extent to which historians have utilized them in constructing a comprehensive portrait, there have emerged a number of generalizations regarding the Klan about which most historians can agree.

The Ku Klux Klan of the 1920s was an intolerant fraternal society composed of white, Anglo-Saxon Protestants. Members located in both rural and urban areas resented blacks, immigrants, Catholics, and Jews. The leaders—in particular the founder, William Simmons, his successor, Hiram Evans, recruiter Edward Y. Clarke, and D. C. Stephenson—were personally corrupt and more interested in power or money than in a cause. Scandals involving these leaders alienated many members and prompted the decline of the Klan. The opposition of Irish and Italian Catholics, funneled through the American Unity League and its tactics of stealing and publishing membership lists, also played a vital role in its decline.

Although most historians can agree with the above generalizations, it is troubling to note that such conclusions rest upon research still sparse in its coverage. Because of the paucity of documents and the tediousness of searching through newspapers, only a few historians have undertaken in-depth studies of local Klans. Thus, a synthesis such as that of David Chalmers rests at times upon incomplete coverage of what was a nationwide movement.[1]

Both Charles C. Alexander and Robert A. Goldberg have produced local studies based on a more intensive use of available sources; both raise questions about our present understanding of the Klan. In Oklahoma, Texas, Arkansas, and Louisiana, the southwestern portion of the Klan empire, Alexander discovered a Klan that flourished in spite of the small numbers of immigrants and blacks in those states. Although Klan rhetoric included more than a sprinkling of prejudice, its growth depended on its moral authoritarianism and its efforts to enforce— even by extralegal and violent means—laws regulating the vices of the community. According to Alexander most Klan members blamed local government officials for failure to enforce the laws properly. Thus, they thought it quite proper to assume the role of enforcer. Laws regulating sex, marriage, and drinking were their primary concern. They took little direct action against Catholics, Jews, or blacks unless they were involved in violations of the law.[2]

Goldberg has studied Colorado, an area remote from the flood of immigration affecting the eastern industrial states, yet the Klan was as powerful there as in Indiana, long considered one of the Klan strongholds. Because of the availability of evidence, Goldberg limited his study to five cities, each of which differed in its response to the Klan. It is Goldberg's contention—indeed, it is his main point—that the Klan fed on local, rather than national, concerns and that each appearance of the Klan requires intensive study of local documents to understand its appeal.[3]

This study of the Ku Klux Klan in the Mahoning Valley, located in northeast Ohio, represents an effort to continue the work begun by Alexander and Goldberg. It is hoped that its conclusions will become part of a more comprehensive synthesis regarding the Klan of the 1920s.

Historians have often treated the Klan as peculiar to the twenties. Following Arthur Schlesinger's model of alternating cycles of liberalism and conservatism, these historians have cited the Klan's rise as evidence of the lessening ability of religious, ethnic, and racial groups to live together in the "Tribal Twenties." They also cite the passage of the Immigration Restriction Act of 1924 as a culmination of the movement to maintain white, Anglo-Saxon supremacy in the United States. Their studies point to World War I and its nationalistic tendencies, the Red Scare after the war, and the labor strife of 1919 as generators of the frictions that produced the Klan.[4] This study would suggest, however, that, although the war and subsequent events were certainly irritants, the Klan is best seen as a consequence of a cultural conflict that resulted from the overly rapid mixing of divergent cultures within a society already undergoing the wrenching changes of industrialization. The conflict became evident in the 1890s and intensified during the Progressive Era. The passage of a literacy test—blocked by presidential vetoes until the advent of World War I—and the activities of the Anti-Saloon League were indicators of the escalation of the conflict. The Klan was a culmination, not a sudden flowering.

This study has benefited from the work of Richard Jensen and Paul Kleppner regarding pietistic Christianity and its involvement in politics. Both men have moved beyond traditional interpretations that highlight economic explanations for membership in political parties to a synthesis that includes moral and ethnic reasons as well. Their most important theme is the idea that pietistic Protestants have continuously involved themselves in midwestern politics as a means of imposing a conservative moral code on American society. Methodists, Baptists, Presbyterians, Disciples of Christ, and Scandinavian Lutherans constituted the pietistic sects; they emphasized personal conversion and revivals over the doctrinal and liturgical emphases of the Episcopalians and German Lutherans. Less concerned about achieving perfection in this world, these liturgicals relied on the moral authority of the church rather than the legal imperatives of the state to transform individual members. Jensen noted also that in 1890 pietists outnumbered liturgicals by two to one in Ohio and Indiana, later the centers of midwestern Klan activity.[5]

The efforts of these pietists to serve as "their brother's keeper" began with Puritan New England and continued in the new republic.[6] Having accepted the principle of religious freedom, pietists assumed the role of inculcating in the population those values considered important in the preservation of a democratic society. Through revivals they sought the perfection of individual moral habits; by the late nineteenth century, they had designated control of the desire to smoke, drink, or dance and the willingness to spend all day Sunday in a prayerful fashion as the hallmarks of Christian character and a sound democracy. Pietists were not content, however, with revivals as a means to spread personal holiness; they turned also to the passage of prohibitory legislation.[7]

In the 1870s pietists formed the Prohibition party, which advocated federal action to outlaw liquor, as well as legislation to promote a Christian Sabbath, use of the Bible in the public schools, and curtailment of prostitution. Many pietists, however, were unable to sever their loyalties to the mainstream parties—they tended to be Republican— and thus resorted to nonpartisan organizations, such as the Women's Christian Temperance Union and the Anti-Saloon League, to pressure mainstream parties and politicians to take action on behalf of Protestant moral legislation.[8]

Many women participated in this pietistic crusade. By the mid-nineteenth century, the rate of participation of women in organized religion had fostered an image of them as morally superior to men. It was the role of moral guardian that encouraged them to join temperance and social purity societies. Eventually, one of the key arguments on behalf of suffrage drew on the belief that the participation of women in politics would purify the society.[9]

Although the United States was a multicultural society, most pietists advocated their moral code as a universal imperative for all citizens. They usually did not challenge the principal of freedom of religion, but they did believe that their moral insights represented what was best for America. Such arrogance would inevitably lead to clashes with ethnic groups that did not agree with, much less practice, the strict pietistic code. As a result, Irish Catholics found the Democratic party a much more receptive home for their cultural inclinations in the late nineteenth century.[10]

With the advent of industrialization and the drawing of unskilled workers from southern and eastern Europe, it was inevitable that pietists would question the new immigrants' morality. As Catholics and Jews, who belonged to culturally distinct nationality groups, their mores differed from the majority and sometimes led them to violate the law of the land. By the 1890s discontented white Anglo-Saxon Protestants formed organizations such as the American Protective Association and the Immigration Restriction League to protest overly loose admission of immigrants.[11]

During the Progressive Era, new and old immigrants engaged in what John Buenker has labeled an "American Kulturkampf."[12] Pietists sought to impose their moral code regarding Sunday closing, the Bible in the public schools, and gambling on resistant ethnics. These pietists, as well as other progressives, derided immigrant participation in corrupt political machines, which they hoped to uproot in favor of more honest and efficient city governments. It was Prohibition, though, that garnered their biggest efforts; Prohibition, they believed, would improve both the moral and political climates.

After 1895 the Anti-Saloon League became the primary organ to secure passage of the pietistic moral code regarding alcohol. The

league relied on pietistic Protestant denominations for support and included many ministers among its officers. League propaganda regarding the weakness and corruption among politicians and its demand for
full enforcement created an attitude among its followers that the Klan
was able to exploit—the belief that committed Christians could convert the world through law enforcement. Although pietists constituted a
majority in the Anti-Saloon League, the league did approach other denominations, as well as Catholics, in its crusade to rid the land of the
evils of drinking.[13]

As a successor to the league, the Klan was a much more blatant
attempt to impose the mores of the white Anglo-Saxon majority upon
all who did not practice them. Although rooted firmly in the pietistic
tradition, the Klan was only one of many such efforts. Many pietists
agreed with the Klan's moral goals but disliked its divisiveness. Others rejected it because of the violence in the southwestern United
States; some recognized the corruption of its leadership and left.
There is little doubt then that pietism was no guarantee of Klan
membership.

This study has also benefited from the discovery of a membership
roster for Mahoning County. Such a find lends itself to quantitative
analysis and aids in the creation of a comprehensive portrait of the
typical Klan member. The results of that analysis challenge the contention of Kenneth T. Jackson that Klan members were for the most
part lower middle class in origin and threatened by economic competition from immigrants. In fact, in the Mahoning Valley, Klan members
belonged to all social strata and most often joined the Klan to preserve
"American" cultural dominance over the new arrivals.[14]

Much of the information regarding the Valley Klan came from newspapers. Fortunately, both the *Youngstown Vindicator* and the *Youngstown Telegram* provided extensive coverage of the Klan, thus serving
as a check on one another.[15] Moreover, the availability of newspapers
in Warren and Niles and cross-coverage of each other's community was
a great aid in substantiating the reports. Where possible, interviews,
court records, and other public documents served as an additional
check on reliability. Unfortunately, sources such as gubernatorial or
mayoral papers, the Niles riot grand jury hearing, and the riot trials
were destroyed or lost.

This project was obviously very time consuming, but the assistance
of numerous friends and colleagues speeded its completion. I would
like to thank my graduate assistants, Robert Fabian, Robert Kuhl,
Jeanne Ontko Suchanek, Scott Van Horn, Dale Vojtus, and Robert
Whiteley. A special debt of gratitude is owed to the following for di-

rect assistance in the research: Philip Bracey, Dr. Thomas G. DeCola, Dr. Martha Pallante, Steven Papalas, Dr. Jack Patrick, Paul Zimmerman, the Mahoning Valley Historical Society, the Reuben McMillan Public Library, the Ohio Historical Society, and the Youngstown State University Oral History Program. I would also like to thank the late Bil Holt for providing the membership roster, Hildegard Schnuttgen for her assistance in obtaining interlibrary loans, and Youngstown State University for a research professorship and sabbatical, as well as professional colleagues, Dominic J. Capeci, Jr., Robert A. Goldberg, James P. Ronda, and Agnes Smith, who have read and commented upon a part of, or the entire, manuscript. Finally, I would like to thank my wife, Patricia Rizzollo Jenkins, for her intelligence, writing skills, and insight into ethnicity, all of which contributed greatly to the final manuscript.

Steel Valley Klan

The Klan's Resurrection

Any order or organization that stands for . . . the uphold-
ing of the Constitution and the religion of Jesus Christ,
ought not to be kicked in the face . . . but ought to be investigated and the ranks swelled.

—The Reverend Richard R. Yocum,
St. Paul's Reformed Church

ifty thousand Klansmen and Kamelias were milling around the field
at Dead Man's Curve on 10 November 1923. Seven kites held an
American flag some five hundred feet above hastily constructed
booths and tents serviced by representatives of local Protestant
churches. The crowd anxiously awaited a parade from the field through
the south side in celebration of Klan victories in the mayoral, city
council, and school board races.

A few years before, such a parade would have seemed impossible in
a city like Youngstown, Ohio, remote from southern influences and a
hotbed of abolitionist activity prior to the Civil War. In fact, at the first
rumors of the Klan's appearance in September 1921, the city council
had angrily passed a resolution denouncing the Klan as "un-American,
lawless, and a menace to the peace and security of the United States."
Mayor Fred Warnock promised black citizens that his administration
would not allow the Klan to take the law into its own hands.[1]

By November 1923, however, the Klan had changed Warnock's
mind. He became not only a member but eventually a grand titan
(district official). Warnock and many other local residents had assumed that the Klan would duplicate the violent and disruptive activities of the earlier organization. Gradually they came to view the Klan
as a protector, rather than a violator, of the moral and legal order, an
organization worthy of northern Protestant Christians' support. In their
minds the Klan of Reconstruction was dead. A new Klan had arisen.

The Klan of Reconstruction had sought the control of race relations
in the South after the Civil War. The granting of political rights to
freed blacks posed a threat to white supremacy and might lead, the

1

Klan feared, to social equality. The beatings, whippings, tar and featherings, and lynchings used to intimidate blacks politically and socially eventually caused the federal government to outlaw the Klan in 1871. Members then joined similar organizations, such as the Knights of the White Camelia. By the 1890s the North had grown weary of intervention, thereby permitting southern states to pass laws disfranchising blacks and segregating them from white society.

Refounded in 1915 by Colonel William J. Simmons, the new Ku Klux Klan also emphasized white supremacy but differed from the earlier Klan in its emphases on fraternalism, nativism, and moralism. After failing as a clergyman and salesman, Simmons had found some professional success as a district organizer for the Woodmen of the World, one of the many fraternal societies joined by Americans of that era. Realizing the popularity of a secret society with elaborate rituals and passwords, Simmons fashioned a Klan that would appeal to the fraternal sentiments of American society—a Klan with acronyms functioning as a secret language, strange-sounding titles like kleagle, grand goblin, and imperial wizard, and a system of rituals known only to members. Simmons's charter, obtained from the state of Georgia, described the organization as a "patriotic, military, benevolent, ritualistic, social and fraternal order." Once a month local meetings, complemented by family picnics and parades, created a sense of camaraderie that appealed to native-born, white, Anglo-Saxon, Protestant men.[2]

Unlike the earlier Klan, which focused primarily on southern whites, the new charter limited membership to a "white male Gentile person, a native-born citizen of the United States of America," and "a believer in the tenets of the Christian religion." The provision that members could not owe any allegiance "of any nature or degree whatsoever to any foreign government, nation, institution, sect, ruler, prince, potentate, people or person" served as a bar to Catholics, who owed allegiance to the pope. Although the charter did not expressly endorse nativism, the continuous use of "100% Americans" as an official slogan in Klan pamphlets and newspapers suggested a connection between the ethnic and religious backgrounds of Klan members and the principles upon which the United States was founded. Nativist underpinnings were readily apparent in the charter's call "to conserve, protect and maintain the distinctive institutions, rights, privileges, principles, traditions and ideals of pure Americanism."[3]

Finally, Simmons's Klan differed from the earlier Klan in its commitment to respect for established law and morality. The charter called

Men, women, and children participated in this Trumbull County Klan rally in 1924. (Courtesy of The Mahoning Valley Historical Society, Youngstown, Ohio.)

on Klan members to defend the Constitution and "to aid and assist in the execution of all constitutional laws." Prospective Klan members were only those men "whose reputations and vocations are respectable" and "whose habits are exemplary." In an effort to extend moral obligations beyond the personal, the charter called on Klan members "to protect the weak, the innocent, and the defenseless from the indignities, wrongs and outrages of the lawless, the violent and the brutal."[4]

In spite of the charter's delineation of the principles of fraternalism, nativism, and law and order, it was inevitable that the leadership would shape the delivery of the Klan message to new members. The Klan's founder and imperial wizard, Colonel Simmons, emphasized the fraternal aspects while he was in control. Though he was an effective one-on-one salesman, he lacked the organizational skills to spread his organization beyond the South. Subordinates, such as a trusted organizer in Alabama who absconded with several thousand dollars from initiation fees, often duped the colonel. By the end of the war, Simmons had attracted only 5,000 to 6,000 members, primarily from Georgia and Alabama; he was searching for a way to expand his operation. In the summer of 1920, he discovered the Southern Publicity Association, a small advertising firm located in Atlanta and operated by Edward Young Clarke and Elizabeth Tyler. Simmons hired this organization to provide a sense of direction to the faltering fraternity.[5]

Clarke and Tyler were hustlers who had founded the Southern Publicity Association as a fund-raiser for such prominent organizations as the Anti-Saloon League, the Red Cross, and the Salvation Army. It is unclear how Simmons met them, but he impressed Mrs. Tyler as "a minister and a clean living man."[6] Eventually Simmons relinquished control of recruitment to the association. Once established as the Propagation Department of the Klan, Clarke and Tyler recruited 1,100 kleagles or salesmen—and an unidentified number of speakers—to scour the country for members.[7] These men carried with them a statement of the Klan platform that included the following principles:

> Tenets of the Christian Religion
> White Supremacy
> Our Free Public Schools
> Just Laws and Liberty
> Protection of Pure Womanhood
> Separation of Church and State
> Limitation of Foreign Immigration
> Upholding the Constitution of the United States
> Freedom of Speech and Press
> Suppression of Vice and Lawlessness
> Preventing the Cause of Mob Violence and Lynching
> Law and Order[8]

Clarke and Tyler were enormously successful: they added more than 90,000 members in a little more than a year to an organization only five to six thousand strong in 1920. Newspaper editors from all over the country pressed Clarke and Tyler for information. Ironically, one photographer who was refused a picture hired some blacks to pose in Klan costumes lest he lose the immediacy of the story.[9]

As the Klan organization expanded precipitously, the Propagation Department made few checks on newly found members or kleagles. Little is known of the type of men enrolled as kleagles—their backgrounds, personalities, or status—but it is evident that the commission of four dollars for every new member was an attraction to recruiters that might easily prove more powerful than any principles the Klan might espouse. Henry Fry, one of the early kleagle recruits and eventually an informant for the *New York World,* admitted in his book about Klan operations in Tennessee that he received very little indoctrination relative to the goals of the Klan. He joined "partly because I was a joiner" (he belonged to the Masons, Knights of Pythias, Odd Fellows, Junior Order of United American Mechanics, the Elks, Eagles, and Owls) but also because he "could see no reason why a fraternal order commemorating the deeds of the original Klansmen should not fill a need in the country today." Fry characterized the information he received as "meager" and suggested that his decision to join was a matter of faith in the similarity of the Klan to other fraternal orders. [10]

That faith soon proved to be misplaced. The day after his naturalization into the Klan, the kleagle asked Fry—to his amazement—to serve as the kleagle's assistant in eastern Tennessee; three weeks later he became the kleagle. In his efforts to recruit, Fry confronted questions for which he had no answer. Worse yet, the king kleagle (Klan-appointed state organizer) could not provide them either. Fry "at once saw that any movement built along such a line was dangerous, regardless of its intentions, because secrecy of this sort places upon the organization the vital necessity of receiving as members only men of the highest character whose positions and reputations in the community would be an absolute safeguard against mischief." "It made me very careful," Fry asserted, "of the class of people whom I permitted to become members." With the king kleagle advising Klan members to "clean up their towns," Fry foresaw mob rule as the eventual outcome of indiscriminate Klan recruiting. In disgust he quit the Klan, labeling it as a moneymaking scheme built upon base appeals to religious and racial prejudices. [11]

Fry was correct in his observation about the potential for the spread of indiscriminate Klan violence. Throughout Texas local chapters heeded the advice of the Propagation Division to "clean up the town" by intimidating moral slackards and degenerates; Dallas witnessed innumerable floggings. In Mer Rouge, Louisiana, two anti-Klansmen, Watt Daniel and Thomas Richards, were kidnapped and killed, allegedly by the Klan. [12]

In many instances the violence was related to what the Klan perceived as examples of a postwar moral decline. Most often attacked were bootleggers, gamblers, wife-beaters, adulterers, and deserters. In the states of Texas, Oklahoma, Arkansas, and Louisiana, the Klan tried to reimpose a moral code that it felt the local officials could not enforce. A residue of vigilante justice from the less settled days of that region contributed to the extralegal atmosphere. [13]

The escalating violence did not seem to concern Clarke and Tyler; they were having enough trouble controlling their own behavior. In 1919 Atlanta police arrested them in a house of assignation not fully clothed and under the influence of alcohol. They were charged with disorderly conduct. Mysteriously, the incriminating page from the police docket disappeared. [14]

Both violence and the shenanigans of Clarke and Tyler came to public attention in September 1921 when the *New York World* published a three-week series on Klan outrages. Carried in eighteen leading dailies, including the *Cleveland Plain Dealer*, the series culminated in a list of 152 murders, floggings, and tar and featherings. Public concern resulted in congressional hearings conducted by the House Committee on Rules. Simmons, however, countered the charges in a masterful performance before the committee. Ill with tonsilitis and bronchitis, he suggested that a few criminals or troublemakers hiding behind Klan robes had committed the violence. Protesting that such actions violated Klan principles and that it was primarily a fraternal and benevolent society, Simmons swore that he would disband the Klan if it was guilty of even a small measure of the charges. He then collapsed in a faint. [15] Simmons's dramatic appearance was effective; Congress took no more action. Ironically, the congressional hearing and national newspaper exposure, both of which were calculated to undermine the Klan by revealing its part in violent incidents around the country, had served only to make the Klan more popular.

Internally, though, the Klan still suffered from divisions within and a lack of leadership. Some northern grand goblins (regional directors) put pressure on Simmons to fire Clarke. Heady from the rapid expansion, Simmons did not take any action; instead, for the last six months of 1922, he took a vacation and left Clarke in charge of a national office that allowed local chapters to spin out of control. [16]

Simmons's lack of supervision created a void that other men began to fill. One of those men was Hiram Wesley Evans. Born in Ashland, Alabama, in 1881, he had come to Dallas before the war to set up a dental practice. A charter member of the Dallas Klan, he became the exalted cyclops (an elected position to replace the appointed kleagle) of that organization once Atlanta gave it a self-ruling charter. Under Evans, Dallas Klan No. 66 was a stronghold of vigilante activity. According to congressional testimony, Evans led his Klan in the abduction of black bellhop Alex Johnson for pandering. The Klan flogged Johnson, branded the letters KKK on his forehead with acid, and left him in front of his hotel.[17] Ironically, after Evans had gained the attention of national headquarters and assumed the position of imperial kligrapp (national secretary), he returned to Dallas in early 1922 to discourage the floggings and other forms of violence that were attracting so much national attention and condemnation.[18]

It was Evans's Atlanta experience that enabled him to see that what worked in Texas might not work nationally. Congressional investigation of the violence, along with the concern of goblins and dragons about Clarke's handling of funds, convinced Evans that national headquarters needed a cleanup. He also had dreams of making the Klan a political power—a focus not shared by the fraternally oriented Simmons. To realize those dreams, he had to replace Simmons and undermine Clarke.[19] Thus, Evans devised a scheme with Fred Savage and D. C. Stephenson to trick Simmons into stepping aside.

Colonel Simmons was used to being in charge, but it was now 3:00 A.M., the morning of 27 November 1922, and he had been out drinking with some of the conventioneers. Tomorrow they would elect him as imperial wizard at the first Klonvocation, or Klan convention. At least, that was the plan until David Stephenson and Fred Savage knocked on the door of Klan Krest, Simmons's Klan-financed home at 1840 Peachtree Street in Atlanta. Fred Savage was a former New York detective, who had risen to a key administrative position, imperial night hawk, in the Atlanta headquarters. David C. Stephenson, a native Texan transplanted to Indiana, was a coal dealer and a very successful organizer of the Evansville Klan. Simmons admitted to these men that he was not a politician and had not organized the formal presentation of his name to the Klonvocation. Like many nineteenth-century candidates, Simmons expected others to speak on his behalf; obviously, he would accept the nomination if offered.

Stephenson and Savage responded with feigned concern. Were someone to present Simmons's name on the floor, trouble would result, they warned him. Numerous men were ready to attack Simmons, and, according to Stephenson, "the moment your character is attacked, there is going to be somebody killed. I have got men placed and have given them orders to shoot and kill any damn man that attacks the character of Colonel Simmons." Simmons was bewildered. His nomination might mean violence and negative press coverage for his beloved Klan.

Before Simmons could respond, both men suggested that he relinquish the office of imperial wizard and create a new position of emperor for himself as a kind of general overseer. They recommended Hiram Evans, former Dallas dentist and current imperial kligrapp, to fill the post of imperial wizard, at least on a temporary basis. According to the Klan Konstitution, Simmons possessed the power to create the new office, but he first met with his cabinet and secured their approval. The next day Hiram Wesley Evans became the imperial wizard, and the colonel's days were numbered. Evans and his aides, Stephenson and Savage, had successfully plotted to wrest the Klan from Simmons.[20]

Once in control, Evans canceled Clarke's contract. National headquarters denounced local chapters that engaged in violence and ordered all chapters to keep Klan robes and hoods at the klavern (the Klan meeting hall) in order to discourage their use for night-riding. These attempts to purge the violence from the organization were based, as indicated by Charles C. Alexander, "strictly on political ambitions and a desire to improve the organization's public relations; it did not mean that Imperial Wizard Evans and his associates at Atlanta were any more humanitarian than their predecessors." Evans's efforts had the desired effect on the states of the Southwest.[21]

Evans was not able, however, to bring peace to national headquarters. Part of his scheme regarding Simmons was simply to ignore him—to accord him little respect and to hope that he faded away. Simmons finally turned to the courts, obtained a control order, and seized the Imperial Palace in April 1923. Evans returned from Washington to file a countersuit. The fact that Simmons had a copyright as exclusive owner of the Klan name, ritual, regalia, constitution, and charter forced Evans to seek an out-of-court settlement. Simmons agreed to exchange his copyright for a $1,000 per month pension for life. But Simmons's dissatisfaction with the money he received as compared with the Klan's waxing income, plus battles over who would run the women's Klan, resulted in further lawsuits that same year. Eventually, Evans offered Simmons a flat sum of $146,500 in return for the cessation of all suits and Simmons's disaffiliation with the women's Kamelia. Simmons accepted the offer but only received $90,000 from his aide, an Atlanta real estate broker who absconded with the remainder.

THE KLAN'S RESURRECTION   9

The gullible colonel returned to court the following year in an unsuccessful effort to recoup the embezzled share.[22]

Though Evans was to bring more control and focus into the Klan organization, its loose methods of recruitment meant that the nature of its appeal can only be judged by investigations into local communities and an identification of the issues it espoused. It was readily apparent that national leaders were willing to tailor the Klan platform to local concerns that would attract the largest number of dollars to Klan coffers. Many kleagles would find it hard to resist this ploy because they earned four dollars out of every ten-dollar initiation fee.

In the Southwest (Oklahoma, Texas, Louisiana, and Arkansas), Alexander has contended that with the decline of the black population in these areas—apparently a result of migration to the North—and the paucity of foreign-born immigration, the Klan turned the focus of its activities toward law and order. "There more than anywhere else, the Klan transcended the limits of a nativist and racist organization and became a device for the ruthless dictation of community morals and ethics." Although various Klan agents and newspapers flooded the area with material emphasizing prejudices against blacks, Catholics, Jews, foreigners, and radicals, Klan activities, including violence, most often focused on moral disorders within the society. Klan members expressed, in Alexander's words, "a passion for reform."[23]

In Colorado, remote from the effects of immigration and with a small black population, Robert Goldberg has found differing emphases in the five cities he studied. In Denver "Protestant anxiety concerning crime waves, Catholic organizing, Jewish distinctiveness, immigrant criminality, and black violation of inferior status" combined to attract a sizable following. In Pueblo enforcement of the vice laws became the Klan rallying cry. The nonpolitical Grand Junction Klan never advanced beyond fraternalism as its organizing principle. Under severe attack from anti-Klan opponents, the Colorado Springs Klan "manipulated the Catholic menace" and aroused "anxiety about moral laxity," but failed to take strong root in a hostile environment. The Canon City Klan won elections with a platform based on civic reform and anti-Catholicism. In spite of the diversity of appeals used by these Klans, Goldberg suggests that "a common Protestant frame of reference toward minorities and lawbreakers" united Klan members in defense of their communities. Insofar as local officials did not respond to crime waves and pleas for civic reform, or to grievances regarding minorities, the Klan was able to marshal its forces; the weaker the official response, the stronger the Klan. Thus, Klan growth was not built on abstract prejudice, but on local conditions, upon ample evidence that grievances were indeed real and not imagined.[24]

The Mahoning Valley, located in the iron and steel industrial belt between Pittsburgh, Pennsylvania, and Cleveland, Ohio, was to be yet another example of the ability of the Klan to prey on local communities. Although the initial reaction of officials in Youngstown, the largest city in the valley, was negative toward Klan penetration, the Klan cast off its identity from Reconstruction days and assumed a new form so attractive to residents that it came to dominate the valley's politics.

No one knows when the first kleagle crossed the Ohio River or perhaps the border from Indiana. By the fall of 1920, though, the Klan had appeared in Cincinnati and in Springfield in the southwestern part of the state. By the time the Cleveland police chief interviewed the grand goblin of the Great Lakes region, Charles W. Love of Indianapolis, in September 1921, the Klan had established a headquarters in Columbus and claimed a following of 15,000 members. In the spring of 1922, Dr. C. L. Harold of Columbus, another dentist, became king kleagle of the state. But D. C. Stephenson quickly replaced him during the summer as a reward for his successful organization of Evansville in early 1922. Stephenson resided in Columbus during that summer but removed his headquarters to Indiana in the fall.[25]

Stephenson's tenure as king kleagle of the state and then grand goblin of the Great Lakes region was to leave a major imprint on the organization. Only in his early thirties at the time, Stephenson was a master salesman immersed in the reading of books on salesmanship and psychology. His use of the sobriquet "The Old Man" to hide his age and the installation of a fake direct phone line to the White House in his office in downtown Indianapolis revealed his emphasis on impression over substance and his ability to hoodwink unsuspecting candidates for membership.[26]

Stephenson could upstage even Hiram Evans. At his inauguration as grand dragon of Indiana, in July 1923, he waited until festivities were well along and Evans had given his speech before sweeping down to the field in an airplane, alighting in a silken purple robe, and apologizing for his late arrival because "the President of the United States kept me unduly long counseling upon vital matters of state."[27]

As the leader most responsible for Klan successes in the Great Lakes region, Stephenson attracted members by emphasizing the preservation of Protestantism and the building of a political machine oriented around enforcement of laws that reflected a Protestant moral code. His most important tactic in developing the character of the organization was the tendering of honorary membership to all Protestant clergymen. Just how many of these clergymen accepted the offer is not clear, but the many who did usually received a visit from the local Klan. Hooded knights would enter services silently, present a monetary offering, and leave. In numerous communities these ministers would encourage their parishioners to participate in the work of the Klan; others would speak out publicly and even serve in leadership roles.[28]

It was Stephenson's appeal to the nativist element in American Protestantism that gained the support of numerous ministers. America, after all, was a Protestant country. And, although the Constitution had proclaimed the existence of freedom of religion, morality and ethics were still subject to the regulation of the government and to the guidance of a common Protestant code. Indeed, Protestant denominations were numerous and often unable to agree on doctrine, but sufficiently unified in the mid-nineteenth century to create free public schools in which children could read the Bible and learn about the contributions of Protestantism to the rise of democracy. The blue laws were another example of Protestant cultural domination; Sunday was the Lord's Day, and many states permitted only prayer and church-related activities away from the home. By the late nineteenth century, the Baptists and Methodists were also uniting against the evils of intemperance by urging the passage of prohibition laws as an essential addition to the prevailing moral code.

In the twentieth century the national conventions or assemblies of pietistic sects, such as the Baptists, Disciples of Christ, Methodists, and Presbyterians, continued their support for the legal imposition of their moral codes on American citizens. The Methodists, for instance, established a Board of Temperance, Prohibition, and Public Morals. "Strenuous effort has been made," according to a 1924 report, "to arouse sentiment against the return of prize-fighting, to protect our public schools from the demoralizing influence of dancing, to promote the safety of the Christian Sabbath while avoiding a fanaticism, to secure the suppression of gambling and commercialized indecency."[29]

In their conventions the Presbyterians (divided at this time into two denominations, the United Presbyterian Church of North America and the Presbyterian Church of the United States of America) indicated as wholehearted a desire as the Methodists to secure proper enforcement of legislation regulating morality. The United Presbyterian General Assembly of 1918 worried in particular about the encroachments on the Sabbath "by the movies, the baseball parks, the ever-defiant saloon, theaters and dance halls, the varied forms of business, the Sunday newspaper, Sunday joyriding, Sunday labor-enslaving, and Sunday golf playing, responsible, it is alleged, for 150,000 caddies being employed on the Sabbath." In 1920 its Special Committee on Reform lamented the post-war "loosening up in the morals of our people." It cited "a wave of gambling, thieving and profiteering," "immodesty in dress," and "uncleanness of life" as threatening the moral life of the nation. As a means of protecting boys and girls from degradation, it recommended keeping every community as free as possible of these vices. It also applauded passage of the Prohibition Amendment; the issue, the committee suggested, was no longer political but rather "one of respect for and the enforcement of the law." The Board of Temperance and Moral Welfare of the Presbyterian Church of the United States of America expressed similar concerns, as well as an additional interest in the need for state regulation of drugs, cigarettes, and motion pictures.[30]

At their 1920 convention the Northern Baptists worried about the "time of unrest and change." Of particular concern were "the forces of reaction and greed . . . trying to restore the old order of things and defeat beneficent measures." The Committee on Social Service concluded that Northern Baptists should unite "all the forces of good will on behalf of a better and more Christian world." It suggested in particular that Baptists must avoid relaxing after passage of the Prohibition amendment; their new goals were to influence legislative assemblies to retain Prohibition and to inspire other Baptists to comply with the law. At the 1921 convention the Northern Baptists passed resolutions to support passage of laws to control drug traffic, to censor motion pictures, and to create a national system of divorce. The report further condemned what Sabbath desecration and "decadence of moral standards in the dress and behavior of women and girls" were doing to the country.[31]

The Northern Baptists, unlike the other denominations, tied their concerns about a deteriorating moral climate to the rise of a new type of immigrant. Such newcomers, the Committee on Social Service contended, came from unfortunate circumstances. They were uneducated, illiterate, and prone to interpret liberty as license; some were criminals. America could not afford the existence of such traits, nursed as they were by the formation of protective neighborhoods and perpetuation of the native language. The committee suggested the need for efforts both to Christianize and to Americanize these new immigrants.[32]

The Disciples of Christ, although less well-known and much smaller than other denominations, also exhibited a pietistic proclivity. Founded in northeast Ohio nearly one hundred years before, the Disciples downplayed doctrine and emphasized instead the practice of a Christian life. In 1917 President C. B. Reynolds spoke to the annual state convention on their obligation to "hunger and thirst after justice and to make justice prevail in the world." Thus, they were "to build their intelligence, their conscience, their religion and their faith into social sentiments, community regulations, social institutions and national policies." Their Board of Temperance and Social Welfare was to lead them in such efforts. Thus, the major pietistic denominations in the North appeared to agree on the need for a moral cleansing of the nation through evangelization and law enforcement.[33]

The liturgical denominations, the Episcopalians and the Lutherans, displayed less interest in the enforcement of a Protestant moral code. Lutherans focused instead on personal salvation. In their theology it was the leavening effect of regenerated individuals rather than state laws that improved the moral climate of society. Historians, however, must be cautious in assuming that all Lutherans adopted this theology. Ethnicity, time of migration, and rate of assimilation affected their adoption of "American" pietistic concerns. Scandinavians, for instance, brought with them a concern about Prohibition not shared with German Lutherans. Eastern Lutherans, who were more prone to use English in their services and to be less isolated from other ethnic and religious communities, were also more likely to support pietistic reform. Thus, both the General Synod and the Scandinavian synods condemned alcoholic abuse and supported the Prohibition movement. They were, in addition, more likely to support strict Sunday observance.[34]

It is also necessary to look within the Progressive Era for an explanation of Stephenson's success in building up the Great Lakes Klan. The so-called Progressive Movement was oriented toward reform, yet it was not so much a movement as a coalition of various interest groups. Elements in one part of the movement might very well oppose measures advocated by another segment. The solutions offered were diverse insofar as they reflected the socioeconomic, political, and religious values of competing reformers.[35]

Generally speaking, though, most Progressives formed organizations and entered politics to achieve their own vision of order. The rise of big business had severed the personal relationship between owner and employee; it fostered strikes and labor violence. The rapid influx of immigrants to work in the factories brought people whose culture differed from most native-born Americans. The speed of these changes, especially in urban areas, provoked many Progressives to propose moral, economic, or institutional reforms as a means of imposing order on what appeared to be a chaotic society.[36]

A common goal shared by many Progressive reformers—perhaps a result of the bond of Protestant values held by its leadership—was the need for cleaner cities, purged of vice and offering honest government. Ever since revelations about the machinations of Boss Tweed in the 1870s in New York, urban reformers had condemned the graft available to an ambitious boss and his machine. The late nineteenth and early twentieth centuries were replete with political battles between reformers and bosses. In that era reformers stymied, moderated, and limited urban political corruption, but seldom maintained their sway over an extended period of time.

Prior to 1900 reformers had directed their efforts toward winning elections; after 1900 structural reform of local government became the major goal. They hoped that civil service, nonpartisan ballots, the Australian ballot system, and initiative, referendum, and recall would retard the opportunity of the boss to retain or to regain political control. Campaigns also occurred to strengthen the powers of city government through the institution of a strong mayor, the addition of a city manager, or the creation of a commission with joint administrative-legislative powers. This movement did not cease after World War I, often cited as the end of the Progressive Era.[37]

The campaign against urban corruption was a recurrent theme in Progressivism and certainly a vibrant one in such Ohio cities as Toledo, Dayton, Cleveland, and Cincinnati. The Ohio Anti-Saloon League, founded in 1893 in Oberlin, Ohio, was a prime example of how Protestant moral values could combine with the urban reform movement in an effort to restore order to the centers of industrial change. By 1895 the "Ohio Idea" (paid professional organizers, monthly dues as a financial base, political agitation and concentration on the liquor issue only) had become the basis for a national organization formed in Washington, D.C., and located in Westerville, Ohio. League literature portrayed the saloonkeeper as a member of a corrupt political machine and warned against use of the saloon as a site of polling activities on election day. Eliminate the saloon, the league cried, and eliminate both a source of gambling and prostitution within the community, as well as a center of political corruption. In short, the saloon was "the storm center of crime; the devil's headquarters on earth; the school-master of a broken decalogue; the defiler of youth; the enemy of the home; the foe of peace; the deceiver of nations; the beast of sensuality; the past master of intrigue; the vagabond of poverty; the social vulture; the rendezvous of demagogues; the enlisting office of sin; the serpent of Eden; a ponderous second edition of hell, revised, enlarged and illuminated."[38]

The Anti-Saloon League tried to work through the Protestant churches. Not only were ministers on its board of directors but many individual churches affiliated on the state and local level, offering their membership rosters for league use. The Methodist church was one of the few to associate on a national basis, designating the league as its official lobbyist for temperance legislation. The United Presbyterians, on the other hand, passed yearly resolutions at each convention that supported work of the league. Since the remaining Protestant churches did not want to become directly involved in politics, the league functioned more as a secular institution "organized to give church people an effective political organization to fight the liquor traffic."[39]

Thus, Stephenson had read the political and religious currents and then laid plans to tap into the mainstream of pietistic Protestantism. Although there was much of the charlatan, as well as the criminal, in Stephenson, he knew how to make his organization appear as a savior of morality and a positive contributor to American social order—unlike the Klan of Reconstruction. The residents of the Mahoning Valley were ready for such a savior.

2

A City Is Reborn

God in these days is not sending fire down and wrecking
cities, but He has His methods of cleaning nevertheless
when His patience is too far taxed.

—The Reverend William Hudnut,
First Presbyterian Church

Successful was the kleagle who accurately gauged the anxieties of
the community in which he kluxed. With the approval of national
headquarters, the kleagle adjusted his message to the area's ethnic
composition, the level of religious strife, a perceived breakdown in
law and order, the assertiveness of the black community, or a desire for civic reform. Well before the arrival of the first kleagle,
Youngstown had evolved into a society ready to receive the Klan
message.[1]

Youngstown traced its Protestant heritage to New England. An un-
developed plot of land on the Mahoning River when John Young purchased it from the Connecticut Land Company in 1797, Youngstown
served as a way station and trade center for migrants crossing the Al-
leghanies via Pittsburgh. The first settlers from New England brought
with them a penchant for a well-ordered society; pioneers had often
laid out the town and chosen their minister before leaving for the Western Reserve. Although the frontier quality of life tempted many settlers
to stray from the tenets of Congregationalism or Presbyterianism, practice of these faiths continued. Especially persistent was adherence to a
strict Sabbath as observed in much of New England. An undocu-
mented story has survived that officials fined one settler for hunting on
the Sabbath in spite of the fact that he had killed a marauding bear.[2]

Between 1800 and 1840 Youngstown was a small village outdis-
tanced by nearby Warren, which had secured designation as the Trumbull County seat. When the canal era came to Ohio in the 1830s,
however, a spur completed in 1840 connected the main artery at Akron
to Pittsburgh via Warren and Youngstown and opened trade opportuni-

ties for the entire Mahoning Valley. A thirty-five-year-old man named David Tod—eventually one of Ohio's governors—saw the potential in developing the area's mines and shipping coal over the canal. By 1846 the first blast furnace, the "Eagle," began operations within Youngstown Township.[3]

The growth of the iron industry attracted 5,000 inhabitants to Youngstown by 1867. By the 1870s the Mahoning Valley was the site of twenty-one blast furnaces, which made extensive use of local coal and iron ore in the iron-making process.[4] As the mines began to peter out, iron producers were able to turn to the Connelsville fields for coal and the Mesabi Range for ores. Ready access to these raw materials, adequate railway transportation, and sufficient capital generated from mining and iron furnaces, as well as a base of experience in the industry, enabled Youngstown to expand into steel manufacturing by the 1890s.

Youngstown's conversion to the steel industry began in 1892 when local investors Henry Wick and Joseph G. Butler, Jr., revealed their plans to build a steel plant that used the Bessemer process. City officials offered them $25,000 and an exclusion from taxation. The Ohio Steel Company began operation on 4 February 1895, in the midst of a depression. Once the depression ended, the superiority of the steel bars rolled in this new plant guaranteed success. Not, however, in time to convince the owners of the wisdom of their investment, so they sold the plant to the National Steel Company in 1899. In 1901 United States Steel Corporation took over National Steel.[5]

The merger movement within American industry around the turn of the century also brought Republic Iron and Steel Company to Youngstown. Republic purchased three local iron mills and converted them to steel production. The executive offices of Republic remained in New Jersey and New York, where the company had been founded in 1899, but the general offices moved to Youngstown in 1911, at the same time that the mills switched to the open-hearth process.[6]

The most important new steel enterprise in Youngstown, though, was the locally owned and developed Youngstown Sheet and Tube Company. Organized in 1900 and promoted by James A. Campbell, the company grew within twenty years into the largest industrial concern within the state of Ohio. During the war years it achieved vertical integration with the purchase of coal and ore fields, the construction of twelve open-hearth furnaces, and the establishment of internal railroad services. With resources exceeding $100,000,000 in 1920, the company produced pipe, plates, bars, sheets, rods, wire, nails, fencing, hoops, and cable. Its payroll of 15,000 workers made it the largest

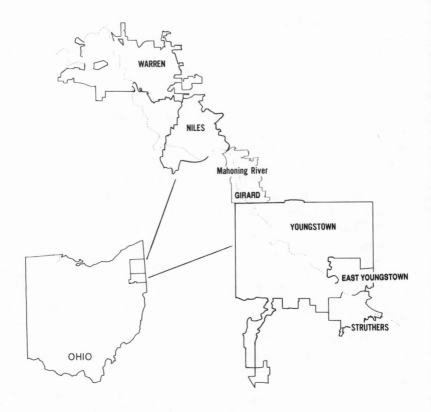

The Mahoning Valley

employer in the city and in the state of Ohio. Although these three companies dominated steel production within the valley, there were numerous smaller companies, as well as fabricating plants that transformed steel into a myriad of finished products. Despite many efforts later to diversify, Youngstown's growth became dependent on a single industry.[7]

The development of the steel industry in Youngstown and surrounding areas transformed the Mahoning Valley. Within the first twenty years of this century, the population tripled in Youngstown (from 44,000 to 132,000); it had passed 170,000 by 1930. The advent of such large numbers of newcomers was a disruptive force, partially because of the size of the immigration but also because of the cultural diversity of the immigrants.

As of 1900 Youngstown was predominately Welsh and German. In the 1850s the coal mines and the iron industry had attracted the Welsh, who were noted for their industry, frugality, and dogmatism in religion (the majority were Baptists or Congregationalists). The Germans came more evenly over the years from Pennsylvania, where they had lived on farms in enclaves that perpetuated German culture. According to Joseph Butler the descendants of the Pennsylvania *Deutsch* in Youngstown no longer kept their children out of public schools or insisted on the preservation of the German language and customs. Although the German language newspaper, the *Rundschau*, folded in 1908, there were still many sick and benefit societies, as well as a singing society called the Maennerchor. The German and Welsh populations had outstripped the older Scotch-Irish and English settlers.[8]

A significant Irish population, the unskilled victims of Ireland's poverty and drought, had also come to Youngstown to work on the canal and in the mines. Although a few Catholics had been among the original settlers in Youngstown, the area remained a missionary outpost of the Catholic church until after the Irish migrations of the 1840s and 1850s. The first church, St. Columba's, now the seat of the Youngstown diocese, was built in 1853, and the first resident pastor was appointed in 1858. By 1890 there were four other parishes: St. Anne's, St. Joseph's, Sacred Heart, and Immaculate Conception.[9] The influx of the Irish generated some anti-Catholic reaction during the election of 1896 when Democratic mayoral candidate Edmund Moore accused the Republican candidate, Fred Hartenstein, of belonging to the anti-Catholic American Protective Association. Moore won the election in spite of Hartenstein's letter to the *Youngstown Telegram* denying that he was a member.[10]

Starting in 1880 and escalating after 1900, the arrival of immigrants from southern and eastern Europe dramatically altered the composition of Youngstown's population and of the entire valley. The jobs available in the steel industry—Republic and Sheet and Tube hired between 23,000 and 24,000 workers in 1920—drew them to Youngstown in such numbers that by 1920 two-thirds of the population was foreign-born or the children of foreign-born (see table 1). The payroll of one local mill consisted of one-third native and two-thirds foreign-born workers.[11]

As with other immigrant groups, these workers tended to form nationality neighborhoods, both as a source of comfort and mutual acceptance and as a way to perpetuate Old World customs. The poverty in these areas located close to the mills, coupled with violations of the

TABLE 1
Youngstown's Population Composition

	1880	1900	1910	1920
% of foreign-born residents	30.8	27.2	31.4	25.6
% of foreign-born and native white with foreign-born parents	NA	68.2	65.2	59.8
% of foreign-born from southern and eastern Europe	0	26.3	65.6	69.9
% of blacks	2.1	2.0	2.4	5.0
Total Population	15,435	44,805	79,066	132,358

SOURCES: U.S. Bureau of the Census, *Tenth Census of the United States, 1880*, Table 6, 423, and Table 9, 454; *Thirteenth Census of the United States, 1910*, Table 2, 418–19, and Table 5, 430; *Fourteenth Census of the United States, 1920*, Table XIII, 809; *Abstract of the 12th Census of the United States: 1900*, Tables 81 & 82, 103–8.

vice laws, led the Welsh and German populations to view the newcomers with trepidation. These people did not assimilate but continued their strange ways, even building institutions to maintain a separate identity.

The signs of stress were most apparent in the labor strife that erupted from time to time. In January 1916 workers on strike against Youngstown Sheet and Tube rioted in nearby East Youngstown and burned down the entire central business district. Of the eighty-one young men arrested—their average age was twenty-seven—only seven were listed as Americans; most came from southern and eastern Europe. The association of the radical Industrial Workers of the World

(IWW) with the strikers generated nativists' fear of the revolutionary tendencies of the foreign-born. This fear was bolstered in the fall of 1919 when William Z. Foster and the National Committee to Organize the Iron and Steel Industry struck against the major producers in Youngstown. The Secret Service interrogated more than two hundred persons and uncovered a revolutionary society at work in East Youngstown. A petition circulated by the local merchants in the midst of the strike objected to Bolshevik influences on the strikers. Though they were initially impartial regarding the strike, the mayors of East Youngstown and Youngstown became so alarmed that they prohibited meetings to discuss the strike and actually arrested one of the participants simply for holding a business meeting.[12]

The immediate response of the companies during the strike was to stir Youngstown's cultural mix even more by bringing in southern blacks as substitute workers. Blacks already constituted 2 percent of the population of the area, but the influx raised that figure to 5 percent. In spite of layoffs after the strike, blacks continued to come to Youngstown in the 1920s, generally to be hired for the least healthy and lowest-paid jobs in the mills. Having suffered from the southern approach to race relations, these black immigrants did not openly challenge the northern system. During the 1920s there was no locally active chapter of the NAACP. Although there was a chapter of Marcus Garvey's United Negro Improvement Association, it was philosophically opposed to racial integration.[13]

In a postwar effort to restore order to worker-management relations, Youngstown Sheet and Tube encouraged workers to learn English and the principles of American government by taking advantage of free night classes. Through the Buckeye Land Company, a subsidiary, Sheet and Tube offered its employees an opportunity to rent or to buy housing at cost. More desirous, though, of creating a docile labor force than in producing homogeneity, the company divided the housing into American, foreign-born, and black sections. The company also attempted to absorb worker energies—whatever were left over after a seventy-two-hour work week—in company-sponsored athletic activities; parks and playgrounds were available for family outings. In order to give the workers a semblance of participation in the determination of working conditions, the company established an employee representation plan in 1920 by which worker-elected representatives from each department could present grievances to management.[14]

The important fact to note about these programs is that Youngstown Sheet and Tube constructed the programs on the premise that foreign workers could blend into American society, that cultural differences could be overcome. Joseph Butler, vice-president of the Brier Hill Steel Company and member of the Youngstown Sheet and Tube board of directors, boasted of the efforts to Americanize the new immigrants. Although admitting that there may be "an inherent difference in the Latin and Anglo-Saxon characters," he blamed the "damning effect of despotism" for narrowing their vision to "mere physical existence" and for the fact that "they had never mounted to spiritual heights or learned to yearn for the better things that, with liberty and opportunity, men of any race may soon acquire for themselves and for their children." Moreover, the journey to the United States had "a tendency to overturn former conceptions of duty, loosen the bonds which held these immigrants to such standards of life as they may have had, and make them more than ordinarily susceptible to unsound social and political propaganda." The churches, he lamented, had lost their power of persuasion because they had to ask for financial support from former peasants used to a state-supported church. The fact that so many immigrants were single young men or men without their families Butler cited as facilitating "the rather low standard of morals to be expected among them." And yet he was optimistic about their future and about their progress toward American citizenship. According to Butler, these new immigrants were "industrious and frugal, amenable to instruction and eager to improve their condition." Many mill owners shared Butler's faith. [15]

It was the pietistic Protestant who viewed these Catholic and Jewish immigrants with a more jaundiced eye, perhaps because of a perceived link between their non-Protestant values and the labor strikes of 1916 and 1919. Pietists' concentration on the salvation of society as the means to save one's soul required the purging of sin through law enforcement, an effort made easier by the fact that the laws of the land reflected Protestant dominance. Sunday observance, vice, and Prohibition laws were all on the books but not yet in the hearts of all residents.

Such attitudes were apparent in the state and local records of the various pietistic denominations. The Disciples of Christ, for example, warned through a monthly paper entitled *The Ohio Work* that World War I had not brought the millenium as predicted; hence, Christians had to engage in "prolonged and intelligent effort" to earn such a reward. The fields needing the greatest attention were in the city and among the immigrants. Predicting that "Christianity will take the cities or the cities will ruin the race," editor L. J. Cahill called on the Disciples to increase their missionary work to create "cities of God" in Ohio. Within the walls of the cities, Cahill found innumerable immigrants in need of Americanization. Since he regarded Christianity as a fundamental undergirding to the preservation of democracy, he exhorted the Disciples "to instill in the hearts of our immigrant peoples the same Christian ideals that have made America the world's hope today."[16]

Cahill was proudest of the Disciples' contribution to the passage of the Prohibition amendment. Although he endorsed the work of other Christian denominations and the Anti-Saloon League, he felt that the Disciples "were an indispensable factor in the temperance campaign." Cahill also noted the cooperation of the Disciples with fourteen other religious bodies in June 1922 to discuss "how to bring the influence of Protestantism to bear upon the moving picture situation and to provide wholesome pictures for the public," as well as how to influence the state legislature regarding "purer morals."[17]

The Methodists, on the other hand, pursued moral reform through a direct alliance with the Anti-Saloon League. In 1910 the East Ohio Conference of the Methodist Episcopal Church commended the League, extended "the use of our pulpits, and ask[ed] them to call upon us whenever we may be of assistance to the cause." After the war its successor, the Northeast Ohio Conference, continued such support. After securing the passage of the Prohibition amendment, the conference turned its attention to electing public officials who supported Prohibition and to organizing "public sentiment back of enforcement officers." They were fearful lest indifference undermine the work entailed in passage of the amendment.[18]

The strongest statement from Ohio Methodists regarding the need for moral regeneration occurred at the Ohio Annual Conference of 1921. The Committee on Reforms demanded "a more stringent censorship of moving pictures, and the enforcing of our Sunday laws with reference to theatrical entertainments." It also applauded "the efforts of our National Government and Social Hygienic organization to suppress licentiousness" and condemned "the widespread increase of gambling today." The committee's report concluded with a ringing endorsement of the U.S. attorney general's appeal for more law and order.[19]

Both Presbyterian denominations joined in the clamor for a regenerated Ohio. The Synod of Ohio (Presbyterian Church of the United States of America) established a Board of Temperance and Moral Welfare, which reported annually to the convention. Labeling itself an example of "Applied Christianity," the board considered its work as essential in the promotion of the millennium. Besides continuing support of the Prohibition laws, Presbyterians, it noted, must also concern themselves with divorce, veneral diseases, censorship of motion pictures, tobacco, and the rising traffic in drugs and narcotics. Samuel Stophlet, chairman of the board, called for a law enforcement campaign to deter bootlegging, Sunday violations, and immoral motion pictures lest the enemies of moral reform turn back the tide. The convention of 1920 adopted a resolution that urged Presbyterians to elect only those officials willing to stringently enforce the laws relating to temperance and moral reform. The First Synod of the West (United Presbyterian Church of North America), covering western Pennsylvania and northeastern Ohio, appointed a Committee on Reform, which endorsed all efforts to secure enforcement of the Prohibition and Sunday observance laws. In addition, the Synod of the West appointed trustees to serve on the boards of the Anti-Saloon League and the Lord's Day Alliance. [20]

Although the Lutheran Church did not traditionally involve itself in politics, it is important to remember that Youngstown was in eastern Ohio, close to the Pennsylvania border, and that approximately half of its Lutheran churches belonged to the recently formed (1918) United Lutheran Church in America (ULC). The ULC had brought together the General Synod, the General Council, and the United Synod of the South. Generally speaking, these groups were more assimilated, more prone to use English at services, and more open to the pietism of other denominations. As a result, the Synod of Ohio (ULC) appointed a Committee on Social Reform, which criticized the existence of widespread disrespect for Prohibition and called for Lutherans to support government efforts to enforce such laws. A subordinate body, the East Ohio Synod, echoed these sentiments when it referred to the efforts of its followers on behalf of Prohibition as "applied Christianity." [21]

The other major Lutheran body in the Mahoning Valley, the Joint Synod of Ohio and Other States, was more traditionally Lutheran. Thus, there were no resolutions at the conventions of the Eastern District of the Joint Synod regarding Prohibition or other moral laws. Its president, the Reverend J. F. C. Soller, in his report for 1917 reaffirmed the commitment of the Lutheran church to building a better world through preaching. "Just as little as the State should meddle into the affairs of the Church," he asserted, "even so little the Church should meddle into the affairs of the State." Although Soller was applying this principle to the war effort, it served as an indication of how it might also be applied to moral legislation. The other liturgical body, the Diocese of Ohio of the Protestant Episcopal Church, exhibited some pietistic influence when it endorsed Prohibition legislation during the war, but such resolutions disappeared in the 1920s. There were no resolutions on other vice legislation either.[22]

Supported, then, by the fervor of numerous pastors and laymen who had attended the state or local conventions, Protestant moral reform appeared in Youngstown in many forms—sometimes a denomination, such as the Methodists or United Presbyterians; sometimes a union, such as the Federated Council of Churches; sometimes a secular organization, such as the Anti-Saloon League; and sometimes just the individual citizen—but always with the belief that God's kingdom could flourish here on earth with committed public officials and concerned citizens in support. These Protestants were advocating moral reform, rather than the more subtle devices of the mill owners, to secure social and industrial order.

Within Youngstown there were at least three organizations that combined elements of the above. The most visibly involved in the moral crusade was the Mahoning County Dry League. The Anti-Saloon League's suspicion of politicians and government had prompted the formation of such leagues to oversee the enforcement of the Prohibition laws. In October 1921 more than five hundred people attended the formation of the Mahoning County Dry League at Trinity Methodist Church; they set a goal of overseeing the enforcement of the Prohibition laws. Within each precinct one man and one woman began to watch for violations. When their reports failed to secure a sufficient response, the Dry League established an extralegal force of its own agents, as permitted by Ohio law, to obtain warrants, lead raids, arrest violators, and take them to court in Struthers, a nearby suburb with a reputation for stricter enforcement and a policy of remitting part of the fine to the agents.[23]

The Federated Council of Churches, composed primarily of pietistic churches, did not think it appropriate to act as an alternate police force, but instead chose to "raise a voice against lawlessness in all forms." Placing the responsibility for better enforcement upon public officials, the council's Social Betterment Committee urged ministers to speak from the pulpit at frequent intervals on the "importance of obedience to and respect for all law."[24] In December 1922 the Federated Council ventured so far as to urge Mayor William Reese to consider moral character in the appointment of a new safety director, a cabinet position that supervised the police force.[25]

Harriet Ritter, usually identified as Mrs. J. F. W. Ritter in local newspapers, headed the third organization, the Federation of Women's Clubs. Under her direction the federation became a major proponent of a home rule charter for Youngstown under which, it was hoped, corrupt politicians could not function. Women, of course, had only recently received the right to vote, and one of their major arguments had been that women's sense of morality would cleanse politics of its male-related corruption. In 1923 Ritter acknowledged the propriety of this role when she commented that Youngstown "may need a woman mayor on moral grounds." For unexplained reasons no female candidates were forthcoming.[26]

The concern of these groups with lawlessness was not fanciful. The commission of crimes in Youngstown had risen sharply since 1900. Felonies, which averaged 136 per year between 1900 and 1910, increased over 73 percent by 1913. From 1914 through 1920 the yearly average was 537 felonies, almost a 400 percent increase over the first decade.[27]

Dissatisfaction with law enforcement in Youngstown came to the surface in the mayoral election of 1921. Fred Warnock, the Republican incumbent, was running for his second term. Although he had won the office in 1919 with a pledge of maintaining law and order, the public expected more than he could deliver. In the spring of 1921, E. H. Moore, the Mahoning County Democratic chairman and former mayor, played on the public's disappointment when he suggested that the existence of forty-six houses of prostitution and the commission of fifteen murders since January were ample proof of the ineptitude of the Warnock administration in the postwar era. By late 1921 Warnock's hopes for a second term were fading.[28]

The Democrats did not inspire a greater measure of public confidence. As a matter of fact, if elections were to serve as a gauge, they inspired much less. Many voters turned instead to a political ingenue, George Oles, the owner of the Fulton Fruit and Meat Market. A native of Riceville, Pennsylvania, Oles had come to Youngstown in 1907 after operating grocery stores in New York, Pennsylvania, Indiana, and other parts of Ohio. The peripatetic Oles changed the site of his market several times before finally settling on the southwest corner of Public Square, where his high volume, low prices, and colorful advertisements attracted many shoppers.[29]

Oles's campaign received a boost from several embarrassing incidents involving the Warnock administration. Within a month of the election, Warnock's safety director was convicted for accepting a bribe not to enforce the Prohibition law. The *Vindicator* contended that Warnock was not directly involved but questioned his lack of knowledge regarding his subordinate. The only action that might save Warnock, it suggested, was a raid on the Oaks, a notorious club and likely speakeasy, located in the downtown area. While Warnock chose to await evidence of actual violations, federal Prohibition agents conducted a raid on Friday, 4 November, and seized fifteen barrels of beer as an Oaks attendant was opening the door for delivery. The timing of these events must have been frustrating for Warnock, who had little opportunity to respond before the election.[30]

Meanwhile, Oles's campaign jabbed incessantly at politics and politicians. "Oles doesn't know anything about politics," he bragged, "and he doesn't want to know anything about politics."[31] This ingenuous statement implied that a political innocent could succeed while experienced politicos failed. Oles presented himself as a strong-willed candidate with simple answers to complex problems.

Oles's image captured the public imagination and brought him an unexpected 11,136 to 10,691 victory over Warnock.[32] Claiming that he had "enough evidence from my friends to tell each man what his politics are and what he has done since birth, where every still is located, where every gambling joint is, the name of almost every bootlegger and every sporting house, the name of every politician who is busy framing Oles for his downfall," Oles promised action when he assumed office in January. He then left for a two-week vacation in Florida prior to his inaugural.[33]

Female support for Oles appears to have been a vital factor in his election, especially since the mayoral contest in 1921 was the first local election in which women voted. Recognizing the significance of female votes, Oles constructed a campaign to appeal to their interest in a clean city and purified politics. Many of these women called the *Vindicator* election night for results and responded, "That's good!" when informed of Oles's victory.[34]

Oles's first month in office was indicative of his lack of experience and of the frustrations that could result from an expectation that reform required only willpower. Two weeks after ordering Police Chief James Watkins to close down the city as one of his first official actions, Oles suspended Watkins. He charged that "there is too much booze in town, too many complaints are coming in and there are too many immoral women." But the mayor had overlooked the necessity of obtaining a civil service board review. Within the week, in spite of Oles's additional charges that Watkins had allowed a prominent attorney to secure an illegal release of several young women from the Foster Detention Home, and that he had failed to raid an establishment pointed out by the mayor, the Civil Service Commission acquitted Watkins. The *Vindicator* noted the flimsiness of the mayor's charges and cited his propensity for bragging, yet it decided to overlook the Watkins fiasco because of Oles's "good intentions."[35]

His administration stumbled along for another five months before falling. Beset by a lack of adequate funding—the city was paying for operating costs through bond issues—and by his inability to fire those he perceived as incompetent or corrupt, Oles quit in late June; City Council President William Reese assumed the office. The incident that precipitated the resignation was his firing of twenty-five policemen in an economy move. The policemen appealed, and the court ruled that the policemen had to be hired back because of a lack of proper notification.[36]

Oles's resignation drew mixed reactions. The *Vindicator* called Oles a half-child, a boastful, vain, and foolish man, who nonetheless had made a sincere effort to govern Youngstown. Some prominent businessmen and clubwomen, on the other hand, appeared before city council on 30 June to appeal for his return. Harriet Ritter, speaking for the General Federation of Women's Clubs, focused on Oles's intentions rather than his oftentimes embarrassing actions. She contended that a faulty political structure had hampered Oles in securing his goals and suggested serious consideration of revamping city government through a charter commission.[37]

Oles's resignation enabled Ritter to resurrect the charter issue.[38] After the *Telegram* joined Ritter in her call for a home rule charter, more than fourteen hundred citizens turned out for a mass meeting at Moose Hall on the evening of 3 July.[39] They selected William J. Williams, an advocate of a strong mayor plan, as chairman. Because there was little unity among the speakers—some even opposed the whole idea—the only agreement reached was to request the city council to place a resolution on the ballot for the appointment of a charter commission. The council agreed, and in November the people voted in favor of its creation.[40]

After numerous meetings of the fifteen commission members in council chambers—they selected William J. Williams as chairman— the commission recommended a federal charter whose provisions, it was hoped, would purify the city of the effects of political machinations. The charter barred political parties from nominating candidates for city offices and limited the mayor to one term as a means of forestalling the erection of a political machine. With faith in the common sense of the voter, charter members provided for initiative, referendum, and recall as an additional check on those elected to public office. Ironically, the Civil Service Commission, which urban reformers had advocated as a means of undercutting the appointment of political hacks, was eliminated. The experience of George Oles with the stifling effect that civil service review could have on the removal of incompetents had produced this provision. Instead department heads would establish their own tests and remove recalcitrant employees for cause. Employees' only redress was to a board of appeals composed of the mayor, the president of the council, and the presiding judge of the municipal court.[41]

After mailing copies of the charter to all registered voters, the commission placed it on the ballot for final approval in May 1923. With only 22 percent of the electorate voting, the charter passed 4,938 to 2,637. Although less than 15 percent of the electorate had supported the charter changes, the *Telegram* chose to emphasize the positive side of passage, a ringing two-to-one endorsement that would put city government on a business basis.[42] Its work over, the charter commission reorganized itself into a voters league, whose purpose was to endorse the best candidates on a nonpartisan basis.[43]

The structural reform evident in the new charter benefited from, and then added to, a wave of moral reform just reaching its crest. The Federated Council of Churches was an important part of that wave. Because numerous Protestant sects often saw cooperation as a threat to their independence, the council in Youngstown had limited its program to evangelization and to the creation of a strong moral climate in the city in the hope that this was a plan around which Protestants could rally.

As part of that plan, the council conducted a yearly census of a quarter of the city, reporting residents' religious preference to the appropriate church and assigning those without preferences to the nearest church. Between New Year's Day and Easter, some churches conducted "an intensive evangelistic campaign with the assistance of evangelists or neighboring pastors"; others engaged members of their congregations in a program of home visitations.[44] The *Federated Churches Monthly Bulletin* reported that evangelism had added 1,700 new members to local churches in 1923 and 2,600 in 1924. The council also supported adult Bible classes in all churches, and reported in 1923 that a five-week session had attracted 8,990 women and 7,389 men.[45] The appearance of the Reverend Charles Clayton Morrison, editor of *Christian Century*, one of the leading organs of liberal Protestantism, as the keynote speaker for the start of the period of evangelization in 1924, was an indication that the council's evangelism represented a broad-based call to all Protestant churches rather than an outgrowth of fundamentalism.[46]

The council issued a call to personal holiness that attracted many residents, who were then encouraged to work for others' holiness by securing stricter enforcement of the vice laws. Condemning "lawlessness in all forms," the council bragged that it was "behind our city officials in every effort to make Youngstown a law-abiding community." By reprinting a message from the Pittsburgh Ministerial Union, the council indicated its belief that lawlessness permitted by public officials "was far more dangerous than any other kind." Suggesting that the fault of the offender was less than that of the winking public official, the union called for less attention to petty offenses and more "to lawlessness on the part of those who occupy positions of influence and power."[47]

In 1923 the Social Betterment Committee of the Federated Council of Churches met on numerous occasions to discuss deteriorating moral conditions within the city. Of particular concern for the committee was Sunday observance. "Roller skating rinks have been closed on Sunday," the committee reports crowed, "and the basketball teams have been persuaded to discontinue Sunday games." But meetings with the mayor, chief of police, and theater managers had not produced any results regarding Sunday vaudeville performances. Carnivals were an additional sore spot because of their reputation for illegal gambling activity.[48]

There were many local ministers from the Baptist, Disciples of Christ, Methodist, and Presbyterian denominations who participated in this crusade, but one of the most prominent and certainly most successful clerics was the Reverend A. C. Archibald of the First Baptist Church, founded in 1860 and located on Public Square. First Baptist had acquired the services of the Reverend Archibald from the pulpit supply as an interim pastor in the summer of 1921. Impressed with his vitality and oratorical skills, the church had offered him a full-time position, which he initially declined. Repeated importuning on the church's part led to negotiations in which Archibald suggested that he would come only if the church was "sympathetic with the forward-looking policy of enlargement at the earliest moment." Once established in office, Archibald fulfilled the hopes of his parishioners as his sermons drew packed houses each Sunday. Archibald also initiated men's Bible classes, which attracted 1,000 men weekly. "The response to Dr. Archibald's dynamic leadership," according to C. Glen Anderson, church historian, "was sufficient evidence that the church needed larger, better and more efficient quarters." On 8 March 1925 First Baptist laid a cornerstone for its new church; its dedication took place on 18 October. By the time he left in 1928, Archibald had personally accounted for the addition of 1,200 new members to First Baptist, a remarkable expansion from an initial base of 500 parishioners.[49]

The first indication of a link between pietistic Protestantism and the Ku Klux Klan occurred in November 1922, when Archibald presented a sermon in response to the appearance of the Klan in Youngstown. Rumors of its existence had frightened the city council in September 1921; thereafter, the Klan had worked surreptitiously to attract members from fraternal societies, such as the Masons, and from Protestant congregations. To an overflow crowd Archibald gave an ambivalent answer to the question, "Has the Klan a legitimate place in American life?"[50] Although he espoused what he considered the principles of the Klan (the preservation of the Constitution, white supremacy, separation of church and state, and the sanctity of the American home), Archibald opposed its methods. "I do not believe in the Klan oath," Archibald asserted, "and I can conceive of no good that can come from an organization that emphasizes bigotry, class hatred and force." A *Vindicator* editorial, however, questioned Archibald's sincerity. He had, for instance, accused the Associated Press of being in the control of Catholics and of emphasizing the wrongdoings of non-Catholic ministers. He also questioned the Knights of Columbus's misuse of government funds for the purpose of fighting Methodists in Rome during the war. Finally, Archibald characterized the Jew as the "world's master manipulator."[51] Such charges implied that Protestants were innocent victims of other religions and needed a protective organization.

Archibald was also very sympathetic to the Klan position on immigration. Referring to America as a Christian government, Archibald portrayed that government as besieged by foreign dangers. In particular, he feared the effect of "the emptying of European riff-raff on our shores." "Some of them," according to Archibald, "are anarchists, some nihilists, but infidels all." For years, he believed, Europe had dumped its undesirables on American shores, and Archibald no longer wished to tolerate their coming.[52] Although Archibald apparently never joined the Klan, his inability to resolve his belief in the principle of love of neighbor with antagonisms and resentments that he felt toward Catholics, Jews, and immigrants was typical of many a member. It was an ambivalence that the Klan was to play upon masterfully to its own advantage.

Within days after Archibald's sermon had stirred up a furor, representatives of the Klan took a *Vindicator* reporter to their headquarters, where a number of prominent businessmen and leading Protestant clergymen identified the Klan as a "Protestant defensive organization" and cited the "insidious attacks of other religious orders" as a reason for its formation. Particularly annoying to Klan members were the alleged depictions of Protestant ministers on stage and screen as comic figures.[53] Thus, the Klan began to exploit local issues, rather than the more general platform provided for kleagles.

The Klan's public appearance in Youngstown provoked many negative responses. Bishop Joseph Schrembs, of the Cleveland diocese, which oversaw the Mahoning Valley, condemned the order for its secrecy, its violation of the Constitution, and its vigilante activities.[54] The local chapter of the Knights of Columbus asked First Baptist to remove Archibald, a request quickly denied by his parishioners.[55] War veterans censured Archibald and formed an educational committee of the Private Soldiers and Sailors Legion to distribute pamphlets about the Klan. They also attacked Mayor William Reese for allegedly accepting a portrait of George Washington from the Klan and hanging it in his office.[56]

The *Vindicator* had already indicated its official opposition to the Klan in June 1922, but now that the Klan had appeared publicly, it took the opportunity to place the Klan in historical context for its readers. The Klan, according to the *Vindicator*, resembled the Know-Nothing party of the 1850s and the American Protective Association of the 1890s, a chapter of which had appeared in Youngstown. The *Vindicator*, however, opposed the efforts of the Akron and Youngstown city councils to suppress its meetings. "Evidence has proved," suggested the paper, "that such essentially unsound movements, if left to run their course in public, live short lives, but, if suppressed, and as their friends will claim, persecuted, may live longer and do vastly greater mischief." The Klan, then, should be free to meet and to express its ideas—a position agreed with by the local chapter of the American Civil Liberties Union. Publicity and reason, the *Vindicator* predicted, would ultimately check its growth.[57] The other local newspaper, the *Telegram*, a Scripps-Howard paper, chose to remain aloof editorially, yet continued to report on Klan activities.

With such formidable opponents and in a city of diverse population, the Klan found it difficult to use appeals to prejudice as a basis for organization. It also had to take Archibald's concerns into account. Hence, the Klan attempted a veneer of cooperation with other faiths when it sent a letter to the school board in December 1922 calling for religious instruction in the public schools. Citing an assertion by Dr. Charles Eliot, president of Harvard University, that the failure of the nation's schools had caused the recent breakdown in moral standards, the Klan suggested that a committee of Protestants, Catholics, and Jews be formed to recommend a program of religious instruction. The board accepted the letter and proceeded to form such a committee. The superintendent, Dr. O. L. Reid, admitted that there was scattered Bible reading in Youngstown schools, usually without comment, but noted that "if the great faiths could get together on some program, it would be a fine thing." The Klan even received support for its proposal in a *Vindicator* editorial.[58]

The Klan's mask of toleration was ripped away, however, in March 1923, when the police arrested a kleagle named Doyle Glossner, a thirty-year-old man from nearby New Castle, Pennsylvania, on the charge of working with a fake constable. Although they never pressed formal charges, the police had searched Glossner's room at the Tod House and found a book of names and addresses—allegedly a list of prospective Klan members—a copy of a speech, and other Klan materials. The speech contained a hodgepodge of prejudiced charges: the establishment of a seminary for black priests in Greensville, Mississippi, a statement by Cardinal Gibbons that the United States would be a Roman Catholic country within ten years, and a characterization of Jews as money-grabbers. Glossner reminded his audience to be wary of Al Smith because of his Catholicism and of James Cox, former governor of Ohio and Democratic presidential nominee in 1920, because he had visited the pope while in Rome. Glossner apparently prided himself on having asked Cox what talcum powder the pope used—an indirect implication that Cox must have kissed the pope on the bodily parts where he used talcum powder.[59]

Glossner's response in a letter the day after his arrest was an indication, though, that the Klan recognized the lack of appeal in straightforward prejudice. Though he admitted that the Klan was composed of Anglo-Saxons and oriented toward patriotism, he denied hatred or malice toward anyone; he focused instead on the need for law and order. The Klan, according to Glossner, stood foursquare against bootlegging and prostitution and called on men to protect pure womanhood. Thus, the public focus of the Klan would remain on moral order, a unifying theme that would allow the Klan to deny prejudices and yet permit its followers to take action against allegedly prime offenders of the moral order, the immigrants.[60]

In late 1922 and early 1923, it was not apparent, however, that the moral crusade and the Klan would link together. The Klan continued to work behind the scenes, its only semipublic appearances being the burning of crosses on 1 March and 1 April of 1923 as an indication of its growing membership and an invitation to join. Meanwhile, the Federated Council, with a membership of 25,000 Protestants, suggested to Mayor William Reese that his appointment of a new safety director would be an indication of the seriousness of his desire to clean up the city.[61] Though the appointment of George Scheible, a local contractor, as both service and safety director seemed to satisfy critics, the Reverend George Ford, executive director of the Federated Churches, continued in early 1923 to attack Reese for his willingness to permit basketball games on Sunday. Ford also cited skating rinks and vaudeville shows as "commercialized" encroachments on the blue laws. Shortly thereafter, Reese would ban skating, basketball, and other organized sports on Sunday.[62]

Reese also made efforts to enforce Prohibition laws, but rarely did those efforts satisfy his critics. As a matter of fact, critics felt it necessary to supplement—for some critics, supplant—the efforts of the Youngstown police department. They turned to state Prohibition officers, agents of the Mahoning County Dry League, and even some detectives from Pittsburgh to lead raids on local offenders. Ohio law permitted such raids as part of a campaign to direct all possible resources toward the control of alcohol. Perry Robison, chairman of the Dry League, labeled the initial raid in February 1923 as "just the first raid of a number we intend making if the law is not enforced to the letter."[63] Reese's efforts paled in comparison and opened him to charges of inadequacy.[64]

Finally, in July the Reverend George Gibson, of the Mahoning Avenue Methodist Church, took these complaints to the governor, Victor Donahey, and asked for Reese's removal, as permitted by Ohio law. Gibson charged that the Reese administration tolerated open gambling and that the city was in a state of "lawlessness." The governor responded with a thirty-day suspension of Reese during which formal charges were to be presented and a final disposition made. Proclaiming himself innocent, Reese attacked Gibson for never providing him with information regarding violations of the law.[65]

While awaiting the hearing, Gibson assumed the reins of leadership in the burgeoning vice crusade. On Monday, 6 August, Gibson chaired a meeting of 10,000 area residents held in Wick Park. Verses of "Onward, Christian Soldiers" filled the air. Gibson called on the audience to launch a crusade for "civic righteousness" that would rid the city of incompetent and negligent officials. He claimed to have evidence to support his charges, evidence gathered since he had come to Youngstown four years earlier. A ring, he suggested, was running the city, and had threatened him when he spoke out. Helpers collected more than $1,300 from the crowd; Treasurer D. C. Hamilton promised to use it "in getting evidence against vice conditions which prevail in Youngstown and in prosecuting those found guilty of breaking the law." Gibson then proclaimed the formation of a Civic League to work against Mayor Reese.[66]

There was little doubt that the Civic League was a front for the Klan. The key figures, Gibson and Hamilton, were both members of the Klan. Moreover, Gibson, in a sermon given one week earlier and entitled "Sin of Tolerance," had indicated his support for an unidentified national organization of "15,000,000 men" that was going to "open the eyes of the nation to the evils now sweeping the land." It stood, Gibson asserted, for a united Protestantism unwilling to tolerate illegal activities. It would appear that the Klan ploy was to draw in supporters that might be suspicious about the Klan and its record elsewhere, or that might be unwilling to associate with the Klan. The Civic League also appealed directly to the Federated Council and the Federation of Women's Clubs for support, but no direct support was forthcoming.[67]

The Civic League's immediate task was to rid the city of Mayor Reese. Desirous of embarrassing Reese, it joined forces with Acting Mayor Robert Backus, who appointed a vigilance committee composed of interested citizens with full power to raid and to arrest potential violators. Paul Morris, also a Klan member, undertook a photographic tour of the city to gather evidence of the open conditions allegedly existent in Youngstown. Morris was prepared to take these pictures to Columbus for Reese's hearing with Donahey.

The well-attended hearings began on 22 August. The Civic League paid the transportation costs of twenty-one witnesses, including Morris; J. N. Carrothers, a state liquor investigator who was collecting $425 each month from Struthers; Cal Huffman, another state agent; and Kedgwin Powell, a young law student. Each witness contended that Youngstown was a wide-open city and cited their raids as evidence of ineffectiveness. Under questioning, however, Carrothers had to admit that he had not sought the aid of the Youngstown police in any instance, nor had they blocked his work. Morris also admitted that he had not reported specific instances of drunkeness or prostitution to the police. [68]

When questioned, Reese admitted that conditions were not good in Youngstown, but he claimed that he had followed through faithfully when reports were forthcoming. Reese also cited the difficulties of enforcement as a major problem in securing total shutdown throughout the city. Pete Sirbu's place, for instance, had pipes for rapid disposal of any incriminating alcohol; police simply could not get inside fast enough to gather incriminating evidence. [69] Moreover, Reese noted, the Youngstown police force was too small, having borne the brunt of recent budget cuts provoked by huge deficits. In the previous year the police force had declined from 197 to 125, and only three members remained on what had formerly been an eleven-man vice squad. [70]

Governor Donahey apparently believed Reese, cleared him of the charges, and praised him for his efforts in difficult circumstances. Even more insulting to the ministers and reformers who had presented the charges was his general condemnation of the "commercialization" of private law enforcement. "We cannot," Donahey asserted, "and will not tolerate the establishment of an enforcement body conducted on a business basis and not responsible to the voters and the elected officials of the state, county or municipality." Furthermore, Donahey recommended that the Dry League cease taking its cases to Struthers and stick with what Donahey described as an effective municipal court. [71]

Donahey regained a small measure of esteem from the reformers when he fired Police Chief James Watkins. Watkins attributed the firing to Reese's testimony that he had refused to go on a raid; he labeled Reese's story a lie. The *Vindicator* defended the efforts of Watkins in regard to major crimes but hinted that he had overlooked Prohibition enforcement, partially because of a smaller police force. "Men in his position," it suggested, "usually fail to recognize how the public, when aroused, will let the demand for a clean city override every other consideration." [72] Public intolerance of shortcomings would affect many more politicians and police chiefs before the tide ebbed.

Although the hearing in Columbus had exonerated Reese, it permanently damaged his reputation. He made an immediate effort to placate the moral forces by writing letters to the Federation of Women's Clubs and the Dry League promising to emphasize the creation of a strong moral climate in Youngstown.[73] Any efforts he might make, however, were limited by inadequate funds, a smaller than average police force, the existence of corruption and payoffs, and the cunning of the ordinary criminal.

The *Citizen*, a Youngstown weekly founded in 1914 and owned by D. Webster Brown, assisted the Civic League's campaign to oust Reese. The newspaper had originated as a trade publication for the Youngstown Auto Club and the Youngstown Real Estate Board. It was also staunchly Republican in its politics and critical of the independent movement that accompanied the rise of George Oles.[74] Its initial reaction to the Klan was negative. In August 1922 it condemned the Klan's attempts to designate itself as patriotic and commented that "patriots do not go about masked, whipping men and women." As with many other Youngstowners, however, the editor of the *Citizen*, Web Brown, would come to change his mind about the Klan, to see its potential as an agent of pietistic moral reform.[75]

Throughout 1922 and early 1923, the *Citizen* encouraged the improvement of Youngstown's moral climate. A consistent supporter of full enforcement of the blue laws, it suggested that a community with a majority of Christians should not tolerate infractions of those laws. The Reverend A. C. Archibald received special commendation from the *Citizen* for his attack on "filth and rot in the news, such as divorce scandals, murders, escapades of debauchees, and the scum of the news generally." To the *Citizen* such reports directly influenced the decline in morals. It also noted the beguiling influence of movies and suggested that Will Hays's appointment as movie censor was little more than a ruse. The decadence of modern society was a recurrent theme, as the editor cited "these days of frivolous flippers and flappers" and the "tendency toward disrespect for government and law in the United States."[76]

The transformation of the *Citizen* into a Klan newspaper culminated during the effort of the Civic League to oust Mayor Reese. Originally a supporter of Reese—probably because he was a Republican—the *Citizen* applauded the Donahey suspension of Reese and called for the election of a mayor who would "have the backbone to give the bootlegger short shrift, the tin horn sport and pimp the 'gate,' and the woman of loose morals an immediate outbound ticket from Youngstown, and likewise the lightfingered gentry and careless handlers of other people's money." It praised the nearby community of Girard as an example of what a "community of churches" could accomplish. In mid-August

1923 the *Citizen* proclaimed its support for law enforcement and for all groups attempting to improve community morals in Youngstown.[77]

In late August the newspaper finally revealed its Klan ties, as the content of the paper began to include allegations regarding the Catholic church. Citing the advice of a Catholic newspaper to mothers not to send their boys to the YMCA, the *Citizen* protested the Catholic church's "unfriendly, hostile and unclean attitude towards American Protestants." It promised that "Protestants will organize, and will organize in a manner that will teach Catholic editors and official spokesmen that such attacks and reflections shall not be made in the land of the free and the home of the brave." One headline even proclaimed that the Catholic church "hates Methodists." By mid-September the newspaper was braying about the Klan's belief in "clean politics, clean administration, clean officials," and reprinted on its front page a local sermon entitled "The Good in the Klan" delivered by the Reverend Richard R. Yocum, of St. Paul's Reformed Church.[78]

The situation was ready-made for the Klan. Its leaders had accurately read the local conditions. Rapidly expanding industrialization had attracted new immigrants to the city and had disturbed the social, economic, and political order. Tensions were most evident in Protestant defensiveness toward Catholic and Jewish faiths and the quest to impose pietist moral order on city residents. The lack of responsiveness of the city government to enforcement of those laws angered potential Klan members and made them susceptible to appeals for reform. The Klan worked surreptitiously to take advantage of the opportunity; both the Civic League and the *Citizen* were little more than Klan fronts.

But the other reform organizations also added to the opportunity when they secured the passage of the home rule charter that effectively eliminated political parties. Such a void meant that any well-organized group might sway the next election, and the Klan stood ready to act, much as the Anti-Saloon League had, by endorsing candidates of either party that represented its values. In July the Klan approached mayoral and council candidates. With a newspaper-estimated membership of 2,000 to 5,000, the Klan was ready to lead the moral forces within Youngstown to victory in November 1923.[79] The tide of moral and cultural reform would finally sweep over Youngstown.

3

The Election of 1923

We want a real man for mayor, a man with a passion for
high moral standards, and with executive ability, no freak.
—The Reverend Levi Batman,
First Christian Church

The Disciples of Christ had abandoned the Corner House Church,
founded more than one hundred years before by the Reverend Alexander Campbell. It was one of the first Disciple churches in the
Mahoning Valley, but had fallen into disuse. Colonel Evan A. Watkins, pastor of the First Baptist Church in Girard, saw its possibili-
ties—on 14 September he opened the building and welcomed at least
one hundred Klan members, who donated money to the church. "I am
pleased," Watkins said, "to see such an orderly contingent of men in
white robes enter a religious house. Their actions are contrary to press
reports of other cities. If this is the way hooded men act in the house
of God, the sooner others follow the better." And thus began Watkins's
campaign to acquire respectability for the Klan so that it might assume
leadership of the moral reformers and elect the next mayor of
Youngstown.[1]

Watkins's star had risen rapidly on the Youngstown political scene.
A recent arrival in Youngstown, he first came to public attention for
his speeches on the Holy Land in the spring of 1923. He was a native
of Wales, and claimed to have acquired his extensive knowledge of the
Holy Land when he accompanied General Edmund Allenby in his famous wartime capture of the holy city, Jerusalem. At his first public
appearance in April at the Warren Masonic Lodge, he identified himself as a medical missionary on leave from the Congregational church.
Although reasons for his appearance in the valley were not cited, his
presence as a speaker at a meeting for "100% Americans" in Warren
on 7 May suggests that he was a Klan-employed lecturer.[2] Eventually
Watkins became a key figure in the Klan campaign.

The passage of the charter provided some welcome assistance to Watkins in the achievement of Klan goals. With the elimination of partisan elections, the Klan could hide behind the cloak of fraternalism and yet endorse candidates. It could also spend money, organize its followers, and create a campaign difficult for other candidates to reproduce.

Though the charter had extinguished the party system, it had no obvious effect on the continuing desire of politicians to seek office. At least eight of the twelve candidates had some experience in an elected office. Minor candidates included George Snyder, former postmaster, and David C. Hamilton, former city safety director and treasurer of the Civic League that had met at Wick Park in August. Seeking vindication of their tenures in office, Mayor William G. Reese and former police chief James Watkins also filed. Thomas Muldoon, an Irish-Catholic lawyer, was the strongest candidate from the Democratic party. Other important candidates included Charles Scheible, former service director under George Oles, William J. Williams, former state legislator and chairman of the Charter Commission, and Fred Hartenstein, former mayor and county treasurer. [3]

The final candidate was the Reverend George Gibson, pastor of the Mahoning Avenue Methodist Church. His friends had encouraged him to seek the office, but he fell afoul of the charter requirement that he be a resident and a voter for five years. Although Gibson would have resided in Youngstown for five years as of 1 January 1924, he had not registered as a voter until thirty days after his arrival in 1919. When Gibson withdrew from the race on 1 October, the *Vindicator* commended him for his crusade against vice. It suggested that his decision was a wise one because his aging appearance revealed the burden of such work. [4]

Amid such a welter of candidates, it was evident that the candidate most able to distinguish himself from the crowd in a manner acceptable to the voters would have the best opportunity for election. All the candidates realized that the most important issues in the election were law enforcement and efficient fiscal operation, and each had promised an effective administration in both areas. Thus, the Klan endorsement became the central distinguishing factor of the campaign. After a secret round of interviews and straw polls in the precincts of the city, the Klan publicly endorsed Charles Scheible for mayor in early October. [5] Within the week other candidates linked to the Klan, such as David Hamilton, withdrew and endorsed Scheible. [6] The Klan had thereby strengthened its position and its candidate; it also guaranteed that the central issue of the campaign would be the Klan as an agency of moral reform and social order in Youngstown.

Klan endorsement of, and subsequent unification behind, a single candidate placed pressure on the remaining candidates to follow a similar course, especially if they were to compete with a Klan that might have had as many as 10,000 members by the fall and the potential to attract additional voters through the broad appeal of the Scheible candidacy.[7] Unfortunately the anti-Klan candidates found it impossible to establish a cooperative campaign.

After the withdrawal of several minor candidates, four anti-Klan candidates remained (Williams, Muldoon, Watkins, and Reese). On 1 October, before the Klan endorsement of Scheible, Williams announced a plan to reduce the field to two candidates. He suggested that all twelve candidates submit to a straw vote by a variety of community organizations, including the City Federation of Colored Women and the Crispus Attucks Unity League, as well as the officers and trustees of nationality clubs. Williams explained further that the "two who stay in the race pledge themselves that if elected mayor, no discrimination will be made against any citizen on account of race, nationality, religion, or party, either in appointment or removal of officials and employees, or in the execution and administration of the law." The composition of the voting organizations probably would have guaranteed the elimination of the Klan candidate, a feat Williams undoubtedly hoped to accomplish, but it was all rather obvious. None of the candidates came to a meeting called by Williams for 4 October in his downtown office.[8] The discouraging development for Williams was not so much the absence of potential Klan candidates at the meeting as the lack of response from those opposed to the Klan—an indication, unfortunately for Williams, that factionalism was stronger among the anti-Klan forces.

On 23 October the *Vindicator* made a final effort to unify the anti-Klan forces in a front page editorial calling for a single anti-Klan candidate. Citing the "calamity of religious and racial strife," the *Vindicator* warned that a Klan victory "would be a great misfortune for Youngstown. It would mean a city government greatly influenced, if not controlled, by men meeting in secret, beyond the reach of public opinion and the law, and bent on sowing discord in the community." Furthermore, "it will set neighbor against neighbor, and will utterly ruin the business prospects of the city." The *Vindicator* urged the necessity of citizens' uniting on one anti-Scheible candidate since the five other candidates were unable to do so.[9]

Such urgings did not, however, override the determination of each of the remaining candidates to stay in the race. Reese and Watkins wanted to vindicate themselves against charges of corruption; Muldoon wished to protect his fellow Catholics. His leading supporters and workers—former mayoral candidate Jerry Sullivan, Edward Peebles, Joseph Kennedy, John McEvoy, and John Callan—were all Irish Catholics. With such a narrow base, they decided to pitch his campaign towards the "Catholics, coloreds and foreign-born," a strategy that might have worked if the foreign-born had become naturalized and had registered to vote. It seems evident from voting patterns, however, that the foreign-born procrastinated in assuming the full rights of citizenship and that the Muldoon forces did little to register them.[10]

Muldoon was successful in attracting support from the black community. The Colored Ministerial Association endorsed him, several of them even appearing at his rallies. The Reverend W. O. Harper, of the Third Baptist Church, labeled the Klan anti-black and only interested in keeping the "'nigger' in his proper place." A black woman identified as Mrs. George Bell also appeared at Muldoon rallies. She carefully distinguished between social equality, which she claimed blacks did not want, and their rights as American citizens. "If whites stay in their place," she cried, "so will the Negro."[11]

Thus, Muldoon's campaign had built a secure base among the black and foreign-born communities, but he needed to broaden that base into the white Protestant communities. To do so would have required him to ally with William J. (Jack) Williams, a man with such connections, especially in the upper-class areas of Youngstown. As late as 24 October, Muldoon rejected an offer from Williams to have the two of them and Watkins withdraw from the race in favor of a fourth candidate. According to Muldoon, "no capitalist that controls money is for the people, so keep your eye on Jack."[12] Thus, class differences played a part in the fragmentation of the anti-Klan forces.

Indeed, they were so strong that near the end of the campaign Muldoon directed his fire more at Williams than at Scheible. Muldoon chose a questionnaire sent to all candidates from the Veterans of Foreign Wars as his point of attack. To questions such as "Are you opposed to the Ku Klux Klan?" and "Would you accept their support if same was offered?" Williams made no response, which Muldoon interpreted as support for the Klan. Contending that the best man—as indicated by his own negative response to the questionnaire—had opposed the Klan from the beginning, Muldoon charged that "Mr. Williams was not opposed to the Klan 6 weeks ago and may not be opposed to the Klan 6 weeks from now."[13]

Despite Muldoon's misgivings, Williams did direct his campaign against the Klan. Expecting to "wage a campaign that will break the backbone of this anti-American organization in the Mahoning Valley," Williams spoke insistently about the history and nature of the Klan. He called Colonel Simmons "mentally warped" and labeled the Klan as the "emanation of one man's diseased brain . . . promoted as a purely money-making proposition." Clarke and Tyler, he suggested, were primarily interested in the Klan as a business proposition. According to Williams the good people of Youngstown were "the victims of a highly organized and commercialized system, which capitalizes the troubles of each individual community to put more money into the coffers of kleagles, dragons, wizards, kluds, etc."[14]

Williams warned the citizens that Klan success politically would lead to racial discrimination and a divided community. Labeling the Klan as "unAmerican and unChristian," he suggested that Protestants did have a constitutional right to organize if they did so in a tolerant fashion, as they had in the Federated Council and the Masons. Thus, Williams tried to appeal to the "intelligent Protestant citizens of this city" to open their eyes to the menace he saw looming over his beloved Youngstown.[15]

Williams was the most able of the anti-Klan speakers, but that was only one source of his strength. Williams was also a prominent lawyer who had taken an active role in the city's politics. He had been elected to several terms as a state representative and had worked with both parties in promoting the idea of a federally financed canal to reduce transportation costs in the Youngstown area for its steel producers and in securing a congressionally authorized survey.[16]

Williams also had chaired the Charter Commission, which had recommended a home rule charter for Youngstown. His work for the charter had given him exposure among the reform elements of the city and a base of support. Those desirous of making the charter work (Williams claimed that the new, nonpartisan government, if properly run, could save the city $100,000 per year) formed a Voter's League to screen candidates for mayor. After the league received refusals from many leading contenders, Williams agreed to run with the endorsement of the Voter's League.[17] In its proclamation the committee cited as its reason for endorsement the fact that "the whole government of the city fundamentally depends upon the election of a mayor who is in full sympathy with the spirit of the charter and home rule, and who has the judgment and courage to surround himself with executive officers of like character, and the industry and perserverance to conduct the city government accordingly."[18]

Although Williams's endorsement by the Voter's League would seem to have been an important asset, it must be remembered that such leagues have often represented upper-class interests in urban politics. Business principle and efficiency, rather than machine politics tainted with corruption, became the battle cry of such organizations. Prior to deciding on Williams, the league had sought prominent businessmen as candidates, including department store owners Lucius McKelvey and George Fordyce, before finally settling on Williams when such candidates were not forthcoming. Prominent businessmen on the committee included local steel magnates Joseph G. Butler, Jr., former vice-president of the Brier Hill Steel Company and a director of the American Iron and Steel Institute; James A. Campbell, president of Youngstown Sheet and Tube Company; T. J. Bray, president of Republic Steel; and Julius Kahn, president of Truscon Steel, as well as a host of investors and directors of prominent businesses and banks. His campaign manager, Charles H. Booth, was a director of Youngstown Sheet and Tube and General Fireproofing, a vice-president of both the Republic Rubber Company and United Engineering and Foundry, as well as a board member of the Youngstown Country Club. Their advertisement on behalf of Williams in the local newspapers, accompanied by a list of names, would have served to indicate to the public Williams's base of support among the prominent and to open him to charges such as that leveled by Muldoon that his class interests would betray the people.[19] Clearly, the interest of the leading financiers and industrialists of Youngstown, who had brought in the immigrant and black workers to fill the unskilled, backbreaking positions available in the steel industry, lay in opposition to the Klan. They could ill afford potential conflicts begotten out of prejudice. Williams's support among the upper class was eventually evident in his strong showing in the First Ward, home of the wealthy and prominent.

To win, Williams needed to broaden his base to other classes and to ethnic voters, but charges that he had covertly sought Klan support plagued his campaign. On 14 October the kleagle, Colonel C. A. Gunder, after refusing to debate with "Jack" Williams, claimed that Williams had been offered support by the Klan, had accepted that support, and then had backed out. Labeling Williams a "turncoat," Gunder advocated that the Klan was better off seeking to build its membership than debating Williams.[20]

Williams, of course, denied the Klan version of their meeting. He contended that he had visited the kleagle in his offices a month earlier, upon the advice of some friends, in the hope that the Klan might assume a neutral stance in the mayoral race. The kleagle, however, suggested a poll of the city to determine the one candidate seen as most likely to run a clean government—all others would drop out. It was then that Williams came up with his own plan, never to be implemented, for narrowing the field. Gunder allegedly boasted that "the real and only issue in the coming election is between Christ and Satan, between Heaven and Hell, between Protestantism and the Pope of Rome" and that he could easily defeat Williams or any other candidate.[21]

The Klan newspaper, the Youngstown *Citizen*, published the Gunder story. It editorialized that "Jack had been willing to flirt with the Klan and the Kamelias, and he did flirt with them." Editor D. Web Brown continued the attack with a warning about the "murderous intent of our local Jack Walton Williams." Williams cried libel and at one point sought the arrest of Brown.[22]

Whether the Klan was employing "dirty tricks" against one of its stronger opponents or the meeting itself created misunderstanding, both Muldoon and Watkins chose to take advantage of Gunder's charges. They repeatedly tied Williams to the Klan because of his neutral response to the questionnaire from the Veterans of Foreign Wars. How could anyone against the Klan not answer negatively, they asked. His defense was to claim that he wanted to keep the Klan issue out of politics altogether by ignoring it. By early November, Williams was speaking to a half-filled hall at the Moose Auditorium instead of a turnaway crowd.[23] His isolation as a candidate of the Voters League was apparent.

The factionalism and infighting among the anti-Klan forces lightened the work of the Klan. Having concentrated its energies on a single candidate, the Klan was able to operate as a political party under a charter that forbade Democratic or Republican nominations for office—a possibility overlooked by charter reformers in their zeal for nonpartisan elections. Not only had the Klan nominated a candidate for office but it also had an organization of two men and two women in each precinct to canvass families. The women's organization, the Kamelias, assisted with their own "parlor" visits.[24]

The Klan's candidate, Charles Scheible, was also a source of strength. Picked after the Klan had conducted a straw poll throughout the city, Scheible had established an impeccable reputation for his previous political service. He had served as service director under George Oles in an administration whose foolishness appealed to Youngstowners because its heart was in the right place. Scheible continued under William Reese, but Reese fired him amid rumors that he was considering running for mayor. An irritated city council responded with a resolution thanking him for the "splendid and efficient manner with which he handled the affairs of the Service Director's office during his term as director." Even the *Vindicator* admitted that "there will be no objection to the candidate the Klan has chosen. Mr. Scheible is a clean-cut, capable man, experienced in public affairs and with a record to which no one can take exception." Naïvely suggesting that there was no reason why he should not accept the Klan endorsement, the *Vindicator* believed that Mr. Scheible could serve all of the people. It expressed relief that the Klan had been so straightforward so early in the campaign.[25]

Charles Scheible had no previous experience in an elected office but had utilized his appointment as service director to impress the local electorate and opinion-makers of Youngstown. Because of his business background, Scheible seemed capable of bringing the two most mentioned qualities of honesty and efficiency to the mayor's seat. Scheible's physical appearance was stolid and respectable. Some might have labeled him colorless, but the packaging provided by the Klan enlivened his campaign with marches and monster rallies. Scheible's appearances were numerous, his words sparse. He was prone to blushing, yet the Reverend Gibson contended that the women admired this trait.[26] A reticent Scheible could not stand alone, however, and so the Klan surrounded him with enthusiastic orators, including the Reverend Gibson, an ambitious local attorney named Clyde Osborne, and, most flamboyant of all, Colonel Evan A. Watkins. At a time when people appreciated the skills of oratory and were willing to listen for hours, Watkins captivated and controlled his audience. His stories from the Bible, the Middle East, and Europe, his familiarity with a variety of subjects, and his energetic presentations drew in large audiences interested in learning about the candidates and seeking entertainment.

Watkins did not allow his credibility to rest solely on his oratorical abilities, however. He claimed to have resided and married in Youngstown some forty years earlier. Watkins's sister-in-law, Mary Dyer, was still alive and a lifelong resident of Youngstown. Watkins also used his birthplace (Blaina, Wales, near the family farm of the Reverend R. E. Williams, of the Wilson Avenue Baptist Church) as a basis for a very close and supportive friendship.[27]

Local residence, local memories, and local relationships served Watkins well, but the final mark of acceptance came with his appointment as the pastor of the First Baptist Church in Girard. Allegedly a

Congregational minister on leave, Watkins assumed the pastorate in July 1923, thus securing a privileged position, a salary, and influence with his fellow ministers. His weekly sermons attracted overflow crowds into the small but attractive edifice. Disappointed members of the congregation stood outside the open windows to be nourished by the word according to Watkins.[28]

The thrust of the Watkins campaign was a well-designed effort to project Scheible as an upright Christian businessman concerned about the morality of the city and the efficiency of the government. According to Watkins, Scheible had no desire to discriminate against anyone on any basis, but he did want to enforce the law—to display the determination necessary for a government official to clean up the city. When Watkins appeared, along with Scheible, at a prominent black church, Bethany Baptist, his nine-point program included

1. civic and public improvements without adding to taxes;
2. honest and economical expenditures of monies;
3. strict law enforcement;
4. suppression of the liquor trade and other immorality;
5. an honest, efficient police force and "a clean, fearless chief";
6. equal treatment for all regardless of race, color, or creed;
7. no cabinet appointments based on political favors;
8. selection of employees based on fitness;
9. a promise to campaign "with malice toward none" and to "do my duty as God and man have a right to expect me to do it."[29]

Clyde Osborne and Fred Warnock, former mayor and future grand titan of the Klan, would echo these themes of honesty, morality, law enforcement, efficiency, and nondiscrimination in other speeches given on behalf of Scheible throughout the city.[30]

Although Clyde Osborne would assert that if he "thought that Scheible was intolerant, I should not support him and would not ask you to," his speeches at times revealed the underlying resentments and prejudices that attracted many to the Klan. Osborne, for instance, voiced his opposition to parochial schools and to Muldoon "until certain things happen to bring his people into Americanism." Jews, he noted, had a right to sell their wares, but the money they earned should be spent in the entire community, not just among other Jews.[31]

On 22 October an unidentified Klan leader met with the *Vindicator* to discuss Klan goals. He expressed grave concern that parochial schools taught children the principle of church rule, thus violating the

constitutional principle of separation of church and state. The best solution in his mind was the required attendance of every child (age 6 to
16) in a public school, where the values of Americanism and patriotism could be taught. The Klan leader also advocated laws to ban racial intermarriage and to segregate schools and teachers.[32] After
reading the *Vindicator* report, it should have been difficult for anyone
to see the Klan as an organization that promoted brotherhood.

It should have been even more difficult for close observers of the
campaign. Fifteen hundred Kamelia women packed the Epworth Methodist Episcopal church to hear Miss Dorothy Nickols, a former Catholic, who claimed she had been held captive at the House of the Good
Shepherd in Chicago. "Storms of applause" followed her description of
life in that convent: severe punishments, inadequate food, and even
recycled, but unpurified, bath water—obviously, a variant of the
escaped-nun tales that arose during previous anti-Catholic crusades.
Rumors also abounded: classic tales of Catholic fathers who purchased
a gun to be placed in St. Columba's basement whenever a child was
born and of Catholic efforts to build a palace in Washington for the
pope.[33]

These resentments and prejudices enabled the Klan to focus on itself as a defensive organization. To many Klan members it seemed that
other religious bodies had organized themselves as a way of promoting
their religion and its followers. The Catholic church, with its hierar-
chical structure, constituted a unified and threatening force to Protestants with a divided constituency. The Federated Council of Churches
represented only a very recent development in Protestant unity,
whereas Catholics long had joined the Knights of Columbus and Jews
the B'nai B'rith.

Why couldn't Protestants form an organization too?, asked Colonel
Watkins—not to discriminate against other religions but to protect
Protestantism. After all, the Constitution guaranteed the right of freedom of assembly; Protestants were simply exercising that right by joining the Klan. Watkins's charge that "a sect may find its way into
political power and so exercise and usurp the privilege of office as to
make themselves unbearable to others" hinted that Catholics controlled
Youngstown's politics, but he would have been hard pressed to prove
the charge. The leading Democrats were Catholic, but the Republicans
usually won the elections. Although Watkins publicly acknowledged
the example of Father Edward Mears, of St. Columba's, the seat of the
Catholic hierarchy in Youngstown, in the promotion of Protestant-
Catholic toleration, he warned "that is not the spirit today and the Klan
will remain until it passes away."[34]

The tie of the Klan campaign to Protestantism was most apparent in the widespread support of Protestant ministers, especially from the Presbyterian, Methodist, and Baptist faiths. Such support lent the Klan an aura of respectability and access to a wide audience dependent upon, but not necessarily controlled by, ministerial leadership. Numerous ministers, such as A. E. Griffith, of the Pleasant Grove United Presbyterian Church; John Heslip, of the Tabernacle United Presbyterian Church; R. E. Williams, of the Himrod Avenue Baptist Church; and, of course, George Gibson, joined the Scheible campaign and spoke from his platform. Other ministers indicated support from their pulpits. In the Brier Hill section, Scheible's neighborhood as a child, the Reverend I. H. Amore, of the Grace Evangelical Church, placed two portraits of Charles Scheible near the altar.[35]

The ministers generally reiterated a defensive posture as the cause of Protestant support for the Klan, and yet they discounted the notion that the Klan would discriminate. The Reverend Mr. Heslip was an archetype of this posture. Although not a Klan member because of his foreign birth, Heslip defended the Klan against attacks that it was lawless and cited press reports as a "propaganda of lies." He countercharged that an unidentified "invisible organization" was penalizing Christians "for being an American and obeying the laws of God and the State." A Christian grocer, he noted, might observe the Sunday closing law, but his competitor stayed open with impunity. On the other hand, Heslip labeled the Klan as not truly Protestant if it opposed people because of their race or religion, if it denied basic rights, or if it took the law into its own hands.[36]

Heslip's attitudes appear self-serving, and yet he was seemingly sincere in condemning the failure of a Protestant to love all human beings without prejudice. The key to understanding Heslip is his contention that the Klan would be truly Protestant if it "stands for free American institutions, for maintenance of the public school and for the teaching of the Bible in all the schools."[37] Free institutions implied rights, such as freedom of speech and religion, admitted Heslip, but also imposed the obligation to obey and to enforce the laws. In citing the Sunday blue laws and other laws relating to morality as the most important laws needing enforcement, however, Heslip was obviously unable to distinguish between what was Protestant and what was American. Although Protestants had disavowed the establishment of religion in America, they nonetheless had enacted laws that reflected what Protestants considered to be the moral life. What Catholics or Jews might see as Protestant culture in America was viewed by Protestants as a universal moral code. Failure to obey was not a cultural difference, then, but disobedience to the law of the country—a morally reprehensible act requiring punishment by the legal authorities. It was Heslip's hope that Charles Scheible would fearlessly enforce that law because "there are certain citizens of Youngstown who have been strongly discriminated against, and they are American citizens who believe in obeying the laws of God and man."[38]

Many ministers who did not support the Klan shared Heslip's views. Dr. W. H. Hudnut, of the First Presbyterian Church, who condemned the Klan and argued for the equality of blacks, chastised his flock for tolerating the European Sabbath. Other laws, he charged, were also selectively obeyed; "as a city we are standing by and allowing the wanton disobedience of the laws to be flaunted in our face and saying nothing."[39] Protestant law and order, then, was a rallying cry for the general public in Youngstown and a goal divorced in their minds from religious prejudice. This frame of reference enabled Watkins to portray Charles Scheible successfully as a Christian candidate capable of enforcing the law and not a bigot. It also enabled Youngstowners to change their minds about the Klan.

As the campaign heated up in the few weeks before election day, the candidates appeared more and more frequently. Mistakenly believing that the Klan was reprehensible in the public eye, Williams tried to discredit Scheible by claiming that he was a Klan member. Scheible denied the charge, but Williams countered with Colonel Watkins's description of the Warren Klan parade on 6 October as being led by an unmasked candidate for mayor of Youngstown. Since Scheible was the only Klan candidate, it was logical, Williams argued, to assume that he was a member at least in substance if not in form.[40] Williams's other trump card was the appearance of U.S. Supreme Court Justice John Clarke, a native Youngstowner, on a stage "filled with honorary vice-chairmen from the ranks of the best citizens of the community." Some of the "best citizens" were from eastern Europe. Williams also received an endorsement from the Slovak-American Political Federation and from the Mahoning Valley Dry League—an important indication that some of the leading Prohibitionists rejected the Klan, yet felt confident in Williams's desire and ability to enforce the Eighteenth Amendment.[41]

Meanwhile, Muldoon and Watkins continued to believe that attacks on Williams would constitute their best chance of winning. After Williams secured the endorsement of the Slovak-American Political Federation, Muldoon managed to secure withdrawal of that support by some of the subsidiary federation clubs and an endorsement of Slovaks for Muldoon.[42] Such infighting improved Muldoon's position with regard to Williams; but Muldoon was still a Catholic, and, as the *Vindicator* had already pointed out, many Protestants and Catholics feared for the ability of a Catholic to govern under such circumstances.[43]

The overall Williams campaign strategy was a simple one: expose the Klan, reveal its misdeeds, examine its prejudices, and the public would withhold its votes. Williams fulfilled his part of the premise, but the public lagged behind. As the campaign progressed, Williams drew a much smaller audience. His misreading of the size of Klan support in Youngstown, as well as his inability to unite the anti-Klan candidates, meant his defeat in the general election.

Despite the emotion-charged atmosphere generated by the mayoral campaign, it was surprisingly free of fights and violence. Still, some incidents did occur. On 30 October at a Scheible rally, while Watkins was speaking, a group of men and boys appeared at the open windows hooting and jeering. As some men tried to close the windows, rotten apples and vegetables pelted the audience. Watkins, however, quieted Scheible supporters with an assertion that rival candidates had played no part in the attack, only some rowdy boys. At nearly the same time across town at St. Anthony's Church, Thomas Muldoon was asking his supporters to remember that "if we can't lick them by ballots, then we'll lick them with bullets." The statement was an isolated comment and more an indication of the frustration felt by Muldoon. As a matter of fact, the next day at a Rotary Club meeting Muldoon retreated, denying that he meant the bullet remark.[44]

In contrast, the Scheible campaign took the proverbial high road. Scheible projected the image of a candidate above the fray and above discrimination—in short, a good Christian, an efficient businessman, an honest politician who could without bias bring moral and economic order to a beleaguered Youngstown. Meanwhile, his opponents were less restrained, more vituperative, and more likely to attack.

Unlike Muldoon the local Catholic church avoided the fray. Priests issued no statements and endorsed no candidate. Bishop Joseph Schrembs, however, whose seat in Cleveland extended to Youngstown, visited the city late in October to endorse the *Vindicator* campaign against religious hatred and intolerance. Without mentioning any candidates or organizations, he left it up to the priests to advise their parishioners on candidates.[45] Whether the priests did so is unrecorded; at best, it was done privately and not from the pulpit.

As election day approached, it was evident that this had been the most exciting campaign in years. The Friday night before the election,

the Scheible forces mounted an "impromptu" parade after a rally at the
Rayen Auditorium. Led by the Warren Kilty Band and Kleagle C. A.
Gunder, more than 2,000 Scheible supporters marched or rode in automobiles along a parade route marked by red flares. Fireworks added
to the pageantry and reminded people of the torchlight parades that
had been so prevalent in American politics before the advent of street
lighting.[46]

The campaign had obviously sparked intense interest among the voters. Registration peaked at more than 43,000 voters (43 percent of
whom were women), the highest total ever. The presidential election of
1920 had drawn out 35,000 voters—a number that nearly always ex-
ceeded that of local elections.[47] But this election stirred the apathetic;
it demanded participation either out of fear of discrimination or because an urban millennium and a proper cleansing of the social order
seemed at hand. The possibility of a new order directed by the voters
and not the politicians or parties had replaced the politics of corruption and muddling through.

Tuesday, 6 November, was a sunny day in Youngstown. Despite the
animosity of the contest, no incidents, fights, or brawls occurred. In
the mayoral election Scheible won a surprising majority (51.7 percent
or 20,944) in a field of six. Muldoon was second with 11,367 and
Williams third with only 5,345. The Klan also won five of seven council races, with a sixth eventually decided in its favor by a recount held
by the newly elected council. And, finally, the victory of four endorsed
candidates guaranteed a Klan majority on the school board. In spite of
the fact that Youngstown's population was only one-third native-born,
the Klan had won decisively.[48]

Geographically, Klan support was strongest on the south side of
Youngstown (the Fourth through the Seventh wards), a middle-class
area, with pockets of the poor and immigrants, close to the Mahoning
River. As recently as 1899, few people had resided there, but the
completion of the Market Street bridge in that year invited swift development. By 1920 more than half of Youngstown residents lived be-
low the river. Scheible captured about 60 percent of the vote in each
of those wards, losing only precincts close to the river. Klan council
candidates also captured about 60 percent of the votes cast on the
south side.

Above the river the Klan was less successful. The Second and Third
wards housed the largest numbers of new immigrants and blacks; the
First was the home of the wealthiest residents and of the owners and
managers of the mills, who had supported Williams. Scheible lost the

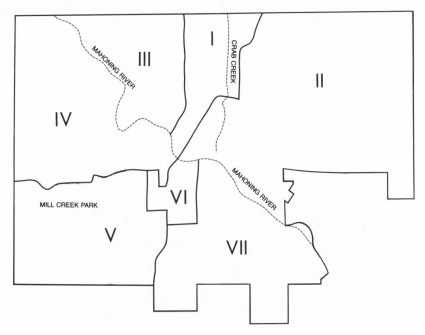

Youngstown Wards—1923

Second Ward to Muldoon with only 24.3 percent of the vote, but un-expectedly won a plurality in the other wards. Williams had been ex-pected to win the First Ward, but finished 500 votes behind Scheible, in second place. This was the only ward in which he beat Muldoon. Scheible's success meant that he had garnered broad-based support from the wealthy and the poor native-born residents, as well as the middle class that lived on the south side.

The broad-based appeal of the Klan was also apparent in the coun-cil races. Besides easy victories on the south side, Klan candidates were plurality winners in the Second and Third wards, primarily be-cause of the number of candidates. In the First Ward several candi-dates, including the eventual winner, Harry Payne, had refused the Klan's endorsement, and so there was no indication of Klan strength, except for the Scheible results, in that ward.

Thus, the Klan victory rested upon broad-based support from all sections of the city. Such widespread support was an indication that its followers were not simple fanatics or unrestrained bigots; rather, they believed themselves to be defenders of a Protestant culture that was essential to the preservation of a moral society. Colonel Watkins had effectively tailored the Klan message to a community not willing to admit its biases. Although Williams campaigned primarily on the theme of Klan prejudices and violence, he did admit that "2/3rds of the membership of the Ku Klux Klan in this Valley is directly attributable to the lack of law observance and to lawless conditions which result."[49] It was unfortunate, Williams said, that an organization such as the Klan "has capitalized the bad conditions in our existing municipal government. Fully 50% of its members have joined because they sought to improve these conditions. After the earnest men and women of this city have worked for years to improve conditions, this organization comes in here and tells the men standing out in the field at night that the Klan alone stands for clean government."[50]

To celebrate Scheible's victory, the Klan organized one of the largest parades ever held in Youngstown. Mayor Reese had denied a permit, but Judge J. H. Lyon, of the Court of Common Pleas, issued an injunction on 9 November to permit the parade.[51] Numerous special railway cars festooned with banners arrived at the Erie Depot in Youngstown on 10 November. More than 50,000 people from Mahoning County and surrounding counties in Ohio and Pennsylvania gathered at Dead Man's Curve, on the Youngstown-Boardman border, in the afternoon. Thirty of the Protestant churches had erected lunch rooms, and the women were busy preparing and serving the food. That night at least 20,000 Klan members marched the streets on the south side of Youngstown without disorder. Some wore masks; most did not. Numerous floats identified the marchers as "100% Americans" and proclaimed the need for nonsectarian schools. A blown-open Klan safe was also on display.[52]

On 12 November, Charles Scheible spoke at the First Baptist Church. "I can not think," he said, "that the Mayor of a large city like ours can afford to be a stranger in a Christian Church." He promised the parishioners that, insofar as possible, there would not be any alliance of his administration with crime or evil, and he thanked them for their support. "The Church," he said, "played no small part in my election. Most of my meetings were held in churches. I appealed to the patriotism of the Sanctuary rather than to the leadership of the slums and as a result I won the battle."[53]

4

Into the Rest of the Valley

Jesus continued his tour of all the towns and villages. He
taught in their synagogues, He proclaimed the good news of
God's reign.

—Matthew 9:35

The crowd cheered as they recognized the exploding portrait of
Doyle Glossner, the Trumbull County kleagle. Glossner had left
Youngstown the previous March after his arrest to klux other parts
of the Mahoning Valley. His success in Trumbull County was now
being celebrated at the county fairgrounds in the evening of 6 October
1923.

Traffic earlier had been at a standstill in downtown Warren. A
crowd estimated at 25,000 had gathered in the public square, and
Mayor John McBride scrambled down from the reviewing stand to restore order. Although the Klan had predicted that 50,000 would participate in its parade, only 8,000 to 10,000 marchers in delegations
from Alliance, Canton, Massillon, Ashtabula, and Cleveland, as well
as Mahoning and Trumbull counties, were taking part. The parade
might have attracted more marchers had the mayor not forbidden a
masked parade, but the numbers were more than enough for a city the
size of Warren.

Klan members had gathered in the late afternoon at the county fairgrounds, where churchwomen provided refreshments. After a round of
music and speeches, the delegations lined up, some carrying banners,
others accompanying floats. The Mahoning County delegation had prepared a float with an exploded safe and a sign warning that "You may
rob our safe but not our spirit. True Americans do not burglarize."
Overhead an airplane circled with an electric cross visible to marchers
and observers alike. The theme of the parade was "One Flag, One
School, One Bible."[1]

55

The success of that day was a heady brew for the Klan to quaff. It was an indication that Youngstown might not be the only valley city to succumb to Klan political control. After all, these cities shared the common bonds of a New England heritage, a dependence on the iron and steel industry, and a rapid influx of numerous southern and eastern European immigrants. Although the valley cities might differ in some particulars, they were all gasping at the speed of change wrought by industrialization. A brief review of each city's history and the activities of the Klan in each community will highlight these commonalities.

WARREN

Warren was a city proud of its tradition. Trumbull County was named after Jonathan Trumbull, one of Connecticut's governors, and the township of Warren after Moses Warren, a member of the party sent in 1796 to survey Connecticut's Western Reserve. Although the land belonged to Connecticut, the largest number of early settlers came from Washington County, Pennsylvania, among them one Ephraim Quinby, who laid out a traditional New England town square in 1800.

In that same year Arthur St. Clair, governor of the Northwest Territory, designated Warren as the seat of Trumbull County government, which at that time comprised the entire Western Reserve. This designation guaranteed Warren's growth based on its role as an administrative center. Although the creation of other counties by 1810 would limit Warren's domain to the eastern part of Ohio, its population continued to grow.

After 1840 Warren profited and grew because of the canal, but not nearly as much as other cities on the Mahoning River. In the late 1840s the southern half of the county separated to form Mahoning County, with its seat at Canfield. Although Warren remained the Trumbull County seat, it now fell far behind Youngstown in population and growth. By 1900 Warren's population was only 8,529, and only one iron works, the Warren Rolling Mill, achieved any measure of success.[2]

And yet Warren retained a reputation as a desirable place to live. Joseph Butler praised Warren for "its culture, its municipal attractiveness and even more for its political prestige." Claiming that Warren was "one of the most beautiful cities of Ohio," Butler cited its New

England design, the public square, and the "stately" Trumbull County Courthouse as evidence. Beautiful elm trees lined many of the streets with shady arches. To Butler's eyes dirt and trash were least visible in Warren of all the Mahoning Valley communities.[3]

Politically Warren was a center of Republicanism. Prior to the Civil War, many of its inhabitants had subscribed to the antislavery cause and joined the Republican party as its leading advocate. Along with Ashtabula, Lake, and Geauga counties, Trumbull County constituted a congressional district upon which the Republicans could count to build a majority that often balanced the Democratic vote in the rest of the state. That district had produced James A. Garfield, who kicked off his presidential campaign of 1880 in Warren. Warren would also serve as a center for the National American Woman Suffrage Association from 1903 to 1910. The treasurer of that organization, Harriet Taylor Upton, was a Warren resident and also the author of a history of the Western Reserve.[4]

By 1900 prestige was not enough for Warren residents. The continued expansion of nearby Youngstown inspired a group of residents to form the Warren Board of Trade in 1905. In 1910, with O. R. Grimmesey as president, the board of trade began an advertising campaign to attract new industries. Backed by a variety of businesses and financial institutions, the board purchased a parcel of land close to railroad facilities, which it donated to businesses that located there. The board recouped the investment by buying more land than needed and selling off the excess. Within ten years thirty-three industrial concerns located in Warren, including the Trumbull Steel Company. Warren's entire downtown was either remodeled or expanded, and the population rose from 11,081 in 1910 to 27,050 in 1920. Optimistic Warrenites predicted that population figures would reach 50,000 by 1930.[5]

Boosterism is a widely accepted phenomenon in American cities. It promises growth and enhanced wealth, as well as recognition and prestige. In the nineteenth century cities fought each other over railroad connections; in the early twentieth century, over major industries. Warren was a belated, but nonetheless serious, entrant into the competition.

The roaring fires and belching smokestacks that appeared along the Mahoning River attracted a new breed of worker, but as in Youngstown, the influx of unskilled peasants from Greece, Hungary, Italy, Yugoslavia, and Romania (see appendix B, table B-1) challenged the customs of that city in a way that would prove irritating to old-line

Warrenites. According to Butler, "the population was largely of American lineage and proud of its record in this respect."[6]

The efforts of Mayor John McBride to upgrade enforcement of the blue laws in the fall of 1922 was an example of escalating irritation between the different cultures. McBride ordered his police force to close all nonessential businesses on Sunday, but he exempted confectionaries, movies, dairies, newsstands, and gasoline stations. A letter from South Pine Street merchants indicating that the majority of them wished to close on Sunday had inspired McBride's directive.[7]

This situation prompted a lengthy editorial in the *Warren Tribune Chronicle*. The editors commiserated with the mayor on the thankless task of satisfying everyone, but then proceeded to criticize his policy of partial enforcement. "Particularly was it a mistake," according to the paper, "to begin it in the 'flats' or so-called foreign section. Our foreign population already has the idea that their chief part in the community is to be arrested and exploited and this move only strengthens that unfortunate feeling."[8]

Blue law enforcement was only part of a developing concern about the morals of Warren. The Reverend C. M. Hare, from Columbus, spoke to the Trumbull County Dry Enforcement League in February 1923. He chided the membership that Trumbull County was "rich enough to lock up every bootlegger in the county," yet had not done so. Many speakers who suggested that light penalties were at fault advocated the replacement of fines by jail sentences with no parole possible.[9]

The conviction that Prohibition enforcement was not working could probably be traced back to an article in the *Youngstown Telegram* in December 1922 that accused Warren of permitting open operation of vice dens. A reporter who visited the Greek American Club claimed to have seen $50,000 in greenbacks and silver. Chief of Police B. J. Gillen denounced the report as "hoakum," and Mayor McBride wrote a letter to the *Telegram* asking for evidence. Gillen contended that the den in question had been raided many times, and the operators fined. The problem of continued operation at that spot, according to Gillen, was the renting of the club to a new proprietor each time an arrest was made.[10] Nonetheless, by January Gillen felt the necessity of responding to the criticism by conducting numerous raids; he also made an unfilled request for twelve more policemen.[11]

Although the *Tribune Chronicle* had chastised those who called Warren "rotten and depraved," it too supported renewed efforts to improve vice law enforcement. In the same editorial that questioned blue laws enforcement, the *Tribune Chronicle* suggested getting "the big gambling places when they spring up." "Let's get the big bootleggers, let's clean out commercialized vice as far as possible," the newspaper cried, "but let's not waste our ammunition on little things like an open ice cream parlor or corner store." The use of "as far as possible" was revealing of the newspaper's evaluation of just how successful such a campaign could be.[12]

Most of the county churches agreed with the *Tribune Chronicle*'s request for a better moral climate. In November 1922 the churches had held a conference under the auspices of the Council of the Ohio Federation of Churches to discuss public morals. The ministers in attendance agreed that there was a need for the churches to work for cleaner motion pictures, international peace, and law enforcement. The following day they formed the Trumbull County Council of Churches to spearhead a campaign of spiritual regeneration during the first three months of 1923.[13]

The Klan's hand was not apparent in the initial stages of Warren's moral crusade, but its presence was lurking in the background. The nearby Youngstown Klan had already made a public appearance, and the first kleagle in Youngstown, Doyle Glossner, had since moved on to the Warren area. He was probably making contacts with ministers, fraternal organizations, and the Warren Automobile Club, from which would come the Klan's exalted cyclops, Dr. B. A. Hart.

The first indication of the Klan's presence was the appearance of Dr. E. A. Watkins as a lecturer for the Warren Masons in April.[14] After another speech at the International Order of Odd Fellows Hall on 30 April, Dr. Watkins asked 100 percent Americans (a codeword for Klan members) to stay after the speech. Apparently the Klan had not drawn the same measure of support as in nearby Youngstown and was proceeding cautiously.[15] These indirect tactics were reminiscent of the Klan's use of the Youngstown Civic League under the Reverend George Gibson.

On Sunday night, 13 May, about 10 o'clock, Klan members from Ohio and Pennsylvania crept from their cars into fourteen different locations throughout the county. They set up and lit crosses anywhere from three to eighteen feet in height, exploded aerial bombs to attract attention, and then melted into the night. Only in Monumental Park in Warren were any Klan members observed. A number of men from a nearby poolroom rushed out to tear down the fiery cross only to be challenged by the surprised Klan members. A pistol was fired, and a bullet pierced the coat of a workman from Trumbull Steel. Within minutes the police arrived to break up the confrontation. [16]

The following evening the Klan held its first public initiation on Cortland Road, just north of Warren. Although newspapermen were invited, there were few security guards to keep the curious out. In front of an estimated 1,500 to 2,000 persons, Klan officials enrolled more than one hundred new members. According to these officials, the Klan had already initiated 3,500 members in Trumbull County. [17]

The appearance of the crosses frightened many Catholics, as well as black families. In response T. H. Deming, the editor of the *Tribune Chronicle*, chastised the Klan for its tactic of engendering fear among Catholics, blacks, and Jews. Although Deming admitted that he had not heard of any attacks on these groups, he suggested that such tactics would lead to retaliation and a possible race or religious war. History, he warned, should have taught the Klan that nothing but harm could come from such wars. He encouraged the Klan not to "let passion and hatred and folly break the bonds of friendship and mutual respect and confidence that now exist between you and all of us." He closed with a plea not to "bring the name of our beloved city into disrepute." [18] This editorial was to be the last written about the Klan. Whether the Klan threatened to withdraw advertising, as done in other cities, is uncertain.

Whatever the cause, Klan activities were not as fully chronicled as in Youngstown. Thus, it is difficult to determine how closely the Warren Klan followed the pattern in Youngstown. Certainly Warren duplicated the industrialization, the type of immigration, and the concern about moral atmosphere that was occurring in Youngstown. Except for the political arena, however, details regarding Klan activities and internal politics were sparse.

Warren was too small to adopt a home rule charter under the Ohio Constitution. Unlike Youngstown, the Klan did not have the advantage of functioning as a quasi-political party in a nonpartisan election; it would have to work within the established parties. The attraction of the Republican party for pietists and old-stock Americans made it a logical organization for the Klan to infiltrate.

The Republican primary of August 1923 attracted five candidates, the most important of which were John H. Marshall and George C. Braden. The influence of Klan-associated issues on the campaign was evident when Braden, a well-known businessman and a longtime official of the Board of Trade, declared his candidacy in May. Absolute

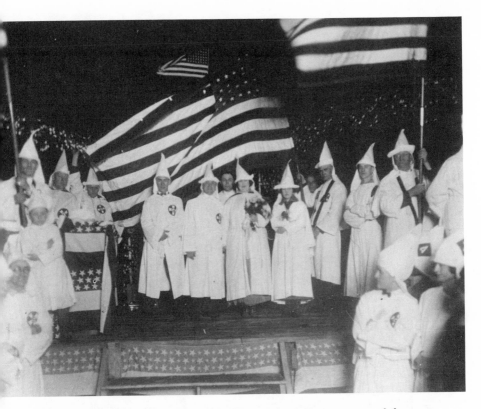

The Klan often held weddings at its rallies and meetings as part of the pageantry to attract more members. (Courtesy of The Mahoning Valley Historical Society, Youngstown, Ohio.)

law enforcement was his thrust, and he suggested that the aliens living in the Flats area must conform, although he promised that he had no intention of preying on the immigrant community.[19]

Braden did not receive the Klan's endorsement, however; Klan support went instead to Marshall, who was a real estate agent. In a rather quiet campaign that emphasized handshaking more than rhetoric, Marshall called for strict enforcement of Prohibition laws; he suggested that "proper respect to our Constitution and American ideals cannot be shown unless these laws are rigidly enforced." On 14 August Marshall won with more than 60 percent of the vote. The total number of votes, 6,786, was at least 3,000 larger than in any previous election. The

Tribune Chronicle characterized the Klan as well-organized and a "factor to be reckoned with."[20]

In November, Marshall's opponent was the incumbent, John McBride, a Democrat who had won the August primary easily. As an elected official attuned to the political tides, McBride had already initiated a variety of attempts to crack down on vice, including Gillen's January raids that closed down eighteen dives. In April, McBride and Gillen banned the sale of baseball and racing pools in Warren. McBride even went so far as to refuse permission for a dance marathon to be held in Warren on the basis that the marathon would ruin the dancers' health.[21]

The results of the August primary caused McBride to escalate his vice crusade. Within the week he sent a letter to his safety director urging a shakeup of the police force. According to reports forwarded to the mayor, policemen were visiting "questionable houses" while in uniform and staying as guests. McBride demanded an investigation into these charges and dismissal of those involved.[22] Whether McBride was sincere in his efforts is impossible to determine. It is important to note, however, that the Klan did not attempt to press charges against McBride before Governor Donahey, as was done in Youngstown and Niles.

Klan efforts on behalf of Marshall peaked a month before the election with a parade on 6 October through downtown Warren. The success of the parade—and the politically inspired presence of Mayor McBride on the reviewing stand—swelled Klan estimates of its power. Having cautiously infiltrated the Republican party as a potential ally and base of loyal voters, the Klan now felt strong enough to separate itself from the party. It published and distributed a Sample Educational Ballot that advised Klan members to vote only for Marshall, Willard S. Eatwell for president of council, and Frank S. Watters for auditor from the Republican ticket, and to cross over to vote for Henry L. Coe, a Democrat, and H. J. Nicolay, an independent, for councilmen. Incensed, the Republican Executive Committee refused to support the split ticket and even went so far as to return the party contributions of Marshall and the other Republican candidates. Republican campaign literature, however, continued to support Marshall, Eatwell, and Watters.[23] The upshot was the formation of a Klan ticket and the creation of a race in which candidates were more appropriately identified as Klan or Anti-Klan.

Mayor McBride ran a two-pronged campaign against the Klan. As an incumbent he pointed to the accomplishments of his three years in office—measured in the number of miles of new paving, sidewalks, sewers, and water lines. McBride was also proud that the expansion of the waterworks (from two million to eight million gallons) had led to a reduction in water rates and a self-supporting plant. For these reasons he identified himself as a "good business mayor." The other prong was an accusation that the Klan was sowing hatred between Catholic and Protestant. "It is the issue of the people, their happiness, their homes, their contentment," according to one Democratic ad, "against the Klan, the 'Invisible Empire,' with all of its MOCKERY, PREJUDICES and HATE." The Democratic Committee suggested to Republicans that Marshall's bolting from the Republican ticket relieved them of the responsibility to vote for him because his loyalty was now to the Klan. A vote for Marshall, according to the Democrats, would bring disgrace on the city of Warren.[24]

A committee of unidentified Warrenites labeled the Warren Good Government League assisted the Democratic campaign. In a series of ads, the league bemoaned the "present intolerable conditions of Hate, Persecution, Proscription, Boycott and Enmity." It chided the Klan that all Catholics, Jews, blacks, and foreigners would not simply leave the country; a fight was the only possibility. It warned businessmen that Klan rule would bring "suspicion, boycott, retaliation and enmity" to disrupt business conditions. And worst of all, the actions of the Klan government would be dictated by the "Grand Lizard" in Atlanta. The only way the league saw to restore the "pleasant, harmonious, friendly conditions and associations that prevailed a year ago" was a substantial defeat for the Klan and its candidates.[25]

As election day approached, few other organizations took a public position regarding the Klan. The *Tribune Chronicle* wrote no editorials and printed no stories of the controversial national activities of the Klan, except for a front-page report on 24 October concerning a speech of Hiram Evans that detailed the Klan platform. In that speech Evans labeled blacks as inferior, Jews as "unblendable," and Catholics as more loyal to Rome than to Washington. It appeared that the newspaper was making a limited attempt to counter the local Klan's claim to be a "religious movement of American brotherhood."[26]

In sermons delivered the week before the election, ministers were surprisingly silent. Only the Reverend M. A. Spencer, of the First Presbyterian Church, spoke on "The Spirit of Intolerance." "Now we come," he asserted, "to the strangest form of Intolerance of all, the rebirth of a hooded secret society to carry out the policies of the Know Nothing Party which flourished in the 50s and of the APA which was strong in the 90s." He condemned the Klan for violating "the spirit of toleration and enlightened freedom which peculiarly distinguishes the American system of popular government." Other sermons urged churchgoers to vote, but did not direct them toward any particular candidate.[27] The absence of pulpit endorsement of the Klan did not mean a lack of ministerial or churchgoing membership in that organization, or a lack of support, as indicated by the churchwomen who provided refreshments at the Klan parade in October. It did mean that secrecy played a larger role in Warren than in surrounding cities.

On election day in Warren, almost 12,000 voters turned out, 5,000 more than in previous elections. Once again the Klan victory was indisputable. Marshall won by a margin of 7,327 to 4,523, and so did three of four Klan-endorsed councilmen. Watters and Eatwell also won. Except for winning only one of three school board seats, the Klan tide was irresistible.[28]

The reaction of the *Tribune Chronicle* was one of amazement and grudging admission that the Klan held the balance of power in city politics. The editors accepted Marshall's campaign denial of any desire to wreak vengeance on Catholics, especially in the police and fire departments and in the schools, and encouraged Marshall to study Lincoln's administration as a guide to healing the wounds of the city. The *Tribune Chronicle* offered "to take him at his word that he will be mayor of all the city for the good of all, and that neither race nor religion will be considered by him in the execution of the duties of the office."[29]

The Sunday after the election, the Reverend C. C. Rich, of the First Baptist Church, gave a homily on the Klan and its goals. Rich asserted that "the ideals of the Klan are to make America predominantly Protestant," but also promised a square deal for all and tolerance of other religions. Rich's ambivalence compares closely to that of the Reverend A. C. Archibald. Rich defended, for instance, the right of Jews to worship on their Sabbath, but found it very offensive that Jews made money on the Christian Sabbath. Obviously he was overlooking the Christian merchant's sales on the Jewish Sabbath.[30] Rich's prejudices were apparently based not so much on opposition to the free practice of religion as to the free practice of morality that differed from conservative Protestant values. In Rich's mind the victory of the Klan ensured that all Americans, regardless of religious persuasion, would practice Protestant moral values or suffer a fine or imprisonment. The following year would demonstrate just how successful the Klan could be in imposing its moral code.

NILES

Founded in 1810 by James Heaton, Niles duplicated the pattern of
Youngstown on a smaller scale. The opening of the Ohio canal system
by the 1840s fostered the development of coal mines and what was
claimed to be the first iron rolling mill in the country. Niles's iron
mills suffered through the depression of the 1870s and recouped, but
the depression of the 1890s, coupled with competition from the steel
industry, produced a life-threatening decline.[31]
Youngstown was the first of the valley cities to switch from iron to
steel manufacturing in the 1890s. By the turn of the century, outside
interests, spurred by the development toward concentration, began to
invest in valley industries. They bought up iron and steel mills and
often closed or moved outmoded plants elsewhere. Niles's mill owners
were very fearful that their iron mills might be absorbed and then
dismantled. Thus, they secured promises from the buyers to reinvest in
the plants and to modernize them. Having completed the deal, however, the new owners claimed that the Niles mills were beyond repair
and closed them. Rather than admit defeat, Niles residents pulled together in a search for new industry. The board of trade offered financial incentives—as high as $44,000—to those willing to locate in
Niles. By 1910 the Thomas, Empire, Mahoning Valley, and Falcon
Steel companies and the Fostoria Glass Company built new plants in
Niles. Republic Steel would eventually take over several of these
mills.[32]
The ethnic composition of Niles was also similar to that of Youngstown. Welsh coal miners and western Pennsylvanian Germans had
come in the nineteenth century. Predominantly Protestant, they had
constructed Presbyterian, Lutheran, Methodist, Episcopal, and Disciples of Christ churches in Niles. Some Irish had come at the time of
the potato famine; enough were present by the 1860s to found St.
Stephen's Church. By the 1920s the Irish population was the largest in
Niles.[33] (See appendix B, table B-2, for population composition.)
There was a very small black population in Niles. A sign near the
Erie Depot—placed there by unknown sources—warned "niggers" that
they had better not "let the sun set on their heads." For the most part
blacks heeded the advice.[34]
Industrialization, however, attracted new immigrants. Many Italians
came to work for the Niles Firebrick plant, founded by John R.
Thomas in 1872. Most of them came from Bagnoli-Irpino, a small vil-
lage near Avellino, in the province of Campania, to settle on the East

Side close to the factory. Naturally they built supportive institutions, such as the Society of San Filippo, a mutual aid society. In 1910 they formed Our Lady of Mount Carmel church. By early 1923 the Italians were the second-largest ethnic group in Niles.[35]

The poverty of southern Italy, the cupidity of absentee landlords, and the corruption of the Italian government had fostered a disrespect for authority and a reliance on family among these peasants. Honor and respect were important to southern Italians, and they were prepared to use violence—even against the government—to protect themselves. Their culture encouraged wine-making, a casual attitude toward Sunday observance (especially among the men), open acceptance of gambling, and a focus on loyalty to the family above all else. Obviously this culture would conflict with the Anglo-American emphasis on emotional control, nonindulgence of the senses, piety on Sunday, and respect for the law. When Anglo-Americans tried to impose their culture, the possibility of a violent Italian response was predictable.[36]

Father Nicola Santoro was the first successful pastor of Mount Carmel. He was born in Italy in 1877, and had joined the Precious Blood Fathers. After serving at a number of parishes in Italy, he was assigned to Spain in 1903. In 1912 he emigrated to Monterey, Mexico, where he was assistant pastor of the Church of the Immaculate Conception. When the Mexican Revolution occurred in 1914, he decided to stay in spite of laws forbidding the practice of religion. After several close scrapes (he had been fined 1,000,000 pesos and threatened with death if unable to pay), he left for the United States with the help of the Italian consul.

When he arrived in Niles in November 1914, Mount Carmel had been without a pastor for three months. The small frame structure could not even attract enough parishioners to fill its one hundred seats. His spirituality attracted so many back to the church that they soon had to add on to the old building. By 1923 it was necessary to construct a new church. With only $6,000 and the bishop's permission, he enlisted his parishioners' help in digging out the basement in November 1923.[37]

Joseph Pallante was one of the early parishioners. He had been born in 1879 in Bagnoli-Irpino, and had come to Niles in 1893 with his father to work for the Niles Firebrick Company. Eventually, he became a padrone and recruited many newcomers from his native village in Italy. Pallante liked his new country and desired to become a full-fledged American. He was the first Italian to move from the East

Side to Hunter Street on the West Side so that his children might learn to speak English. His daughters could date non-Italian boys and did not have to follow the Old World custom of having a chaperone. Joseph even joined St. Stephen's Church, after an argument with Father Santoro, but the Italians generally sat in the last few rows of the Irish church. Assimilation was not an easy road.[38]

The Jennings family was less prone to assimilation. Marco and Rosa DiGenero had come from Naples to New York in the mid-1880s. No one knew how the family name had changed, but it is assumed that some immigration official was responsible. After having a daughter, Theresa, and three sons, Jim, Joe, and Leo, the Jennings moved to the east end of Niles, where they built a grocery store at 600 Mason Street. By the 1920s the brothers had converted the grocery store–home into a speakeasy, gambling joint, and athletic club. The Jennings Athletic Club sponsored boxers and a semi-pro football team that won the Mahoning Valley championship in 1925. The young Italian and Irish men who boxed and played football served as a sort of Praetorian Guard for the establishment. As political brokers for the East Side, the brothers had worked for the election of Vincent Lapolla, the only Italian on the Niles City Council.[39]

The Jennings Athletic Club was just one of many Italian bootlegging and gambling establishments on the East Side. Each street had some activity, with Langley Street being the point of highest concentration. In the Italian moral code, neither activity was wrong, but they were living in a country in which the predominant culture did not agree.[40]

Trumbull County Protestants were already planning to crack down on the notorious East Side. Spurred on by the previously mentioned Trumbull County Council of Churches and the Trumbull County Dry Enforcement League, the new county sheriff, John "Brickey" Thomas, began a series of raids into Niles. Loaded with warrants sworn by W. L. Bence, the district Prohibition officer, Thomas swept into Niles on 26 January 1923, and made thirteen arrests. Councilman Vince Lapolla, from the East Side, provided bond for the men, including Jim Jennings and Joseph Round, the son of the police chief, Lincoln Round. Two federal agents testified that they had bought liquor from Round at his bowling alley, but he claimed they had lied. Round was found guilty and fined $1,000. Jennings received an $800 fine.[41]

The arrest and conviction of Round's son served to verify the growing conviction that the failure to shut down the bootleggers lay at the feet of lax or corrupt public officials. Before this incident, the *Niles Daily News* had cited the statement of the state Prohibition commissioner, Don V. Parker, that "prohibition will become a reality when local authorities start to do their duty," and his call for "such a storm of protest that every negligent or indifferent official would take cover."[42] After Bence's raid, the *Daily News* implied that Federal Inspector Bence must not have had much confidence in Niles's officials since he had given the warrants to Sheriff Thomas. "The day is coming," the *Daily News* warned, "and not far away, when the good citizens of Niles are going to rise up in their might and power and declare that a clean out of this protected business must come, regardless (*sic*) where the chips might fly."[43]

A resident of Niles, Judge Joseph Smith, of the County Probate Court, fired up the crusaders in March when he charged that Niles could have been $10,000 richer, "and the policemen and firemen would not have to go begging for their justly earned salaries," had the city administration done its job. Invited to speak to the Kiwanis Club, Smith charged that he had no standing with City Hall, nor did any citizen. "Instead in the year 1922 the bootlegger, the gambler, the keepers at houses of ill repute have had its call."[44]

The mayor of Niles, Charles Crow, was incensed. After all, he had been elected to four straight terms as mayor since his first election in 1915. Crow had been born in Coal Center, Pennsylvania, in 1870, and had worked as a miner in his youth, but he turned to baseball to escape the dangers of the mines. Niles had a reputation as a good baseball town, and Crow came there to pitch and manage. He also opened a shoe store on Main Street before entering politics at the request of other businessmen. Until Prohibition became such a hot issue, he had been a very popular mayor.[45]

On 10 March, Crow appeared at the city council meeting to lambast his critics. According to Crow, publisher E. R. Smith of the *Daily News* was a hypocrite who took advantage of his position to solicit bribes. Referring to Smith as a "dangerous man to the community," Crow recounted an offer made to him by Smith: $800 in exchange for political support as a gubernatorial candidate. In addition, Smith allegedly had solicited a $5,500 loan on his financially desperate newspaper from Congressman John C. Cooper; when Cooper refused, Smith endorsed his rival in the primary. In a vein of Progressive rhetoric, Crow announced that Smith's newspaper was beholden to the "trusts" for financial support, in particular, Youngstown Sheet and Tube under the guise of a contribution from the Anti-Saloon League. Crow also questioned Judge Joseph Smith's dedication to principle when he had served as Niles's city solicitor; supposedly Smith made no comment and took no action regarding saloons or liquor law violators. Finally, Crow charged his opponents with attempted entrapment, both through detectives employed to shadow him and a woman who tried to lure him into a compromising situation.[46]

Publisher Smith denied all the charges. His editor, J. M. Gledhill, called Crow a demagogue and recounted a story about his own meeting the previous fall with state Prohibition commissioner Don V. Parker, in which Parker had a list of the bootleggers protected by public officials in Niles. The names turned out to be the ones arrested in January in the Thomas raid. Crow responded with a second appearance before council replete with affidavits from two men and a Youngstown judge, W. P. Barnum, who claimed to have witnessed Smith's efforts to solicit a bribe.[47]

This flow of charge and countercharge became all the more intense when the other newspaper in town, the *Niles Evening Register*, took the side of the mayor. In an editorial the *Evening Register* testified to the veracity of Crow's affidavits and accused Smith of ignoring them. The newspaper also accused Smith of being anti-labor as publisher of another newspaper in nearby Newton Falls, and of being involved in shaky real estate deals. Worst of all, according to the newspaper, he could not even spell![48]

For the public the issues must have been confusing, but for the recently founded Law Enforcement League, there was no doubt that Crow was guilty. As early as February, a group of citizens had discussed taking Crow before Governor Donahey to secure his discharge for failing to enforce the law.[49] At least thirteen other mayors were in the process of being so charged as the tidal wave of law enforcement began to roll over Ohio.[50]

In early May the head of Ohio Prohibition enforcement, B. F. McDonald, promised to bring the Crow case before the governor. When Crow was finally summoned to Columbus on 13 June, he brought the city account books. Crow's major line of defense was the accumulation of $11,000 in fines through the first five months of 1923. No one else in the county had collected more, according to Crow. He also claimed that he had contacted state Prohibition officers for assistance in Niles long before local factions began to do so.[51]

For unknown reasons Crow was able to secure a private audience with the governor. Donahey barred reporters and officials of the Anti-Saloon League and excluded State Prohibition Director B. F. McDonald. Whatever Crow related to Donahey, it was successful, for he was exonerated.[52] Donahey was more critical of Chief Round in suggesting that he "could show greater zeal in the enforcement of the laws," and that he should be released from duty unless an improvement was shown.[53]

The governor was far more critical of the Law Enforcement League. According to Donahey,

> It is impossible for any mayor to maintain a proper observance of law unless he has the sincere cooperation of the citizens who want a good town. This is often lacking, and personal or political grievances are the cause of complaints against officials. Possibly petitions for removal of officials could be secured from most any city. The mere fact that liquor can be secured in any city is not proof that its officials are laxer or inefficient, but we ought to have at least a majority of the laws enforced in Ohio.[54]

The governor was very upset by the unsubstantiated charges.

Crow claimed vindication while defending the work of Chief Round. Indignant with Donahey, the chief pointed to an understaffed, six-man force that he had unsuccessfully asked council to increase as the cause of his inability to clean up Niles. In addition, Round claimed, it was most difficult to obtain evidence for warrants and conviction, especially with barred doors and sinks or pipes used by offenders to dispose of the liquor. Obviously, Round's point was well taken, but it was also just as difficult to obtain evidence of bribery. Bootleggers were quite willing to allow token raids that would give the administration an appearance of rectitude. In spite of a setback, the Law Enforcement League pledged to continue its efforts to improve Niles's moral environment.[55]

The linkage between this crusade and the local Protestant churches was once again apparent in the appearance of Dr. John Wean, pastor of the First Methodist Church, at the Crow hearing. Having seen cars parked before Niles's houses of gambling and prostitution, Dr. Wean made no apology for "doing what he thought was his Christian duty." He denied that he was one of the instigators, but prided himself on his association with "a number of blooded men of Niles who wanted to see a clean, moral city."[56]

It is not clear how closely involved the Klan was in this crusade, at least initially. The *Evening Register* recorded the first appearance of Dr. E. A. Watkins on St. Patrick's day. Remembering the city from forty years before, he praised Niles as "always a decent little place to live in." His next round of appearances in April included the Masonic

Lodge and the Kiwanis Club, when he introduced himself as a medical missionary of the Congregational church and a former intelligence officer of the British army. In praise of his oratorical skills, the *Daily News* had encouraged readers to attend his lectures. It was the editor of the *Daily News*, J. M. Gledhill, who introduced him to the Kiwanis.[57] Watkins, it would appear, was covertly laying groundwork for the Klan.

The burning of three fiery crosses marked the first semipublic appearance of the Klan. On 26 April citizens saw the crosses on Salt Spring Road, Deforest Road, and Hartzell Avenue opposite Union Cemetery. No one in Niles seemed to know anything about it, although some people had noticed cars with Pennsylvania license plates headed out to those spots. It was reported, however, that organizers had been in the area for several months, and that one had been in Niles several weeks before.[58] The veil of secrecy would continue to cloak Klan activities in Niles throughout 1923.

The appearance of the Klan did not deter Mayor Crow, who had announced his bid for reelection prior to the inquiry in Columbus. Crow was to face stiff competition in the August Republican primary. His major opponent was Frank Wagstaff, a contractor, school board president, and member of the Board of Health under Crow. Wagstaff's platform included the usual commitments to law enforcement and a business administration.[59] A third candidate, Tom Hall, a steelworker and a Crow appointee to the civil service commission, also promised stricter law enforcement.[60] Neither of Crow's opponents was openly linked with the Klan or the Law Enforcement League. Crow narrowly defeated Wagstaff in the August primary, 2,004 to 1,814, with Hall garnering only 663.[61]

Harvey Kistler won the Democratic primary, although a newcomer to politics. Born in Lordstown, Ohio, in 1885, Kistler had come to Niles when he was twelve years old. His first job was as a telegrapher for the Pennsylvania Railroad. After purchasing the Taylor Insurance Agency, he sold insurance in the mornings while continuing on the railroad's afternoon shift. A strapping six-foot, 200-pounder who wore bow ties and pince-nez glasses, Kistler presented what was described as a "dignified" appearance. He received the Klan's endorsement in the general election.[62]

His cousin, O. O. Hewitt, chaired his campaign committee. Rather than holding huge rallies or massive parades, the Kistler campaign set up committees in each precinct to canvass door-to-door, as the Klan was doing in Youngstown.[63] There were no public debates or forums. The only public appearance of note occurred the Saturday before the election, when Kistler held a torchlight parade reminiscent of the Blaine-Cleveland presidential election of the 1880s.

Crow lost on election day by a margin of 3,014 to 2,552. He carried the Third Ward, the center of bootlegging and gambling activities on the East Side, by 456 to 56, but Kistler won the other wards by almost 900 votes.[64] As with many other incumbent mayors, Crow drowned in the rising tide of reform.

GIRARD

Girard was the smallest of the cities bordering on the Mahoning River. Its population numbered 6,556 in 1920, a 75 percent increase since 1910. Originally a part of Liberty Township, Girard was laid out in 1837 as a result of surveying done for the Pennsylvania-Ohio Canal. Its location on the canal and its later development in the 1850s as the southern terminal of the railroad line to Cleveland brought a growth spurt. The discovery of coal in Liberty Township after 1860 was a boon to Girard's economy and led, as in the case of other valley cities, to the opening of several iron works. With the decline of the coal beds after 1880, the Girard economy stagnated. It would revive after 1905 with the influx of capital from Youngstown investors into an oil cloth company, a leather factory, a truck manufacturing plant, and iron plants now converted to steel production. The location of the McDonald works of the United States Steel Company on the river just above Girard also added to the town's growth.[65]

Until 1920 Girard was considered a village under Ohio law. Having passed the 5,000 population limit, it applied for incorporation as a city and finally held its first elections under an Ohio city charter in November 1921. (See appendix B, table B-3, for population composition.) After the primary a dissatisfied local doctor, W. D. Cunningham, took out petitions as an independent candidate in the general election. Running on a platform of strict enforcement of the laws, he unexpectedly won. The former village mayor, J. J. Cronin, instituted an unsuccessful lawsuit the following October that sought Cunningham's ouster on the basis that his filing of petitions after the primaries was improper. Cunningham identified the supporters of that suit as "the remnant of the old booze ring who are attempting to oust me from office. Some people in Girard don't like reform," asserted Cunningham, "and my methods of cleaning up the town and enforcing laws."[66]

At six feet tall and weighing more than two hundred pounds, Cunningham was an imposing figure to Girard bootleggers. Through his police chief, Roy L. Sanford, Cunningham cracked down on liquor law violators. "That Girard is dry and that folks obey the law and maintain order, and that all visitors are required to do the same, is the opinion and edict of Mayor W. D. Cunningham of Girard," reported the *Citizen* prior to becoming a Klan newspaper, "and he is backed up and his hands upheld by the people of Girard."[67] Reputedly, law enforcement was so strict in Girard that spitting on the sidewalks led to arrest.[68]

The churches of Girard played a leading role in Cunningham's moral crackdown. According to the *Citizen*, "Girard takes considerable interest in her churches, which are largely responsible for the fine moral influences pervading the community." The mayor and Chief Sanford drank deeply from the churches' moral wells; both were members of the Men's Bible Class of the First Methodist Episcopal Church.[69]

Girard was a city prepared for the message of the Klan. Colonel Evan A. Watkins found a receptive audience there and even a pulpit: the First Baptist Church selected Watkins as its minister. It was no surprise when the Klan endorsed Cunningham as its candidate for mayor in 1923, and he triumphed easily over his Democratic opponent, Wade Deemer, in the general election.[70]

STRUTHERS

Struthers was a rural village suddenly subjected to the pressures of rapid urbanization. It had been founded in 1798 by John Struthers at the mouth of Yellow Creek, and it had foundered after the War of 1812. Thomas Struthers, a descendant of John, refounded the community after the Civil War. Until 1900, though, Struthers was farmland dotted by a sawmill, a blast furnace, and several small factories. After 1900 the construction of the Youngstown Sheet and Tube plant across the Mahoning River in East Youngstown and the need for housing for workers rapidly transformed Struthers into a formally incorporated municipality by 1902. Its population of 5,847 in 1920, bolstered by the expansion of Youngstown Sheet and Tube into Struthers, enabled it to become a city as defined by Ohio law.[71] (See appendix B, table B-4, for population composition.)

Unfortunately, Youngstown newspapers provided only sparse coverage of Klan activity in Struthers. From such coverage as there was, Struthers had gained a reputation as a hotbed of dry activity and a place where dry agents could expect a fast trial and a substantial fine for liquor law violators. Youngstowners bemoaned the loss of municipal revenues to this nearby municipality. The first recognition of Klan activity in the Youngstown newspapers came with the endorsement of Hans P. Johnson, a Republican, for mayor in 1923 and three men, including George Mohr, for councilmen. The Reverend A. M. Stansel, of the Struthers Baptist Church, was a vocal supporter of the Klan, as was the Reverend Leroy Myers, of the Struthers Presbyterian church, who would later become the exalted cyclops of the county Klan. Election results, however, were mixed: both Johnson and Mohr won, but anti-Klan candidates took the other seats.[72]

EAST YOUNGSTOWN

East Youngstown was the frontier experience repeated once again, but this time in an eastern industrial setting. Wooded hillside and farmland leading down to the river constituted the geography of the nonexistent East Youngstown in 1900. The construction of the Youngstown Sheet and Tube plant near the river in 1901–2 attracted an influx of immigrants, and by 1920 the city of East Youngstown had 11,237 residents, making it the second-largest community in the valley. (See appendix B, table B-5, for population composition.) The lack of a strong form of government—East Youngstown was part of a township until 1909—permitted random development. Most of the young male immigrants had to live in shacks or in crowded boarding-houses.

East Youngstown quickly gained a reputation for lawlessness. Until 1909 the township trustees had to rely on constables and justices of the peace to maintain order. Joseph Butler blamed the reputed youth-fulness of the population (in which males outnumbered females 6,812 to 4,425) accompanied by the illicit sale of liquor in unauthorized saloons for the problems, although he admitted, "many of the stories concerning East Youngstown's lawlessness in its earlier years are exaggerated."[73]

In January 1916 a strike at Youngstown Sheet and Tube resulted in occurrences that would only confirm many Youngstowners' opinions of their immediate neighbors. The recession of 1913–15 had created widespread unemployment, but wartime orders for steel brought workers back. Demands by the returning workers for higher wages precipitated a strike that began on New Year's Day. In spite of some concessions on the wage issue—officials simply posted the new wage structure because of company policy of nonrecognition of worker organizations—dissatisfaction continued. Numerous fights and clashes broke out, testing the mettle of the village police, and the governor was put on alert to have state guardsmen available.

At 4:00 P.M. on Friday, 7 January, a crowd of workers and their wives gathered at the bridge leading into the plant. The crowd protested when several workmen attempted to enter the factory in defiance of the strike. Someone fired a random shot, which provoked a volley from plant guards stationed on the bridge. The crowd dispersed and returned to saloons and homes in the village. Within the hour a fire broke out, and a mob poured gasoline into surrounding buildings to spread the fire. They proceeded to batter in some of the buildings as the fire raged unchecked. In a riot reminiscent of the commodity riots of the 1960s, some of the bystanders looted the stores but directed no violence at the company. The rioters wreaked havoc for at least six hours before a committee of volunteers and the Ohio National Guard halted their activities. The leveling of the entire business district of East Youngstown left vacant lots and charred buildings that remained five years later as reminders of the excesses of that day.[74]

Butler described the riot as a "drunken frolic rather than a real riot" and blamed the free flow of liquor available in the numerous saloons of East Youngstown. "Whiskey," he contended, "added fuel to grievances," and village officials failed to close the saloons.[75] It is uncertain as to whether Butler's interpretation of the riot was the majority opinion of the Youngstown area, but it is evident that liquor consumption and lawless rioting by foreign workers were issues raised in the Klan platform. The incident could have served only to convince many citizens that prohibition of alcohol and saloons, as well as better law enforcement, could forestall a repetition of such events.

East Youngstown elected its first city government in 1921. Although only 5 percent of the population cast ballots, at least half of the elected officials were of southern or eastern European origins. As of 1920 there existed churches or missions for Slovaks, Ruthenians, and Italians only. Protestants had no churches of their own and relied on nearby churches in Youngstown and Struthers.[76]

Ethnically, then, East Youngstown was an immigrant community. Throughout the Klan years the city provided little, if any, support for the local chapter. It was more a sore spot for Klan officials than a center of recruitment. As a result, the Klan did not endorse any candidates in the municipal elections; they probably would have viewed such endorsement as a liability anyway. In 1923 the city elected T. Lee Gordon, an opponent of the Klan, as mayor.[77]

The day after the election, the newly elected Klan mayors of Youngstown, Warren, Struthers, and Girard—Harvey Kistler, of Niles, was unable to attend—met at the Youngstown YMCA to discuss civic problems. Colonel Watkins had suggested the meeting as a means of coordination among the communities in the solution of common problems, and it was so enthusiastically received that there was talk of monthly meetings. Law enforcement was the key item on the first agenda. According to Watkins, "the police departments of the various cities will work together under the regime. A network for the detection of a crime will extend from Struthers to Warren. There will be a war on the bootleggers."[78] Because of the experience of Watkins as a member of the British army intelligence corps, speculation occurred that he might head an intelligence bureau to engage in secret service operations. The Klan mayors also supported joint efforts on the development of a valley water supply.[79]

Klan victories in five valley communities and the cooperative attitudes of Klan-supported mayors generated optimism among many Klan members that the millennium was arriving. Control of the local governments by Christians would mean stricter enforcement of the vice laws and a police force purged of its corrupt elements; control of the school boards would mean children immersed in a Christian atmosphere and less dalliance with evil as they matured. The Klan program for cleansing Mahoning Valley residents not only of their past sins but also of their future ones was ready for implementation.

5

Many Are Chosen

As individuals they were successful business and professional men, nearly all of them devoted church members,
married men with families, and just the sort of men to make
up a prosperous community.

—Henry Fry, Kleagle

O n 30 September 1923 the Irish Catholic cop was nowhere to be
seen in the vicinity of the Erie Terminal Building in downtown
Youngstown. Burglars took advantage of this mysterious absence to
jimmy a lock and then short the elevator fuse box, a ruse that kept
the nightwatchmen embroiled in the basement. They climbed the stairs
to a sparse fourth floor office, supposedly owned by an insurance company but in reality a front for the Klan. The burglars dragged the safe
containing membership lists, some money, and assorted legal documents down the hallway into another office, "peeled the can," and took
the membership list. The report of the police investigators deemed it
the work of professionals. Behind their work, however, lay a cleverly
concocted plot to steal and to publish the Klan membership list—a
tactic developed by the American Unity League from Chicago. By late
March 1924 a booklet containing a partial list of names would appear
on the city streets entitled "Is your Neighbor a Kluxer?"; it sold for
$1.00 per copy. It was published by The Tolerance Publishing Com-
pany, the printing arm of the American Unity League (AUL).[1]

The AUL was founded in Chicago in June 1922. Composed primarily of Roman Catholics, this organization attempted to get its hands
on Klan membership lists through disgruntled ex-Klansmen, bribery,
or burglary. Its director, Patrick H. O'Donnell, a criminal lawyer, believed that "the publication of the names of those who belong to the
Klan will be a blow that the masked organization cannot survive" because many of them were businessmen dependent on the patronage of
"those groups they classify as alien." The AUL published a weekly
newspaper called *Tolerance*, which printed the names, addresses, and

occupations of Klan members culled from the membership rosters. It ceased publication in 1924 after exhausting its Chicago sources, enduring a number of lawsuits by enraged Chicagoans who denied that they were members (including William Wrigley, Jr., the gum manufacturer), and the defection of one of its owners, Grady Rutledge, to the Klan.[2]

The AUL began to expand its operation beyond Chicago in December 1922, with Ohio targeted as one of the Klan centers needing its attention. Ralph Ewry established an office in Columbus, from which he contacted potential members in Youngstown. In October 1923 a local chapter of the AUL announced a membership of 1,600 as well as its plans to publish a weekly newspaper. It opposed Charles Scheible for mayor and protested Klan plans to parade in Youngstown as something that was intended "only to incite riot and bloodshed." Its officers included two lawyers, Samuel Davidson and John W. Powers; a grocer, P. H. McEvey; and an engineer, Wallace T. Metcalfe. Within this group the plans were hatched to steal and to publish the Klan membership list.[3]

In light of the secrecy surrounding the Klan and the disappearance of most of its membership files, the Mahoning County booklet is an obvious gold mine for investigation into the social composition of the Klan. Contemporary observers were certainly not able to agree about the background of the membership. Henry Fry, a disenchanted kleagle from Knoxville, Tennessee, and a contributor to the *New York World*'s exposé in 1921, claimed that he could not "find anywhere in the country a finer, cleaner or better lot of men than those among whom I worked as an agent of Ku Kluxism. As individuals they were successful business and professional men, nearly all of them devout church members, married men with families and just the sort of men to make up a prosperous community."[4] Stanley Frost, a journalist, agreed with Fry that those joining the Klan were not "always, though sometimes, the best in the community, but they are usually the good solid, middle-class citizens, the 'backbone of the nation.'"[5] Prominent observers of the 1920s, such as journalists Frederick Lewis Allen and Robert L. Duffus and sociologists Helen and Robert Lynd, challenged this middle-class thesis; they suggested that the Klan drew largely from the lower classes. In 1965 historian Charles C. Alexander, in his work *The Ku Klux Klan in the Southwest*, combined these contemporary observations into a sweeping generalization that "people from every stratum of society found their way into the order. Excluding non-

whites and non-Protestants, the membership of the order was remarkably cross-sectional."[6]

The lack of statistical data, however, taints such observations. Admittedly, the contemporary observations are invaluable and suggest the
participation of both the middle and lower classes, but they do not
indicate the level of participation or compare it with the percentage of
each group in American society at that time. In 1967 Kenneth Jackson
tried to correct the impressions of earlier observers and historians in
his seminal work *The Ku Klux Klan in The City, 1915–1930*. Not only
did he effectively establish the thesis that the Klan was an urban, as
well as rural, phenomenon, but he also provided demographic data
regarding the size of Klan membership and its social origins.

From scant lists of four communities (Knoxville, Tennessee; Chicago, Aurora, and Winchester, Illinois) with a blue-collar majority of
63.8 percent, Jackson concluded that the Klan was primarily a lower-
middle-class movement composed of "rank and file, non-union, blue-
collar employees of large businesses and factories." Lacking a high
school education, religiously conservative, and poorly paid, these socially marginal men joined the Klan, Jackson theorized, as a reaction
to the threat posed to their status by the new immigrants. In general,
he described them as less than adequate achievers caught between
individual desires for advancement, the competition of newcomers,
and their own insufficiencies. According to Jackson, status concerns
affected white collar members also. He characterized them as "strug-
gling businessmen, ambitious and unprincipled politicians and poorly
paid clerks."[7]

Particularly galling to these Kluxers was the threat to their neighborhoods. Residing in what Jackson classified as zones of emergence,
Klan members objected to immigrant or black intrusion. According to
Jackson " 'the zone of emergence' was usually made up of working-
class neighborhoods of modest homes and apartments and it was here,
among white laborers, that the Invisible Empire thrived."[8] Klan members, unable to move into the better neighborhoods, satisfied their
frustration by joining a secret society that would reaffirm their status.

Because of its demographic base, the Jackson thesis has held sway
until the 1980s. The appearance of Robert Goldberg's work on the
Klan in Colorado effectively challenged the Jackson thesis. His study
found that "the Klan's membership was highly diversified. Except for
the elite, the Klan drew its membership from all sections of the socioeconomic class spectrum." Having benefited from the availability of

membership rosters from Denver and Canon City, as well as lists of
Klan leaders in Denver, Pueblo, and Colorado Springs, Goldberg's
work provides a more sophisticated and thorough quantitative analysis
of Klan membership.[9]

The key to understanding the difference between Goldberg and
Jackson is what each does with his data. Whereas Jackson focuses on
the larger numbers in the blue-collar classes, Goldberg compares the
numbers in each class with the population at large. In Denver, for
instance, the lower-class Klan members outnumbered those from
higher classes two to one, seemingly a point in favor of the Jackson
thesis.[10] But when compared with the figures and percentages for the
Denver population at large, the upper classes were attracted to the
Klan at a higher rate. For Goldberg, then, the underrepresentation of
blue-collar workers in Klan ranks in Denver raises doubts about the
validity of Jackson's conclusions. According to Goldberg, "The Colorado Klan was not an economic movement or a spokesman for the socially deprived. The Denver case demonstrated that, excluding the
elite and unskilled laborers, the Klan rank and file was an occupational cross-section of the local community."[11] Goldberg thus rejects
the economic and status-preserving motivations suggested by Jackson;
he describes the Klan instead as a social movement built on local
grievances.

The existence of a Klan membership list for Youngstown and Mahoning County is an important test for the findings of both Goldberg
and Jackson. Though Goldberg has the more impressive and seemingly
more comprehensive rosters, the state of Colorado did not duplicate the
eastern experience of heavy industries and a multiplicity of immigrants. Youngstown's rapid growth and heavy influx of immigration in
the period from 1900 to 1920 differentiated it from the Colorado cities
studied by Goldberg. As for Jackson's thesis, the proximity of new immigrants to old-line residents affords an opportunity to measure the
impact of movement into the zones of emergence and to compare rates
of class participation with figures for the population at large.

During the years of peak Klan activity, 1923–24, many Youngstowners joined the Klan. The *Vindicator* speculated that as many as 10,000
may have joined, after Colonel C. A. Gunder, kleagle of the local
Klan, contended that the stolen membership list contained 10,500
members. Obviously, these figures are close enough to lend credence
to one another.[12] Additional support for their validity comes from historian Jackson, who has estimated the participation of as many as
17,000 members in the entire Mahoning Valley.[13]

The published list, however, contained only 2,420 names for Youngs-town and about 900 for the rest of the county, thus making the Klan only one-third as strong as estimated. The validity of the list is attested to by the appearance of known leaders, including Grand Dragon Clyde Osborne, Grand Titan Fred J. Warnock, Exalted Cyclops Web Lentz, the Reverend George Gibson, and the former safety director, David Hamilton; it is also supported by interviews with those on the list who are still alive. It would appear, however, that the list is a partial one at best. Many letters, such as *A* through *D*, are sparsely represented, and some are missing entirely. Altogether the missing or underrepresented letters constitute 43 percent of the alphabetical listings in the *Youngs-town City Directory* for the year 1923. Filling in for each letter propor-tionately would produce an approximation of 4,250 members in Youngstown proper. The discrepancy between this figure and aforemen-tioned estimates may have resulted from the Klan's tendency to exag-gerate its rolls, or perhaps the impending bankruptcy of the AUL led to a publishing decision to eliminate names in order to keep costs down. Without further evidence it would appear that the Klan was at least 5,000 strong in October 1923.[14]

Data regarding average age and marital status suggest that the Klan was broadly representative of the population in Youngstown. The age of Klan members is located in table 2 by five-year cohorts and compared with figures from the 1920 census. Although there are variations at the opposite ends of the age spectrum, the mean for each is extremely close, 34.03 to 34.36—only a four-month difference. Table 3 contains the comparative figures for marital status, again a very close approxi-mation of 62 percent to 63.2 percent.[15]

As a determinant of social class, occupation is the most important variable in evaluating Jackson's thesis about economically marginal men. Jackson, unfortunately, did not attempt to tie together occupa-tional and economic status. His blue-collar figures did not differentiate between skilled, semiskilled, and unskilled workers. If Jackson was correct in his analysis, one would expect the majority of Klan mem-bers to belong to those groups lacking in skills and economically re-warding work, not the entire cohort of blue-collar workers. Fortunately, the stolen roster specified what kind of work each member did; this occupation was then checked against the 1923 *Youngstown City Direc-tory*. In order to classify occupations and social status, I have relied on Alba M. Edwards's *A Social-Economic Grouping of the Gainful Workers of the United States: 1930.*[16] Appendix A provides a listing of the six categories used by Edwards, and some of the occupations in each.

TABLE 2
Age

	Klan Members	Native White Males	NWM%	K%
Under 20	93	1910	7.71	3.95
20–29	835	8393	33.87	35.44
30–39	726	6689	26.99	30.81
40–49	461	4347	17.54	19.57
50–59	178	2126	8.58	7.55
60–69	49	974	3.93	2.08
Unknown	65	Mean	34.03	34.36

Table 4 compares the numbers and percentages of 269 randomly selected Klan members in each of the six categories with the numbers and percentages of native white males and of all males, as obtained from the 1920 census of Youngstown occupational statistics.[17] It would be unwise to compare Youngstown with national statistics because of the fact that the country was still half agrarian.

Because the Klan restricted membership to native-born white males, it is best to compare the Klan figures with those of the native white males in Youngstown. A comparison reveals that the Klan membership came from all socioeconomic categories in percentages that approximate four of the categories. In two of these categories, the percentages differed significantly, with the skilled worker 6 percent higher and the unskilled worker 10 percent lower. There is a 97 percent chance that the unskilled percentage, 5.58, is within 3 percent of the Klan figure at large; for the skilled workers there is an 80 percent chance that the figure is plus or minus 4 percent.

Marginality, of course, is a quality not open to easy assessment. Data is unavailable regarding the exact financial condition of sample members, as well as their mental and psychological attitudes toward status. Categories 1, 2, and 4 do, however, represent the highest so-

TABLE 3
Marital Status

	Klan	%	Youngstown	%
Married	1,505	62.2	30,180	63.2
Unmarried	916	37.8	17,570	36.8

cioeconomic levels. The fact that Klan statistics exceed, albeit not by very large amounts, the native white statistics in these areas suggests that at least 57 percent of the Klan members were not economically marginal. Obviously, the percentage could be even higher depending on what number from category 3 could be classified as economically secure, such as advertising and real estate agents, insurance salesmen, credit men, and accountants. Thus, it can be safely concluded that the majority of Klan members were not marginal in their socioeconomic status.

Another variable that relates to marginality is home ownership: one would expect marginal men to be less likely to own homes. According to the 1920 census, 52.2 percent of homes were owned in Youngstown and 47.8 percent rented.[18] Table 5 compares homeowners and renters among the Klan with the Youngstown data. Klan members who were related to a family that owned the home have been combined with owners in order to compare Klan data with census data, which consists of dwellings rather than people. The figure for the combined grouping (dwellers in housing owned by oneself or relatives) was 50.2 percent, which is slightly lower than the Youngstown average of 52.2 percent. However, the closeness of the figures would suggest that Klan members did not differ significantly from Youngstown's population in the category of home ownership. It is also important to note that renters should not be automatically considered as marginal.

The final variable regarding marginality and a key to the Jackson thesis is residence within a transitional neighborhood. In his book Jackson describes a zone of emergence as a "broad belt separating the core of the city from its outer residential fringe," and as "made up of working class neighborhoods of modest homes and apartments." Unfortunately, Jackson did not correlate transitional neighborhoods as a

TABLE 4
Occupational Statistics for Youngstown

Job Skills Rating	Klan	K%	Native White Males	NWM%	All Males	AM%
High Nonmanual	16.5	6.13	1,404	6.03	1,751	3.96
Middle Nonmanual	32.5	12.08	2,469	10.61	4,269	9.65
Low Nonmanual	51.0	18.96	4,122	17.71	5,768	13.04
High Manual	104.5	38.84	7,642	32.84	10,953	24.77
Middle Manual	49.5	18.40	4,069	17.49	6,452	14.59
Low Manual	15.0	5.58	3,563	15.31	15,026	33.98

variable with the four partial lists he used to engender occupational statistics. Rather, he has relied upon voting records in Chicago, interviews with some former Klan members in Memphis, and another partial list in the case of Indianapolis. [19]

As to Youngstown, it must first be recognized that the city itself was a huge area of transition. Foreign-born whites constituted almost 20 percent of the total population, and even higher percentages in such nearby suburbs as East Youngstown and Niles. These foreign-born whites lived in all the wards (ranging from 14 to 24 percent of the population), and usually close to the river and the steel mills. Some 70 percent of the black population resided on the north side in the Second and Third wards, but another 20 percent were located in wards 4 and 5. [20] Ethnic neighborhoods were clearly identifiable within these wards, but sprinklings of new-stock immigrants, especially Italians, had already penetrated into numerous old-stock enclaves. [21] In short, it

TABLE 5
Home Ownership

	Homeowners	Non-owners	Lives with family
Klan	95	134	40
%	35.3	49.8	14.9

1920 Census: Youngstown dwellings. % owned: 52.2; % rented: 47.8

would appear that rapid change in population and dispersion of the new immmigrants both in and around the city may have generated fears among the old-stock inhabitants of Youngstown.

If one applies Jackson's definition strictly, however, the picture regarding the effect of transitional neighborhoods on Klan members is mixed. Of 288 Klan members, 147 lived on streets that had either none or just a few new-stock residents—approximately 51 percent of the sample. Those who lived in neighborhoods already predominately new-stock (45) numbered 15.6 percent, and those in neighborhoods in the process of change totaled 33.4 percent. It would appear that one-half of the population sampled lived in areas not yet subject to change in ethnic composition; another 16 percent resided in areas that had already completed the transition. On the basis of statistical data, it would seem unlikely that transitional neighborhoods served as a prime motivation for the majority of Klan members; it may have for some, but the evidence is inconclusive.

Psychological data is, of course, much harder to come by. People could live in a virtually safe area and yet feel threatened; the problem is to identify at what point different people become worried. There is some admittedly sketchy evidence from interviews with Klan members still alive sixty years later. For the twenty-nine people interviewed, there was no designation of a transitional neighborhood as a major factor in joining the Klan. Of course, most interviewees were rather young then (18 to 30 years of age), and not as settled, or even worried about their housing. An ill-defined sense of patriotism, civic reform, and the influence of friends were causes most often cited for joining the Klan.[22]

In focusing upon economic factors as primary indicators of why someone would join the Klan, Jackson has overlooked the interrelationship between middle-class status and the values of the Klan. James Q. Wilson, in his work *Political Organizations*, has offered a better model for interpreting the Klan. He contends that such organizations—described more appropriately as pressure groups—seldom represent the lower classes. According to a variety of studies, the economic, social, and psychological pressures placed upon the lower classes force them to emphasize the present moment rather than future goals. Thus, they seldom join such organizations as readily as the classes above them. When they do, however, they expect immediate gains, usually of a material kind, or they undergo a personality transformation "so that the members, though lower class on recruitment, soon become middle class, at least expressively if not economically."[23] Wilson cites Pentecostals or the Black Muslims as examples of such transformations, wherein self-control and hard work become the compelling norms of the transformed member.[24]

The Klan also could not have been appealing to the lower classes because its dues structure was expensive—$10 to join, $6.50 for a robe, plus monthly dues. In essence, it took away, rather than provided, immediate material gains. According to Wilson, lower-class members might have been willing to sacrifice had there been a personality transformation involved. The Klan, however, did not seek to transform its members but to transform the society, to create reforms of the political structure and thereby to impose middle-class Protestant moral standards. It was assumed that those joining were already converted.

Although the Klan would not, and indeed did not, refuse membership to less substantial native-white Protestant males, its broadest appeals were to the middle class. The Klan's strength lay on the south side of the Mahoning River, the most recently developed portion of the city. Although it had a following on the north side, those areas were predominately upper-class in the First Ward, and lower-class, including immigrant and black, in the Second and Third wards. In the election of 1923, the Klan candidate lost only the First Ward, which also failed to elect a Klan-endorsed councilman. In the Second and Third wards, Charles Scheible won, but not with a majority of votes as occurred on the south side. It was to the south side that the majority of the middle-class residents had moved.

Recruitment patterns also reflected the middle-class orientation of the Klan. The kleagles first approached fraternal organizations and then Protestant churches. Fraternal societies, such as the Masons, were well-established and usually predominately middle-class in membership. Protestant churches, such as the Methodist Episcopal, the Baptist, and the Presbyterian, varied in their class appeal; but Youngstown churches located beyond lower-class neighborhoods were the most likely to be Klan strongholds, especially on the south side.[25]

One of the Klan's major efforts to appeal to the middle class was its attempt to build a country club in nearby Canfield. Having purchased the Wetmore farm, the Klan campaigned to acquire for its members the most visible accoutrements of upper-class status—a country club with golf course, swimming pool, dining hall, and meeting rooms. Although never built, partially because of questions regarding Klan financial dealings and partly because of a declining membership base, the country club represented a long-term goal requiring financial support only available from the middle class; the upper class, of course, already had constructed the Youngstown Country Club, and probably would not desire or need to duplicate such facilities.[26]

For Youngstown, then, it is safe to conclude that Jackson's thesis is overstated. The Klan drew broadly from all wards, all sections, and all classes. It was weakest among the semiskilled and unskilled workers—the men that should have constituted a larger proportion of Klan membership were Jackson correct in his observations. Explanation of the motivation of Klan members must move beyond such a narrow economic interpretation.

Trying to explain people's motivations is fraught with danger. Not only was there no sociologist or George Gallup to develop and administer a scientific questionnaire to members of the Klan, but it was also difficult to get Klan members to discuss their participation once the Klan fell apart. Even those still alive some sixty years later and willing to talk might have rationalized, or simply forgotten. And yet some generalizations are necessary.

It is impossible to sum up the reasons for the growth of the Klan in a single motivating factor. James Q. Wilson, a political scientist, has noted that four incentives usually attract members of political organizations or pressure groups: material, specific solidary (offices, honors, or deference), collective solidary (conviviality, exclusiveness, or group esteem), and purposive.[27] The Youngstown Klan offered incentives in each area. For the organizers it offered the possibility of great material rewards; kleagles received $4.00 out of every $10 membership fee. For politicians and status-seekers, it created a bedazzling array of offices with intriguing and mysterious titles, such as grand dragon, kludd, exalted cyclops, kligrapp, and klaliff. Clyde Osborne would later admit to political ambitions as his overriding concern in joining and then leading the Klan in Ohio.[28] But the material and deferential rewards of office are limited to a handful; it is to the last two incentives that we must look for an explanation of the broader membership.

The collective solidary incentive consists of two somewhat disparate categories: exclusivity and conviviality. The Klan appealed to those who sought either. As a "Protestant Defense League" for native-born white Americans, it appealed to those wanting to protect American culture interlaced as it was with Protestantism. For some Protestantism was linked to democratic ideals; for others it represented a universal morality for all Americans. Catholics in particular were pictured as more loyal to the pope than to democratic institutions. Immigrants were portrayed as practicing a morality alien to American Protestantism, whether it involved bootlegging, gambling, or simply not according proper respect to the Lord's Day. Paul Morris, the last editor of the Klan's paper, the *Citizen*, complained about the need for Protestants to unite in defense of America. Indeed, it was an act of patriotism to do so.[29]

Such seriousness of purpose was not usually found in fraternal organizations. Colonel Simmons, however, was steeped in fraternal sociability and the appeal of parties, picnics, marches, parades, and carnivals. Thus, the Youngstown Klan held many events to attract those seeking excitement and conviviality. The Klan might rent the local amusement center, Idora Park, for the day, bring in Vern Rickett's band, and conclude the evening with fireworks. During the political campaigns, parades led by the Scottish Kilty band wended their way through downtown Youngstown and the near south side. Huge picnics with speeches, initiation rites, aerial displays, and even a wedding were common occurrences, all for the purpose of generating a sense of fun with one's own kind.[30]

According to Wilson, a purposive intent takes an organization beyond fraternal goals. Seeking to reform society as a whole, its members are willing to delay immediate benefits for the good feeling of being associated with a noble cause.[31] For many Klan members that noble cause was the salvation of Youngstown, a salvation dependent on strict observance of the vice laws and more Christian education for its children. Many Klan members came to this cause through pietistic Protestant sects and their ministers. From samples taken, the Methodists constituted 32.7 percent of the Youngstown Klansmen registered in churches; the Presbyterians (especially from United Presbyterian churches), 23.9 percent; Disciples of Christ, 17.3 percent; pietistic Lutherans, 7.8 percent; and Baptists 8.6 percent. The total number or percentage of Klan members that did belong to churches is unavailable because not all churches retained their records, some records were incomplete or poorly kept, and some churches no longer existed. Only one church refused to open its records. At least 33 percent of the sample, however, did belong, and it can be legitimately argued that the percentage would be much higher were more records available. Also, as indicated by Jensen's study of Iowa, those acknowledging affiliation with the Methodist, Presbyterian, Baptist, Disciple, or pietistic Lutheran faiths outnumbered registered church members by at least a 2-to-1 ratio. Considering that the Klan restricted its membership to Protestants, it was more than likely that pietistic Protestants, whether registered or not, dominated the organization.[32]

One anomaly in these statistics that requires further explanation was the percentage of Lutherans (13.1) that joined the Klan. It already has been established, of course, that almost half of the Youngstown Lutheran churches belonged to the United Lutheran Church (ULC). A recent (1918) creation of the General Synod, the General Council, and the United Synod of the South, the ULC represented German and Swedish Lutherans, who most often lived in eastern areas of the country and who were more assimilated into American society; they generally supported Prohibition and the enforcement of vice laws.[33]

There were, however, a significant number of German Lutherans who belonged to the Joint Synod of Ohio and Other States. The joint synod's espousal of traditional Lutheran theology regarding state legislation would seemingly preclude its members from joining the Klan. Nevertheless, some did, particularly from the Martin Luther congregation. Without the direct testimony of these individuals, it becomes necessary to offer speculative conclusions about the reasons for their membership. The most likely explanation for this pattern was the rate of assimilation of the Youngstown German population. Mill-owner Joseph Butler noticed, for instance, that most of the Germans in Youngstown no longer isolated themselves or their children in German enclaves. They spoke English and even sent their children to public schools. As the second-oldest Lutheran church in Youngstown (1859), Martin Luther was likely to have followed the pattern observed by Butler. It was World War I, though, that probably played a crucial role in leading Joint Synod Lutherans into the Klan. The questioning of their patriotism, accompanied by book-burnings, boycotts, and beatings in other areas of the country, pressured them to prove their Americanism. Although Youngstown newspapers did not report any incidents locally, the fact that the local school board banned the teaching of German sent a message to German Lutherans. As a 100 percent American organization, the Klan offered many German Lutherans an opportunity to prove their loyalty and affirm their status as American citizens.[34]

The statistical evidence cross-referencing membership in pietistic churches and the Klan is very suggestive but not conclusive. There is additional, less quantitative evidence, however, supporting the portrayal of the Klan as an extension of what Richard Jensen and Paul Kleppner have described as pietistic politics. Numerous local ministers joined or supported the Klan; the most vocal came from the Methodist, United Presbyterian, and Baptist faiths. A Methodist minister, George Gibson, might have become the Klan candidate for mayor had it not been for the residence requirement. Whenever the Klan held its parades, local Protestant churchwomen set up booths; according to a *Vindicator* reporter, at least 30 Protestant churches served food at the postelection victory rally in November 1923.[35] Once one includes the numerous speeches of Klan leaders and the articles from the *Citizen*, it is quite evident that the Mahoning Valley Klan was a purposive organization with pietistic goals and members.

It has become a commonplace assumption among historians that Protestant fundamentalism (often defined incorrectly as the Five Points of the Presbyterian General Assembly of 1910—inerrancy of the Bible, the Virgin Birth, Christ's atonement for our sins, the Resurrection, and the Second Coming) was linked to the rise of the Ku Klux Klan.[36] According to Robert Moats Miller, "though not all Fundamentalists were Klansmen, virtually all Klansmen—aside from the obvious charlatans—were Fundamentalists."[37]

Fundamentalism was a response to doctrinal challenges arising from Darwinism and the new biblical scholarship.[38] Emanating from Germany, the Higher Criticism undermined belief in the inerrancy of the Bible and challenged its historical authenticity, while at the same time attempting to retain a Christian base of beliefs. Darwinism posed an even more serious threat, not only because it postulated a different story of creation, but also because many intellectuals accepted Darwinism as a reason to reject any Christian base.

As these ideas from scholarship and science began to infiltrate Protestant seminaries, to gain sway over numerous ministers, and to affect the laity, a backlash erupted. In 1910, thanks to the contributions of Milton and Lyman Stewart, chief stockholders in the Union Oil Company, the Reverend Amzi C. Dixon began publication of a set of twelve pamphlets, entitled "The Fundamentals." These pamphlets, mailed free of charge to an estimated 250,000 pastors, evangelists, missionaries, theological students, Sunday School superintendents, and YMCA-YWCA secretaries, established a doctrinal core for practicing Protestants that reaffirmed the inerrancy of the Bible. Written by a group of recognized American and British scholars, "The Fundamentals" offered a conservative defense against the inroads of modernism, yet it avoided, for purposes of unity, some of the controversial positions later associated with fundamentalism.[39]

According to most recent historians of fundamentalism, its primary focus was on doctrine and not a response to social or political conditions. Premillennialists, who constituted a major segment of the fundamentalist movement, believed that the world was beyond salvation until the Second Coming of Christ; hence, they were hesitant about engaging in reform causes. Decline in morals or the appearance of false, modernist prophets could be, and often were, read as a sign of Christ's coming by premillennialists; but their path to salvation lay in personal, rather than social, regeneration. As a result, premillennialists had initially opposed American entry into World War I, as indicated by their leading journals, *Our Hope* and the *King's Business*. Modernists then launched an attack, especially through the University of Chicago's School of Divinity, on premillennialism as unpatriotic. Only the identification of the Higher Criticism with German militarism and an interpretation that "corrupt German Biblical scholarship was at the root of the astounding moral collapse of German civilization" finally persuaded the premillennialists to support the war.[40]

After the war premillennialists transferred this newfound sentiment to America, where the war against modernism could be interpreted as a defense of a bastion of Christian civilization. William Bell Riley, a Minneapolis Baptist preacher and premillennialist, organized the World's Christian Fundamentals Association in 1919 to stand against the wave. "The enemy had come in like a flood," its resolutions committee wrote, "and the Spirit of Jehovah had lifted up a standard against him."[41] Instead of awaiting Armaggedon as inevitable, Riley now urged an attack on the "Great Apostasy."

There was nothing inherent in Riley's theology, however, that would lead his followers to focus on immorality in the nation's cities, or on the Klan goal of "cleaning up the town." Although Riley had argued in his early years in Minneapolis that "the Church of God is especially charged with civic reform," premillennialism seems to have put a damper on these sentiments; thus, he avoided the subject in most of his works after 1910. Only one of the more prominent premillennialist preachers, John Roach Straton, pastor of Calvary Baptist Church in

New York, played upon the theme of urban corruption. In a book, *The Menace of Immorality on Church and State* and a published sermon, "Will New York Be Destroyed If It Does Not Repent?," Straton compared the corruption exhibited in New York's hotels and cabarets to that of Nineveh, Babylon, Sodom, and Gomorrah; he called for a return to the Bible as the only means of salvation.[42]

Thus, religious fundamentalism seems to offer little as an explanation of the rise of the Klan insofar as the Klan built on a platform of civic reform. Although fundamentalists did promote a feeling that American society was in crisis and that a return to the Bible was in order, their focus was more on denominational struggles over doctrine than over redemption of the moral order. Fundamentalists may have joined the Klan, but not for doctrinal reasons.

Although it is indeed true that some fundamentalists did join the Klan, perhaps as a reflection of fundamentalist crisis theology and support for a return to the Bible, the most prominent denomination in terms of Klan membership was the Methodist. Although the Methodist Episcopal Church, as it was called in 1920, did face some internal confrontations over modernism, the Wesleyan set of beliefs, not fundamentalism, remained as the underpinning to Methodist theology throughout the twenties. Wesleyanism emphasized a personal experience of Christ and the importance of good works as an indication of salvation. Since most Methodists deemphasized doctrine in favor of holy living, they were reluctant to apply definitions as a criteria for membership. Hence, Methodists were more appropriately called evangelicals than fundamentalists.[43]

It is also important to note that the Methodists were at the forefront of the Social Gospel movement. In 1908 their General Conference was the first such organization to adopt a social creed that translated the Sermon on the Mount into modern-day action. This creed projected a liberal stance not often associated with fundamentalists by historians. Unlike premillennialists, who saw the present age as one of decline, the Methodists felt optimistic that the Kingdom of God was at hand. The good Methodist could bring it sooner by helping the needy and desperate.[44]

The Disciples of Christ also combined an orientation toward the Social Gospel with widespread membership in the Klan. Their Board of Temperance and Social Welfare, founded in 1907, not only participated in the study of the steel strike of 1919 by the Interchurch World Movement but also studied race relations, labor issues, unemployment, and housing. The editor of the *Ohio Work*, L. J. Cahill, suggested that industrial conditions were influencing the Disciples' orientation. Whereas their origins lay in a more theologically based era, it was necessary for them to realize that the new emphasis was sociological, "and the church is judged by its service as much as by the correctness of its intellectual conceptions of Christianity." He also believed that Disciples "have been reared in an atmosphere of reform," supported by the presupposition that "things could be righted." Perhaps it was this presupposition that attracted so many Disciples to the Klan. As observed by Disciple historian Henry Shaw, "because of the nature of its constituency, the Disciples' churches were especially susceptible" to the Klan.[45]

What, then, led some Methodists—as well as some Baptists, Lutherans, Presbyterians, and Disciples of Christ—into the Klan if not fundamentalism? Simply put, it was a campaign to secure full enforcement of those laws that controlled the morals of the community, laws that represented the thinking of most pietistic Protestant denominations as to what constituted the mores of a Christian community. There was more widespread belief in the pietistic moral code among these denominations than agreement over doctrine or church structure. Campaigns to enforce vice laws had become a mainstay of these faiths. Through the temperance crusades of the 1870s and 1880s to the vice commissions established in 102 cities after 1900, Protestant ministers had sought proper enforcement of the law by local authorities—sometimes successfully, but more often without a thorough cleansing of the Augean stables.[46]

It is important to note, however, that many pietists did not join the Klan because of its potential for divisiveness. The Reverend Levi Batman, of the Disciples' First Christian Church, typified the skeptical pietist. On the one hand, he bemoaned, as did many Klansmen, the selective observation of the city's laws. "Today," he observed, "there seems to be a tendency to seek to disregard, to beat the law, and to elect which laws one will obey." Citing Sunday observance and Prohibition laws in particular, he warned of the potential destruction of American civilization. Yet, Batman also called for toleration of other religions lest "the country run red with the blood of religious war." From all indications, Batman did not join the Klan, although many members of his congregation did.[47] In the Mahoning Valley the Klan made inroads into pietistic denominations because of its control by moderates. Had the Klan appealed more to moderate factions nationally, or, more importantly, had it been free of a morally suspect leadership, it might have had an even greater impact on local and state politics.

Though it is easy to prove the existence of different motivations among Klan members, determining the percentages of each is virtually impossible. The majority of members probably joined for exclusiveness, conviviality, or moral purpose, and possibly some combination of the three. The primary focus of these reasons, though, was religious and cultural, not a contest for scarce economic resources, as argued by Jackson.[48] Klan literature and speeches do not refer to the loss of jobs to immigrants, or to a threat to neighborhoods; Klan actions were not directed toward keeping immigrants out of jobs or housing. Rather, there was a constant sense of distress over the moral directions of the city and a fear that American democracy, as buttressed by Protestant morality, might be on the decline.[49]

In short, the Klan was indeed a Protestant defense league, a nativist organization that defined America as a conservative Protestant culture. Its appeal cut across class lines and attempted to produce a unified front, a stiffened resistance to a politically corrupt society. Ethnic prejudices intensified feelings, thereby provoking a cultural clash. Unfortunately, Klan members suffered from an inability to see moral grayness, or to tolerate different moral values within an increasingly diverse American society.

6

The Millennium

"And I saw a new heaven and a new earth. For the first heaven and the first earth passed away, and the sea is no more."

—John, *Revelations*, 21:1

T he achievement of the millennium was almost at hand! Klan electoral successes created great excitement about the governments in the valley now headed by self-proclaimed Christians whose stated intent was to use their offices to effect a more moral society. For many Klan members the defective enforcement practices of the past had resulted from corruption or from a lack of backbone. There was an aura of confidence that the new officials suffered from neither malady. The Klan, however, was underestimating the capacity of its ethnic rivals, the Irish and the Italians, to resist its control; more importantly, it overlooked the human flaws of its members.

Charles Scheible, mayor-elect of Youngstown, had identified his campaign with the Klan, and the Sunday after the election, he reiterated his pledge to distance his administration from criminals or evildoers. His appearances before the First Baptist congregation and the Baptist Ministerial Association reaffirmed the bond that existed between Scheible and his supporters.[1]

The battle to win an election, however hard fought, is always easier than the struggle to deliver on campaign promises. Within the month Charles Scheible was at odds with local ministers over the enforcement of the blue law, even without having served a day in office. Amid rumors that Scheible had told Colonel Watkins that "it is not wise to enforce a bad law" because the ensuing uproar might lead to a recall, the evangelical ministers—a group estimated by these ministers to number about twenty-six out of forty local ministers—issued a statement calling for *full enforcement* of all the laws. "With all due respect . . . ," they reminded Scheible, "you owe your election to the moral law-abiding, God-fearing men and women of this city." "We believe," they continued, "it is time to cease discriminating against the American, law-abiding citizens, and we pledge our united support both from the pulpit and from our private influence in the closing of all grocery stores, all theaters and all movies on the Sabbath, all of which are operating contrary to our law."[2] The Reverend Archibald protested that since the law in question was already on the books, failure to enforce it constituted discrimination against Christians, thereby "allowing citizens of non-Christian faith, not only to plunder our dollars on Our Holy Day, but to plunder our sacred institutions, and to discredit and to nullify in the consciousness of our younger generation of Christian citizens, the great Christian Holy Day that has made American civilization what it is." For the moment, however, Archibald was willing to wait for Scheible's actions as mayor, rather than to require an immediate response.[3] The linking of American culture with Protestant morality was apparent in the comments of the ministers, as was the sense of urgency they felt about maintaining the link.

The ministers considered the selection of a new police chief as a litmus test for the Scheible administration. As a vital cog in the effort to enforce the laws more stringently, the police chief had to be someone above suspicion and yet with experience in the field. The ministers felt fortunate in being able to recommend one of their own, the Reverend Evan A. Watkins, of the First Baptist Church in Girard.[4] Watkins was not only an eminently qualified Christian, they argued, but also experienced as a member of the British army intelligence corps.

A man of infinite talents, Watkins held a press conference in early December to present a twelve-point program revealing how he would handle the position. Boasting that he could "destroy the red light district in one week," Watkins promised to leave the chief's desk for a more visible role in running the department—to sit astride a horse while touring the city. Setting a goal of stopping the "small town horseplay" among policemen, Watkins suggested personal inspections, round table discussions of problems on the beat, and the rotation of assignments as the paths to achievement of that goal. Surprisingly, for someone who supported law enforcement as the means of achieving a moral society, Watkins blamed filth and squalor for producing crime; he even queried reporters as to "how can one expect to lift the foreigner to real American citizenship while he lives in such a vitiated atmosphere?"[5] Nonetheless, the goal remained the imposition of Protestant moral values on all who hoped to become an American.

In mid-December, Mayor William Reese, still stung by the criticism of his administration and his poor showing in the election, decided to place pressure on the Scheible administration by offering to appoint Watkins for the duration of his term. The following day he withdrew his offer after pointing out that Watkins had not taken a police exam. Tongue in cheek, Reese praised Watkins for some good ideas, including one "that the city needed a chief who can ride a horse and jump fences."[6]

By the end of December, Scheible announced that Attorney Kedgwin Powell was to be the new police chief. Powell had participated in the Klan campaign and was closely associated with Clyde Osborne, Scheible's choice as law director. The selection of Osborne indicated his growing influence within Klan circles. Born on a farm in Portage County in 1881, Osborne had moved to Hubbard in 1898. He obtained a teaching certificate at the age of sixteen, and taught at several Youngstown business colleges before being admitted to the bar in 1905. By 1923 Osborne was working with his fourth law partnership. His employment as legal counsel for Mayor Reese during the Columbus hearings and his earlier opposition to the home rule charter created suspicion as to the sincerity of his conversion to the cause of moral reform. Osborne would later admit that he joined the Klan to further his own political ambitions.[7]

The ministers saw the appointment of Powell and Osborne as part of a pattern, as Archibald put it, of "sinister influences on Charles Scheible." The growing rift was apparent in the complaint of one minister that "the men around Scheible are interested only in their selfish ambitions." When Scheible offered the chairmanship of the board of visitors to the Reverend John Heslip, of the Tabernacle United Presbyterian Church, he declined because "I don't want to be numbered among men who are mere office seekers, who are politicians. I don't want to be a member of a cabinet which compromises." It was for this very reason that many had joined the Klan—to seek an end to compromises that undermined principle.[8]

It would appear that Heslip was accurate. Scheible and Osborne were not true believers. Rather, they sought the specific, solidary incentive of holding office and realized that a successful politician could not impose strict enforcement on a cosmopolitan city. Scheible's efforts to seek a livable compromise were apparent in a directive on blue law enforcement issued his first day in office.

Facing the blue law issue squarely, the directive stated that all vaudeville shows and poolrooms were to close, but theaters could show "proper" movies after 1:00 P.M. Drugstores, newsstands, confectionaries, cigar stores, milk depots, restaurants, and hotels could open on Sunday, but gas stations were restricted to the hours of 1:00–3:00 P.M. In an unexpected effort at fairness, the directive permitted Jewish merchants to remain open on Sunday if they closed on their Sabbath.[9] In a letter to the public, Scheible described his actions as corrective measures "to check the tendency of certain elements of this community to make of the day a so-called 'Continental Sunday' with all its attendant evils of open ribaldry, gambling and drunkenness." He pledged to "safeguard the Christian Sabbath from needless desecration and vicious practice."[10]

Scheible's directive drew mixed reviews. Pastors Archibald, Heslip, and Williams were angry, but the Reverend Hawkins, of Epworth ME, and the Reverend Hammaker, of Trinity ME, approved. The *Vindicator* praised the new rules as a good compromise for a cosmopolitan city. Labeling advocates of strict enforcement as Puritans, the newspaper noted that recent European immigrants wanted some recreation on Sunday, such as a movie or a baseball game, and predicted that stricter enforcement would drive them to less innocent pleasures.[11]

In what can be best described as an equal response to an applied force, the gas station owners—some sixty-five of them—demanded that the administration enforce the closing law for all types of businesses. After hiring a local Jewish attorney, Nathan Kaufman, they took out a mandamus petition to require the mayor to take action. Kaufman chided Scheible that he had promised full enforcement of all the laws during his campaign. Judge Gessner, however, dismissed the writ with the argument that courts could not enforce the law, and that relief for delinquent enforcement could only come through provisions in the city charter—an obvious reference to the possibility of a recall.[12]

For Kaufman, who preferred to have no Sunday closing law, the problem was not simply a matter of a Continental Sunday but of technological changes in the society. At the time the blue laws were passed, Kaufman noted, "Youngstown was not much more than a cow trail with its crossroads store and a meeting house," " . . . and it was easy to pass such restrictive laws and equally easy to live up to them." Now there were automobiles, gasoline stations, theaters, streetcars, and steel mills, some of which provided innocent enjoyment on Sunday, and some of which could not be closed down for one day without hampering their operation.[13]

Legally Kaufman still had the option of bringing specific charges against businesses left open under the Scheible directives. Once Kaufman pursued these cases, numerous complaints flowed into Scheible, many of them from local businessmen and bankers, who contended that visitors were staying away from Youngstown on Sunday. They estimated the loss at $100,000 in revenue. The *Vindicator* sympathized with those out for a Sunday ride and their need for gas or service. Changing conditions, the newspaper asserted, required moderation in the Scheible directives and the classification of the auto as necessary transportation, similar to the street railway.[14] Scheible caved in to the pressure in early March and permitted the stations to remain open until 2:00 P.M. By early May further modifications permitted them to remain open all day, a privilege granted to auto repair and accessory shops as well.[15]

Meanwhile, a state supreme court decision provided an opportunity for the Ministerial Association to rally support. In a case brought by a Findlay, Ohio, motion picture operator, the court ruled that the state blue law prohibited movies. The Ministerial Association, apparently with the support of all forty-five members, met with Scheible to demand the closing of all picture shows on Sunday. Arguing that motion picture shows did not involve any workers, Scheible refused to "close motion picture shows on Sunday unless I am compelled to do so." Web Lentz, exalted cyclops of the Klan and city councilman, hesitantly supported the association's demands, but Scheible chose to ignore Lentz's concern.[16]

The crusade for Sunday closing was just as much a disappointment in surrounding cities. In Warren, Mayor Marshall called for sensible observance of the blue law. He opposed vaudeville shows or soft drink stores that operated as saloons, but newsstands, gas stations, and motion picture theaters could stay open. When approached by Klan No. 70 in May with a demand that he close down motion picture shows in accord with the recent state supreme court case, Marshall retorted that his opinion remained the same: that strict enforcement of the law was "unfair and unkind" since movies functioned as harmless entertainment and a deterrent to crime. In nearby Niles, Mayor Kistler also refused to close down movie theaters.[17] East Youngstown, with no Klan mayor and a preponderance of inhabitants who worked in the mills on Sunday, refused to enforce the law at all.[18]

The administration of Charles Scheible had no conflict with the Klan over the enforcement of the other vice laws. As an expression of its confidence in the new administration, the Mahoning Valley Dry

League promised to rein in its enforcement agents.[19] On his first day in office, Kedgwin Powell predicted that "this city can be cleaned up and we are going to try our best to accomplish the cleaning." As Powell was establishing new procedures for the beat policemen to handle vice violations, Clyde Osborne informed slot machine investors that the policy of the new administration was no gambling and no bribes.[20]

There were, however, three potential roadblocks in the path of righteousness. The city was in severe financial difficulties, the police force was poorly paid and thus susceptible to bribery, and the criminal element was practiced in exploiting human foibles. The city's finances had been on a downhill slide for a number of years, ever since the decision was made to issue bonds to cover current operating expenses. Once the bond money was spent, a new issue became necessary. With the state of Ohio's recent ban on such usage, Scheible and his finance director, Arthur Williams, confronted a budget of approximately $2.5 million with $1.7 million already committed to bond and interest payments. City expenses required immediate cuts from the $1.3 million spent the previous year to $875,000 in 1924.[21]

These financial stringencies were to have an adverse impact on police staffing and morale. In the previous year the police, who were paid $150 per month and worked seven days a week, had not received payment for the last three months. Although the new administration was able to resume payment of salary because of the receipt of second-half property tax collections, the Scheible administration had to forgo a promised raise and, in addition, lay off twenty-five policemen, hardly an auspicious way to begin a law enforcement campaign.[22]

Within the year the severity of the financial problem diminished, and a basis was laid for long-term financial stability. After a levy defeat the previous November, the new administration turned in two directions for relief. The city council passed an occupational tax on all those who worked in the city, but near the end of 1924, it had only collected from half of the residents. The city also benefited from prosecution of Prohibition cases within the city; the fines now accumulated in city coffers instead of in those of nearby communities, such as Struthers. Seeking a more reliable source of income, the administration placed another levy on the ballot in August—it failed—and again in November. Its passage then meant that the city could begin to reduce its bonded indebtedness and the proportion of city revenues spent on that indebtedness, as well as to drop the hard-to-collect occupational tax. Financial well-being, though, was still five years away.[23]

Even without these financial stringencies and the concurrent pressure on the police force, the craftiness of vice law violators in the avoidance of detection posed just as many problems for an enforcement-minded administration. Besides payoffs to willing policemen to ignore illegal activities, violators could also rely on informants within the police department who relayed advance information about raids. When the police broke in, they found an abandoned site. Oftentimes lookouts or heavy doors protected speakeasies; by the time the police succeeded in breaking down the door, incriminating alcoholic beverages were hidden away, perhaps in a trap door in the floor, or poured down a sink. Violators were also willing to take some of the heat if the police or a friendly administration was under public attack. In such cases a well-known joint was raided and the bartender arrested. In some instances the owner rented the operation to a flunky who was willing to take the rap and a jail sentence in exchange for a financial reward. Thus, the owner could reopen once the heat was off. Even the most ardent of enforcers would find it difficult to shut down vice operators totally.[24]

And yet the Scheible administration tried. As finances improved, it added more policemen and established two vice squads. Numerous raids and arrests were part of a citywide crackdown on gambling, prostitution, and illicit alcohol. The city's coffers benefited from the prosecution of the cases in Youngstown, but at the end of the first year, Scheible admitted that bootleggers, gamblers, and prostitutes remained a problem.[25]

Despite its efforts the administration came under attack, sometimes from the politician eager to establish a reputation, sometimes from the zealot determined to purge all remnants of evil. City Councilman Owen James battled verbally with Powell over his effectiveness, an attack that served to intensify administration efforts. In March 1925 the Federation of Women's Clubs complained to Powell about unregulated dance halls and their effect on the morals of young people. Powell warned hotels and restaurants that permitted such dances about the consumption of "hip pocket" liquor. "Young girls are being ruined," claimed Powell, "by having liquor dispensed too freely from flasks at dances, both private and public." He promised to seek a council ordinance to require chaperons and to ban noisy jazz music, close dancing or embraces, and suggestive movements. Council took no action after the state legislature passed a bill to ban those under eighteen from attending dances and to prohibit dances on Sunday.[26]

The administration's well-intentioned actions did not quell public dissatisfaction. In September 1925 Governor Donahey once again held hearings after receiving reports of Powell's alleged irregularities, but he later dropped any charges because of insufficient evidence. Meanwhile, the Ministerial Association began passing around petitions calling for more rigid enforcement of the Prohibition amendment. In early December, Clyde Osborne, now grand dragon of the state, held a heated conference with Scheible in his city hall offices during which he related reports coming to him of wide-open operations within the city. Scheible denied the charges and asked for evidence.[27] The Reverend A. C. Archibald stirred the pot further with a sermon that called nonenforcers of the Prohibition law "Judas Iscariots." Federal, state, and local officials, to his mind, had not enforced the law to the best of their abilities, and they, not bootleggers, were the key factor in the ruination of Prohibition.[28]

Amid charges that he was seeking a political office in Mahoning County, Osborne cited a speech by Powell admitting that there were more than 350 bootleggers in Youngstown. Claiming that the administration was unable or unwilling to enforce the law, Osborne called on the Klan and the WCTU to fight for a cleaner government.[29] This call to battle created a recall movement directed by the Klan and assisted by the WCTU. But the Klan had dwindled significantly in size by early 1926, and the movement fizzled.[30] Disillusionment with elected officials was only one cause of that decline.

The lack of support for recalling Scheible also represented a growing realism regarding the limits of strict enforcement. In an editorial the *Vindicator* praised both Scheible and Powell for accomplishing so much with a limited force. The newspaper claimed that Youngstown was cleaner than most cities. Even the Reverend Archibald began to hedge. In a sermon to his congregation, Archibald called Scheible a "disappointment," but admitted the great problems the administration had faced when it assumed office. Archibald rejected the recall movement on the basis that citizens could not expect 100 percent from their officials. As long as they conscientiously did their best, that was all that could be asked. Once again Archibald had pulled away from the implications of earlier sermons; even he did not possess the willpower he so often called for in public officials.[31]

In Warren a similar alienation occurred between the mayor and the Klan. Upon taking office, Safety Director G. L. Reeder reorganized the police force and began an immediate crackdown on bootlegging and gambling. His efforts to stop "gas hawks" from accosting young women and to keep naughty magazines off newsstands in public places drew praise from the Tod Avenue Methodist Episcopal men. They pledged their assistance to "an efficient officer of the law," both as a "Christian as well as civic duty." Even Sheriff John Thomas, of Trumbull County, described Warren as "remarkably clean," a result of the work of the city police.[32]

And yet the Klan opposed Marshall for reelection in 1925, probably because of his compromises on Sunday closing. Although Anne Brooks, a Third Ward councilwoman, received the Klan endorsement, the Klan was too small by then to exert much influence. Brooks finished a distant third to Marshall, who won again by fourteen votes over attorney W. B. Kilpatrick, the Democratic candidate, whose support allegedly included disillusioned churchgoers and civic organizations. In its advertisements the Marshall committee cited its capable handling of law enforcement as more effective than that of previous administrations. Its appeal, though, was to those who now realized the limitations of government. "We realize," the ad commented, "there is an abundance of work yet to do, but as it is something that springs up overnight, we just have to keep everlastingly at it and maintain the highest degree of morality possible." The millennium had not yet arrived.[33]

The achievement of perfection was not just a problem external to the Klan. Overly rapid growth had produced major internal imperfections as well. The only apparent criteria applied to prospective members were a white, Anglo-Saxon, Protestant heritage and the means to afford the $10 membership fee. No tests were taken, no attitudes examined as thousands of people rushed to join this popular organization. It would have been difficult, even if rigorous screening had been applied, to achieve unity, particularly in an organization that emphasized numbers rather than commitment.

It would be even more difficult in an organization in which the commitment of the leaders to stated goals was not as great as that of the newly acquired membership. As the infighting between Simmons and Evans and the scandals regarding Clarke, Tyler, and other national Klan leaders came to public attention, numerous members began to question their leaders' intentions. In Cleveland, Lorain, Sandusky, Canton, and Elyria, there were also reports of dissatisfaction with the local kleagles and their methods of organization. Until the Klan secured a local charter, the nationally appointed kleagle controlled the organization and its finances, and apparently permitted no audits.[34]

In the Mahoning County Klan—organization was on a county-wide basis—newspaper reports from the two months after the election of 1923 revealed stresses regarding the leadership of Colonel C. A. Gunder. A native of Marion, Indiana, Gunder, almost fifty, was an experienced salesman for fraternal organizations when he joined the Clarke campaign.[35] After his appointment to klux Mahoning County, his seeds sprouted into one of the larger organizations in the state and gained him recognition from national headquarters. By the time of Scheible's election, questions had begun to arise locally about finances and the fact that most of the dues went to Atlanta. Friction over possible irregularities in the organization's finances culminated in a drive for a charter that would give the local Klan power to elect its own leaders and to control the finances.

The first indication of friction regarding Gunder's performance occurred in December 1923. Claiming more than 18,000 members, at least 10 percent of the county population in 1923, Gunder had applied for a local charter and had gone to Columbus over Thanksgiving to obtain it. For some unexplained reason, Trumbull County Klan No. 70, under the leadership of Doyle Glossner, received its charter, but Mahoning County did not. According to the *Vindicator*, rumor had it that a board of auditors was investigating Gunder's financial report.[36] At the 3 December meeting of the local Klan, though, Gunder presented the charter and received a diamond ring in return.[37] The next day the newspapers reported that Gunder was to leave for a higher Klan position, earned by his performance in Youngstown.[38] No public report was ever issued regarding the audit of Klan finances; Gunder went on unscathed in January 1924 to head the Klan in the Worcester, Massachusetts, area. When Hiram Evans made an appearance at the Canfield Fairgrounds in June 1924, however, Gunder would return amid rumors that he might once again seek to control the county Klan. One faction, so the *Vindicator* reported, was strongly opposed to him and the possibility of having "any more dissension in the ranks."[39]

Whatever the problems with Gunder, the loss of his services created a vacuum not easily filled. At first it appeared that a multitude of strong leaders, including Charles W. Stillson, of the board of education, the Reverend George Gibson, and former mayor Fred J. Warnock, would seek the post of exalted cyclops, enticed by Gunder's statement that it was a paid position. A revelation, apparently made at the election meeting, that the kleagle had misinterpreted the constitutional provisions about pay for the cyclops caused many candidates to withdraw. Instead the Klan selected Webster R. Lentz, a department manager at the Stambaugh-Thompson department store. Nothing came of the movement to declare the election illegal.[40]

Lentz's consolidation of control as exalted cyclops brought a measure of internal peace to the Klan throughout the first five months of 1924, but the approach of elections on the county and state levels would once again increase tensions. Victories in the races for the governorship and offices of state representative and state senator (one-half were elected every two years) would have enabled the Klan to control the state. A more immediate goal for the Mahoning and Trumbull Klans was victory in their respective counties. Two of three county commission seats were available, but Klan sights were set specifically on the prosecutor and sheriff posts, which would give them control of the law enforcement agencies in both counties.

In mid-May the Klan met at its Kountry Klub field in Canfield to select candidates for the Republican primary, then three months away. The Klan pre-primary attracted from 16,000 to 17,000 voters; women of the Kamelia voted also. The Klan endorsed candidates for every major county and state office, but it was particularly hopeful of capturing the county sheriff's post.[41]

The primary of 12 August was not as definitive as the Klan had hoped. Although it captured all county commissioner seats, the state senate post, and two of three spots as state representatives, the Klan was very disappointed in the defeat of its candidates for county sheriff and county prosecutor since they were linchpins in the law and order campaign.[42]

The sheriff's race served as a good basis for evaluating the location of Klan strength. Adam Stone, the Klan candidate, carried county townships by a 2-to-1 margin, as well as Struthers and the south side of Youngstown; but incumbent Paul Lyden dominated the north side and blitzed East Youngstown by a 10-to-1 margin. The fact that the Klan had concentrated on the sheriff's race and yet lost indicated that the Klan was beginning to decline after the overwhelming triumphs of 1923. The geographical patterns once again held constant, but the number of Klan votes had lessened.[43]

Having lost the most important races, the Klan now faced the quandary of whether to support the entire Republican ticket or to run independent candidates in the November general election. Clyde Osborne, the campaign chairman for the state, commented that the Klan would be neutral where it lost; he spoke against an independent Klan slate. "This primary will teach the Klan a lesson," Osborne hoped. "Candidates can not be nominated regardless of qualifications and sometimes without the careful observation of the character and past record of the aspirant for office." Osborne promised that the Klan would correct such mistakes in the future.[44]

In early September, however, John S. Fye, a south side grocer, filed an independent petition for the sheriff's race. His supporters included Albert Cooper, Klan nominee for county commission; Owen James, Youngstown city councilman; and Sam Fye, the Fourth Ward Klan leader. When William Countryman, mayor of Poland, filed as an independent in the race for probate judge, the Klan went on record in opposition to both candidates. In a lengthy editorial in the *Citizen*, Evan Watkins chastised those who would support an independent ticket and accused them of "sour grapes" over winning only ten of the fifteen Republican races. Though he admitted that the Klan primary at the farm may have been a mistake, Watkins felt that the failure of Klan members to vote in the Republican primary had been the real culprit.[45]

It was during this fracas that Watkins began to experience difficulties with the ownership of the *Citizen*. By October the difficulties had widened into a split leading to Watkins's resignation. The immediate cause of the resignation was an apparent difference over support for the independent candidates. In the same issue announcing Watkins's withdrawal, the newspaper announced its support for John Fye, an elder in the Presbyterian Church and a man of "Christian integrity." Both Fye and Countryman eventually lost in the November election.[46]

The resignation of Watkins represented more than political differences. Since Watkins had assumed the editorship one year before, the newspaper had moderated the harshness of Klan prejudices. In July 1924, for instance, Watkins invited the Knights of Columbus to play a baseball game during the Klan picnic at Idora Park. "A colored referee and 2 Jewish friends on the gate," claimed Watkins, "ought to take out of the day all the usual sting of bigotry which the enemies of the Klan usually attribute to it." The Knights chose not to play.[47]

Watkins also invited Joseph Heffernan to speak from his pulpit on Sunday, 14 September. Joe Heffernan, an Irish Catholic, was a native of Youngstown. Because of his closeness to the ethnic communities— he was a noted orator able to converse in several languages— Heffernan overcame Klan opposition in his attempt to become a municipal judge in 1923. The fact that he garnered as many votes as Scheible suggests that many Klan members voted for him, perhaps because of his commitment to strict law enforcement. In his invitation Watkins alluded to a statement of Heffernan about the shamefulness of

Joseph Heffernan while he was municipal court judge from 1927–31.

religious disputes. Heffernan made the comment during the "tack" case, which involved several young men who had spread tacks on the road leading from the Klan farm in Canfield back to Youngstown after a rally in July at which Hiram Evans, the imperial wizard, appeared. Heffernan refused the invitation.[48]

Watkins's creation of a new organization, the Rams (named after Rameses), capped his efforts to present the Klan in a more tolerant light. Watkins made the membership nonsectarian and encouraged members to wear either short horns or no horns, so that there would be no butting of heads. He even went so far as to advertise in the *Citizen* that brotherhood was the guiding principle of the Rams Club.[49]

By August 1924 Watkins's strained relationship with the Klan became apparent in his editorials. Watkins expressed impatience with the attacks being made on the newspaper: "From the next issue until the cause is removed or we cease to function," Watkins promised, "there is going to be a clean-out-in-the-open fight for loyal, patriotic and Protestant organization in Mahoning County. If there are men who think the only thing we should do is slam the Church of Rome in their pet and ferocious way, they have another 'think' coming." The *Citizen,* Watkins threatened, "will feel it a God-given duty to put the clamps effectively on this type of parasite." An advertisement for a Sons of Italy meeting in the paper attested to Watkins's commitment.[50]

Amid mounting attacks in September, Watkins held his ground. In an editorial on the sixth, he portrayed the Klan as "unalterably Opposed to Religious Intolerance." He admitted, however, that Catholics required watching because they still labeled Protestants as heretics and refused to recognize their marriages as valid. Protection rather than intolerance was his goal. His patience reached its limit the following week. "The complaint is sometimes made," he noted, "that we do not hit as hard as we ought to. Well, we are running a newspaper and not a sewer. We want to run a decent journal and not a personal organ of hate and venom unfit for publication and unsafe to enter an American home." He concluded that it was best for the newspaper "to leave it to others to play the mountebank and to indulge in insane ranting and mental dribbling." By 9 October the owners fired Watkins.[51]

The plight of Watkins revealed the debilitating struggle within the local Klan over what to do about Catholics, Jews, and foreigners. The differences between the cultures of these groups created frictions that were natural and understandable. How to deal with those differences, however, was a much thornier question that festered within the Klan organization. For some Klan members the differences were irresoluble and required removal of rival ethnic groups from posts in the government and teaching positions. The Scheible administration, however, had refused to remove "undesirable" employees. After a visit to City Hall several weeks after his election, Scheible praised the fact that there seemed to be little deadwood and promised to keep all employees. Police Chief Powell also promised to treat officers fairly and equally regardless of race, color, or creed. Although eventually individual employees were let go, there was never a wholesale firing of

Catholics, Jews, or blacks. The same was true of Warren, where Mayor Marshall promised to keep all city employees.[52]

It would appear, then, that there were two Klans. Many of those who joined in 1923 sought Protestant moral dominance only, not Protestant hegemony. They believed themselves tolerant toward other religions and willing to permit their practices; they were also nonrestrictive in regard to jobs and housing. Watkins's campaign for Scheible had attracted these Klan members, but a more militant and more prejudiced faction questioned whether the contrasting cultures could live together at all.

The Youngstown City Council, with the blessing of Mayor Scheible, did attempt, though, to place some limits on aliens. The council passed an ordinance in April under suspension of the rules to make it unlawful for an alien to own or to possess firearms; only Harry Payne, non-Klan councilman of the First Ward, dissented. The *Vindicator* labeled the action as discriminatory; it suggested that similar action be applied to ordinary citizens.[53]

A second ordinance stirred up more of a controversy. If enacted as originally proposed, the ordinance would have denied licenses for operating theaters, restaurants, poolrooms, dances, pawnshops, or as peddlers and junk dealers to those aliens already operating businesses within the city. Both Scheible and Osborne opposed the motion, as did Harry Payne, who presented an amendment to permit those aliens having first papers, but no time to finish the process of naturalization, to receive licenses. The passage of Payne's amendment indicated that at least two Klan council members were sympathetic to aliens engaged in the naturalization process and not simply anti-alien. Obviously they hoped to forward the process of acculturation by encouraging speedy engagement in the acquisition of citizenship. The *Vindicator*, however, considered the entire proposal an injustice committed "under the name of Americanism." Complaining that the ordinance would deprive many aliens of their livelihood yet provide no substitute workers for important jobs, the *Vindicator* condemned this Americanism as "merely narrowness and selfishness."[54]

After considerable debate and public pressure, including threats by Mayor Scheible to veto the bill and attorney Nathan Kaufman to test the ordinance in the Ohio courts, the final form of the ordinance permitted two groups—aliens whose business required police surveillance and aliens with first papers who owned a business prior to 1 April—to purchase a license. The key to unanimous passage of this ordinance seemed to be Clyde Osborne's advice as law director that the state courts would not uphold a more restrictive ordinance.[55] The compromise was an indication of the split between moderate and intolerant factions and of Klan efforts to patch up its internal divisions.

Within the public schools there were also efforts to restrict Catholic access to teaching positions. According to some Klan members, Catholics retained a loyalty to the pope that made them willing pawns in a papal plot to convert Protestant children through Catholic teachers. Their loyalty to the pope raised questions about their commitment to a democratic system of government and about the politics they might teach. Within the Youngstown school system, there was no question raised by the board, at least publicly, about the employment of Catholic teachers. But in nearby Struthers eleven robed Klan members, headed by the Reverend A. M. Stansel, pastor of the First Baptist Church, attended the 5 May 1923 meeting of the board of education, and demanded that "only real Americans" be employed in Struthers schools. Board members admitted that four of their teachers were Catholics, but noted that glowing reports had been received of their teaching. No action was taken.[56]

Although the elimination of Catholic influences within the public schools did not take root in the valley, the movement to reintroduce the Bible and prayer did. The Klan, in its first public appearance in Youngstown, had presented a letter to the board of education at its meeting on 4 December 1922. The letter expressed concern that "our young people are exhibiting each day the consequences of this moral laxness," and cited the schools for failure to stem the breakdown of moral standards. The Klan's solution was a religion course taught to each student, whose curriculum would be agreed upon by Protestant, Catholic, and Jew. Thus, the initial thrust of the Klan was comprehensively moral rather than sectarian; it realistically assumed that it could not impose Protestant instruction. Superintendent O. L. Reid agreed that "if the great faiths could get together on some program, it would be a fine thing."[57]

For the next year there were debates over how to manage such a program. Initially the board examined the Gary Plan, first adopted by the Indiana steel center. Reid opposed the Gary Plan, however, because it allowed the children to meet with their own minister during the school day; public schools, after all, were supposed to unite students. The *Vindicator* complained that the plan would also lengthen the school day.[58]

In December 1923 the Reverend George L. Ford, executive director of the Federated Council of Churches in Youngstown, forwarded a letter citing the importance of religious education, including both the Bible and character development. He was concerned that such education could not be done in the schools "because of the mixed character of our population," nor by individual churches because of inadequate finances. Turn instead, Ford suggested, to the Dayton Plan, which provided for a voluntary release one hour per week for religious education. The Federated Council would construct a program for Protestant children, and the other faiths could do likewise. The board expressed interest in this plan and asked Ford to provide them with more details.[59] In the winter of 1925, the Federated Council started classes with 108 students; in the fall the classes drew 1,500.[60]

Meanwhile, a Klan majority had assumed control of the board in 1924. Within its first month the board passed a resolution ordering teachers to read the Bible at the start of school. "Brief selections of scripture," according to the board's directive, "chosen with reference to the age and understanding of the pupils, shall be read by the teachers without any creedal or sectarian comment whatsoever." Comments were permitted to indicate "the existence of God and human responsibility to Him for the practice of the moral virtues such as truth, justice, reverence and square dealing." The superintendent, principals, and teachers were to prepare a graded course of study. After a year of work Superintendent Reid recommended a course of study that required Bible passages and character lessons on forgiveness, honesty, industry, and kindness; the board accepted the report unanimously.[61]

The overall accomplishments of the Klan after a year of control in the city of Youngstown must be judged as meager at best, if one begins with the premise that the organization was highly prejudiced. Elected officials, whether Klan-supported or actual Klan members, had not chosen to penalize or to persecute members of other faiths.[62] Indeed, their prime emphasis was on moral development in the public schools and enforcement of the vice laws. Obviously Bible-reading, moral development, and vice laws had a distinctly Protestant tinge; but even in those areas, leaders, such as Scheible, Osborne, and Watkins, were attuned to the necessity of compromise in a city so cosmopolitan in composition. As politicians they enacted what they believed would be most acceptable to the majority; after all, continued success in office depended on satisfying the majority.

Despite the fact that the Klan had built its membership and political power on a platform of law enforcement without prejudice, its petty prejudices found their way into its rhetoric and attracted many members less willing to compromise, less willing to live and let live. Osborne, for instance, had accused Jews of keeping their wealth to themselves and Catholics of supporting only Catholics for political office.[63] As editor of the *Citizen*, Watkins had also chided Catholics when he printed a story connecting the Roman Catholic church to illiteracy; statistics gathered from the U.S. Bureau of Education revealed that Catholic nations were 45 percent illiterate, whereas Protestant nations were less than 5 percent. Such statements could only serve to aggravate the fears of Catholics. On the evening of St. Patrick's Day 1924, for instance, the Klan lit crosses throughout Youngstown. Obviously, the day was a well-known drinking holiday for many Irish, but the Irish saw only prejudice and not the moral and cultural judgment being made by Klan members. A near riot resulted in the downtown square shortly before midnight.[64]

The firing of Watkins as editor of the *Citizen* provided an opportunity for those more poisoned by prejudice to vent their anxieties. The new editor was Paul Morris, a well-known participant in Klan activities. Formerly a photographer for the *Vindicator*, Morris had taken photographs of the cheat spots in Youngstown when William Reese was mayor and had presented them to Governor Donahey as evidence in the Reese hearings. An already seated member of the school board, he created a controversy in 1924, along with the Klan-endorsed candidates, over the building of East High, which at that time would have been the third high school. Since Morris came from the west side of Youngstown, he complained about the excessive expenditures and size of East High; he proposed that a junior high be built on the west side as well. The fact that the east side population was more heavily immigrant and close to East Youngstown probably played a part in Morris's opposition. Morris also cited "the dangers of traffic congestion and evil influences" as a problem for west side children in walking to the present junior high. Eventually, East High was downsized and a high school built on the west side named after N. H. Chaney, a former superintendent of schools in Youngstown and a successful candidate for clerk of courts on the Klan ticket in 1924.[65]

Morris turned the *Citizen* into a bitterly anti-Catholic paper, worse even than before Watkins took over. He reprinted a story from the *Voice* which claimed that Catholics controlled the New York executive, legislative, and judicial branches in order to suppress freedom of speech and thought. Another front-page story described how nuns and priests had taken over the Kalida school district in Putnam County,

Ohio, in order to teach students the basics of the Catholic faith. A number of other lay Roman Catholics had been observed in public schools placing pictures of the Virgin in their classrooms or requiring children to make the sign of the cross. Oftentimes these teachers called in a priest to present Catholic teachings.[66]

These stories served to confirm Morris's paranoia concerning the plotting of the Roman Catholic church. In an editorial in October 1925, Morris called on Protestants to unite against their common enemy. The United States was in the midst of its third great crisis, according to Morris, the others being the American Revolution and the start of the Civil War, which he accused Jesuits of fostering. In the present crisis "papal immigrants, herded here from Europe and Ireland by the hierarchy of Rome, in pursuance of a definite policy, have grouped themselves in our great cities. In obedience to the commands of their priests they have propagated large families," all with the purpose of making America Catholic. The Jesuits, he warned, were lulling Protestant Americans to sleep by their usage of catchwords like "tolerance," "broad-mindedness," and "religious liberty." The issue, he claimed, was not religious, since the Roman Catholic church was "a world-wide political system, a terrible parasite which draws out the lifeblood of peoples, holding them in superstition, poverty and degradation, while it takes the livery of religion as the most effective cloak for its real design, which is autocratic political ascendancy." It was imperative, then, that Protestants unite within the Klan, a "divinely ordained" organization for the defense of Protestantism. Through union they could slay "the ancient juggernaut of Anti-Christ," a task beyond the capability of Europe. "The Lord God of Battles," he promised, "will give almighty power to the sword we wield."[67]

Morris's clarion call went unheeded. By the time Morris took over as editor, the Klan had begun to fade. His vitriolic attacks gathered no support, rallied no troops. Instead, in 1925, he faced stiff opposition in his bid for reelection to the school board. The *Vindicator* singled him out and denounced it as "wrong and unpardonable for a member of the Board of Education to make the base appeals to race, class and religious prejudice" that he was making. Morris lost the election.[68] The plight of Morris was a sure sign that the Klan had not built its strength on religious prejudice so much as moral intolerance.

Internal difficulties were not the only explanation for the Klan decline. Rumors of financial irregularities and the publication of the Klan membership roster had also eroded its strength; failure to produce a millennium amid political compromises had generated factionalism that was corrosive. But it was the opposition of rival ethnic groups that finished off the Klan.

Within Youngstown the opposition had formulated early within the Irish community. The Irish, of course, had a deep-seated hatred for Anglo-Saxon culture as represented by the British. Under the control of Great Britain for centuries, the Irish had suffered repression and economic servitude, yet retained their culture, language, and religion. Having escaped British rule, they were well equipped to resist any organization or group that threatened their newfound freedom. They were also ill-prepared to tolerate even moderate forms of prejudice; the Klan statements about Catholics smacked too much of British intolerance.[69]

Within the United States the Irish often entered politics as a means of self-protection and advancement. The most visible form of Irish opposition in Youngstown was the mayoral campaign of Thomas Muldoon. His list of supporters read like a litany of Irish names. Several young Irishmen had also participated in the "tack case" during the Klan parade to Canfield. It was the plot to steal and to publish the Klan membership list, though, that caused the most harm. The Irish dominated the American Unity League, which arranged the burglary. The publication of the membership roster was a blow to the Klan, which had partially built its appeal on secrecy. Though no Klan dues records are available to pinpoint the times at which members left the organization, the spring of 1924, with the publication of the list and inner turmoil over political compromises and strategy, marked the beginning of the Klan's decline within the valley. By the fall of 1924, it was evident in the firing of Evan Watkins that the Klan was losing its moderate base of support.[70]

The appointment of Clyde Osborne as grand dragon of the state was an attempt to bind up Klan wounds and renew the battle. Osborne's appointment came after his skillful performance at the Democratic National Convention in New York City in the summer of 1924. Osborne had met Hiram Evans on his previous visits to Youngstown, and apparently impressed Evans enough to warrant an invitation to accompany him to the convention as his legal adviser. One of the leaders of the movement to denounce the Klan by name in the Democratic platform was E. H. Moore, former mayor of Youngstown and former county party chairman. There was no doubt that the Democratic party would denounce organizations that opposed religious liberty; the question of whether to name any organization specifically, however, threatened to split the party. Moore had managed to wrest control of the Ohio delegation from the state Democratic chairman, W. W. Durbin, and hoped to cast a unanimous ballot in favor of naming the Klan. Osborne, however, was able to prey upon divisions within the delegation—in particular, between Moore and the supporters of Governor Victor Donahey.[71]

Donahey, then only fifty-one years old, possessed qualities that appealed to the typical northern Klan member. He was a Methodist and an ardent supporter of Prohibition, and belonged to the Knights of Pythias, the Elks, and the Modern Woodsmen of the World. He came from the small town of Westchester, in rural Tuscarawas County, and had served as a township clerk, county auditor, and state auditor for two terms. After his victory in 1922, Donahey earned the sobriquet "Veto Vic" for his refusal to pass more than seventy bills forwarded by the Republican-dominated state legislature. Moore, an urban wet, had opposed Donahey in the previous election.[72]

The upshot was a split in the Ohio delegation, with twenty-eight voting to name the Klan and twenty against. Osborne took credit for creating the split, but how, or even if, he managed it is unclear. After all, the factional differences were already there, and Donahey was a cautious politician unwilling to alienate by a direct assault. In an interview with a reporter, Osborne hinted, though, that the Klan's support for Donahey in the gubernatorial race was the Klan's share of a deal struck with the Donahey delegates.[73] Although Donahey would receive Klan support in the fall, he never admitted that he had sought Osborne's endorsement.

What seems more likely is that Osborne took advantage of the situation to improve his standing with Hiram Evans. Osborne could not have struck such a deal since the Klan had already endorsed Joseph Sieber, a lawyer from Akron, in the Republican primary held in August after the Democratic convention. Although Sieber lost to Harry L. Davis, former mayor of Cleveland and governor of Ohio, it would have been embarrassing were Donahey to cash in Klan chips against Sieber. It is also important to note that the Donahey delegates were against naming the Klan out of political considerations rather than out of any sympathy for the Klan. At a meeting of the Ohio delegation, all speakers, including those against naming the Klan, labeled the hooded organization un-American, un-Christian, and unconstitutional. Osborne went out of his way to praise one of the speakers, who called the Klan a bunch of "misguided Christians," because of his moderation in speech.[74]

Whatever Osborne's role, he had impressed Evans. For his work Evans named Osborne to succeed Brown Harwood as grand dragon of the state, the first Ohioan so named. His immediate goals were a reorganization of the state Klan into six provinces, passage of the Klan legislative program by the state legislature, and a thorough cleansing of the city of Niles. It was in Niles that Osborne hoped to rebuild lagging Klan fortunes in the fall of 1924. He was to face the determined and oftentimes violent opposition of the Italian community.

1

The Niles Riot

Set out for the great city of Nineveh and preach against it;
their wickedness has come up before me.

—Jonah 1:2

They stood silently in a field north of Niles at 10:00 A.M. on the morning of 1 November 1924. After Mayor Kistler swore in the nearly one hundred fifty Klan members, it was not clear whether the white ribbons dangling from their lapels designated them as a Klan guard or as police officers. Their assignment was to clear the way for Klan members, to protect their constitutional right to parade through Niles without interference. After dynamite had exploded on his front porch several days earlier, Kistler was in no mood to compromise. A violent confrontation was at hand.

It was a series of events over the previous year that had produced such an unsettling scene. What had begun as a cultural clash was now a war. More than half of the Niles population was Irish and Italian, and they believed that the Klan threatened their way of life. Prejudiced statements from national and local leaders had convinced both Irish and Italians of the need to unite in opposition. The Italians took the lead in Niles; their concept of honor and their experience with governments in Italy that were oppressive and corrupt led them to a more physical—indeed, violent—means of stopping the Klan. And the more physical the confrontations, the more determined the Klan to impose law and order. [1]

Somehow Harvey Kistler had not believed that it would be that difficult to reform Niles when he first assumed office. A political novice, he expected to exercise control over every aspect of his administration, to set high standards for public officials—particularly within the police department—and to crack down on vice in Niles. The willpower of a committed Christian was his strength, the talisman that would guide him on his crusade. Kistler smugly underestimated the staying power of the entrenched bootleggers.

Behind Kistler stood the prayers and moral certitude of local Protestant churches. In March 1924 the Methodists sponsored a revival led by Dr. George Hugh Birney. Before overflow crowds Birney complained of the "no-man's land of warfare in the Mahoning Valley," and questioned the indifference of many churches to the moral conditions that existed in Niles. He challenged the citizenry to "struggle and take risks and sacrifice until victory is assured against the sin that slays the soul."[2] Birney had an ally in the Reverend Robert Ketchum, of the Baptist church, who had come a year earlier from Butler, Pennsylvania, with a reputation as a crusader and a "bear on bootleggers."[3] Ketchum was to assume the mantle of leadership in the moral crusade.

Supported primarily by Klan members, Kistler focused his first reform efforts on the police force. Surprisingly, despite Lincoln Round's troubles with Governor Donahey, Kistler reappointed him as police chief.[4] His ace in the hole, however, was his cousin, O. O. Hewitt, whom he named as the director of public safety. In his forties at the time of appointment, Hewitt was a soft-spoken man of average build, but his prominent jaw projected a sense of determination. A farmer and teacher in nearby Newton Township in his younger days, Hewitt had moved his family to Niles, where he worked for the Niles Forge and Manufacturing Company. As safety director, Hewitt was to be in charge of the allegedly unreliable police chief.[5]

Hewitt undertook a two-pronged effort in the war against vice in Niles. Armed with a Kistler-sponsored ordinance that doubled the fine for liquor violations (from $500 to $1,000), he raided questionable houses repeatedly, usually leading the raids himself. In an effort to avoid leaks, especially from within the police department, he kept the destination secret until the raiding party was en route. Upon arrival Hewitt often wielded an axe to break down bolted doors.[6]

Hewitt's second point of attack was the caliber of the police department. As in many cities, the Niles police force was understaffed and underpaid. Early in 1923 the city withheld pay for two months, a situation that could open even honest policemen to the possibility of graft.[7] The fact that some policemen took bribes was difficult to prove, but widely suspected. In cases tried in 1927 and 1931, bootleggers testified that certain policemen received $10 per week to forgo enforcement of the Prohibition law.[8] Without sufficient evidence, however, to mount a campaign against bribery, Hewitt attacked other signs of ineptitude by firing police officers William Mullen and Joseph Mears for intoxication while on duty and conduct unbecoming an officer.[9]

The pressure generated by more raids, larger fines, and the plugging of informational leaks in the police department provoked a violent reaction. On 17 April 1924 a stick of dynamite wrecked the home of Police Chief Lincoln Round. A time bomb set for 2:00 A.M. blew a six-foot hole in the wall. Fortunately, the explosion's force traveled sideways rather than upward, where the family was sleeping on the second floor. The *Warren Tribune Chronicle* speculated that strict enforcement was the cause.[10] The resort to intimidation and violence was a harbinger of things to come.

Meanwhile, Trumbull Klan No. 70 decided to hold its spring Konklave on Friday night, 9 May, followed by a march through Niles's downtown. The Konklave attracted 3,000 Klan members from the Youngstown-Warren area and also from nearby Sharon, Pennsylvania. As the Klan members and 200 autos moved along the parade route, several cars blocked their way. A well-known bootlegger, "Curley" Sandfrey, and former police lieutenant Joseph Mears were arrested for obstructing traffic as the parade continued. Kistler simply reprimanded and released them.

When the parade made the turn on the "doughnut," a name given to Niles's downtown business section, and passed by Central High School, a very predictable confrontation occurred. The Klan had lit a cross in front of the school, which some of the observers charged and knocked down. As the Klan members sought to recover the cross, bystanders pelted them with stones and bricks; several shots were fired. One young man was hit on the head and knocked out. Two of the Klan tormentors, Michael "Brea" Naples and Anthony Sherro, were swooped up along with the cross and carried out to the Klan field, where they were forced to kneel and kiss the flag. Naples would angrily point out that he was a sailor, although in his civilian clothing at the time of the parade, and that his patriotism should not be in question. Naples was an associate of the Jennings family, and Sherro served as the bodyguard of Tony Nigro (alias White), considered one of the leading bootleggers in Niles.[11]

Mayor Kistler attributed the disturbance to "hot-headed youths from East Niles," but the background of these youths would suggest that there was more to this riot than the reaction of Catholic or foreign-born young men to a prejudiced organization.[12] The confrontation marked the point at which certain East End Italians, noted for their bootlegging and gambling and often connected with the Jennings Athletic Club and speakeasy, assumed leadership of the Italian opposition to the Klan. Though it was to their self-interest to oppose the Klan's moral crusade, they also viewed the Klan's actions as an unwarranted and disrespectful attack on the Italian way of life.[13]

Because Klan leaders saw the attack on their parade as yet another example of immigrant lawlessness, they defiantly announced a Giant Konklave to be held on Saturday, 21 June. It was estimated that fifty thousand Klan members from Ohio, Pennsylvania, and West Virginia would attend as well as a special attraction, the grand dragon of Pennsylvania, Sam Rich. In preparation for the potential confrontation, Mayor Kistler established no-parking-zones to avoid the type of blockade set up by Sandfrey and Mears. The march was scheduled before dark because unknown antagonists had severed the power cable for downtown lighting during the previous parade.[14]

The decision of the Klan to attempt another parade marked a shift in the battleground, away from vice enforcement and onto the streets where vice offenders could muster broad-based support. Bootleggers and gamblers benefited from the displacement of each side's antagonisms onto such a seemingly harmless event as a parade. What to the Klan was a constitutional right to parade was an affront to the honor of the Italian community because of disparaging remarks about the Catholic religion made by Klan members during the previous parade.

Kistler was amazingly confident about his ability to handle the crisis. According to the *Vindicator*, Kistler claimed that "members of the Klan have been cooperating with officials . . . in trying to prevent disorder," and "he saw no reason why the Klan demonstration should be accompanied by trouble." Events prior to the parade, however, made Kistler's optimism look foolish. On Thursday a bomb thrown at a burning cross erected across from the McKinley Memorial blew the cross apart. The day before the parade, a crowd estimated to be one hundred fifty strong tore down a banner hung across Main Street to welcome the Klan.[15]

As an estimated ten thousand Klan members poured into Niles the next day, roving crowds assaulted them with an assortment of bricks, glass, rocks, and pipes hurled at suspected cars. Windshields were broken and American flags torn from their perches on Klan cars. One young man was dragged from his car and beaten unconscious. No one took credit for the assault, but the presence of a flaming tire doused in kerosene in front of Central High School aroused suspicions about the presence of the Knights of the Flaming Circle, an anti-Klan organization from Steubenville. A rumor that a trainload of the Knights had arrived so discouraged Klan members that many began to leave.

By 3:30 P.M. the grand dragon had decided to call off the march. The exalted cyclops of the Trumbull Klan, Dr. B. A. Hart, accepted the decision, but continued the meeting at the Klan grounds off North Road. According to Hart, "it was a good meeting and a large crowd, and the law-abiding spirit of the Klan meeting was shown." Amid speeches and fireworks a ground display, "Down with the Rotten Politicians," burned brightly while crowds continued to line the streets of Niles, more in anticipation of a riot than a parade. Fights and other disorders continued almost until midnight, and Kistler finally had to call Sheriff Thomas for assistance.[16] The local police force had proved once again to be an inadequate agency of the Klan's enforcement campaign.

On Monday, Kistler promised a full-scale investigation. "It has been reported to me," he said, "that American flags were torn from machines during Saturday night's fracas. All American citizens of whatever creed will agree that such action is deserving of a heavy penalty." Kistler did not understand that the Irish and Italian assailants were rejecting not the flag but the Klan's contention that its people and their mores were the American way. The following day eighteen men, including Jim Jennings, "Dude" Murphy, local prizefighter out of the Jennings stable, and attorney Patrick Fusco, were arrested on charges of desecrating the American flag, discharging firearms in the city, destroying property, and using profane language, but the warrants were unexpectedly withdrawn the following day.[17]

Kistler did not feel intimidated by the riot or by his inability to punish those responsible. "No mayor," Kistler lamented, "has ever had to face a more disorganized community. But I'm not the kind of man who will back down because there is opposition." When asked about future Konklaves, he cited once again the right of peaceful assembly. "As long as a Konklave is law-abiding," he asserted, "and lives up to regulations, it will be permitted in Niles." He included any organization, whether Protestant or Catholic, as eligible to exercise that right.[18]

The Youngstown *Citizen* responded with a stinging indictment of Kistler. The people of Niles, according to the *Citizen*, had elected Kistler to clean up the operations of the police force, but "he has failed to do it and is now faced with the most disgraceful episode in the history of Niles." The newspaper blamed his natural timidity for a less than forceful response to riot conditions. The police were even worse, "a serious farce" in the words of the *Citizen*. Round lacked "ability and courage" to direct his men, some of whom stood by and watched the beatings; only Lieutenant Gilbert helped any of the marchers. The newspaper bragged that "no such a hellish game could be pulled off in Mahoning County" and called for Round's immediate removal.[19]

The *Citizen*'s remarks were indicative of tensions not easily controlled by moderate forces or compromise. Klan members were indignant that the anti-Klan forces had escaped punishment, and made threats of violent retaliation. The burning of a cross on the property of James Kaley in nearby Mineral Ridge in the evening of 23 June prompted a frightened call to his Catholic friends in Niles. A detachment of fifty cars arrived within minutes to aid Kaley. Meanwhile, fifteen carloads of armed Klan members were coming from Warren. The rival forces were about to meet in a field near Ohltown Road when Sheriff Thomas arrived with five deputies. He drove into the middle of the five hundred men, stood on his seat, and pleaded with them to disperse. After forty-five minutes, they retreated, taking their antagonisms with them.[20]

Meanwhile, the anti-Klan forces finally were coalescing into the newly formed Knights of the Flaming Circle. After a riot in nearby Steubenville, Ohio, in August 1923, Dr. W. S. McGuigan, a dentist, announced the formation of the organization and his installation as "grand supreme monarch of the central division of the organization." The name referred to the Circle tactic of lighting a gasoline-doused tire to counter cross burnings. Though the organization would attract many Niles members, there did not appear to be any offices, dues, or other appurtenances normally associated with fraternal societies. The Circle was more a response to immediate issues than a long-term, goal-oriented organization.[21] It was also an effort to unite the Catholic population of Niles.

On Sunday, 29 June 1924, the Knights of the Flaming Circle held its first public meeting at the East Side Athletic Club to initiate more than four hundred members. Attorney Patrick Fusco chaired the meeting, rather than the behind-the-scenes leaders, Jim and Joe Jennings and Tony Nigro. Fusco solicited funds to support suits seeking the ouster of Kistler and Round. The Niles Ministerial Association, on the other hand, promised the support of their parishioners in case of attempts to oust the mayor or police chief. The battle lines in the "Niles Civil War" were now drawn.[22]

On Saturday morning, 19 July, at 2:00 A.M., Lt. Charles A. Gilbert and another police officer approached three men laboring over a stalled auto near the Allison Hotel on Main Street. The men grabbed

Gilbert as the other officer mysteriously disappeared. A broken bottle shredded his face and scalp, and produced deep gashes in his right eye and mouth. Bleeding profusely, he was left in the street to die. Gilbert would recover, but the incident reopened Niles's wounds. The *Citizen* thought that the beating of Gilbert was related to his actions during the riot, a retribution for taking the part of the marchers, an act of intimidation of a police officer who dared to enforce the law. Incensed once again with Chief Round, the Niles City Council blamed him for the Gilbert beating.[23]

The fact that Klan opponents had effectively neutralized the Niles police force made the Klan more determined than ever. On 3 August the Klan held a meeting in Mineral Ridge that precipitated a series of violent confrontations. Leaders described the Klan meeting on Saturday evening as spiritual and orderly, but on Sunday a burning cross in front of the local Catholic church provoked the Knights of the Flaming Circle to respond by burning tires in front of the houses of suspected Klan members. As crowds gathered and fights seemed imminent, Sheriff Thomas arrived to dismiss the potential combatants. Hostilities had dissipated only because of his presence.[24]

To the north in Niles, Circlers had gathered in front of the McKinley Memorial and set fire to another tire. Steve Martin, a roll-turner at the local Thomas mill, was standing across the street, on the steps of the Presbyterian church. He refused an invitation to join the revelers, which sparked a fight in which Martin was outnumbered. He fled with the Circlers in pursuit, finally dashing into a confectionery store. The mob gathered outside the store, pushed the door in, and hit Martin on the head with a watermelon. He was then thrown through the door. Some unidentified persons came to the unconscious man's assistance and carried him home.[25]

The mayor's response on Monday was to ban all cross or tire burnings; jail was to be the penalty. The administration also arrested six Circlers for causing the Mineral Ridge disturbance, but the pressure of Circle supporters' surrounding the police station resulted in a quick hearing and bonded releases. Late that night, about 11:45, Circlers reported to the police that they had seen Klan members in cars carrying guns to a meeting at Joseph Rummell's pool hall. As the police entered the hall to search for those carrying arms, an estimated two hundred Circlers followed. Shouting ensued, followed by some jostling. The police re-created a sense of order when they arrested six Klan members for carrying weapons. The Klan then tried the same tactic as the Circlers—surrounding the jail—but the chief refused to release the men until after a hearing scheduled for Tuesday. Crowds continued to gather on street corners the entire night despite the entreaties of Sheriff Thomas.[26]

Merchants in the city were distraught. They told a *Vindicator* reporter that they wanted the governor to stop playing politics and impose martial law. Meanwhile, Kistler fought to maintain local control by hiring twenty-four special police to patrol the city. By Wednesday, Chief Round would claim that "Niles was as quiet and orderly as any city in the state last night and we don't need any outside help in keeping it so."[27]

In spite of a more restrained atmosphere, bitter feelings remained, and the hearings for arrested individuals promised further inflammation. On Wednesday, Kistler scheduled a hearing for Frank Sundae, allegedly the one responsible for the beating of Steve Martin. Sundae's lawyer, Patrick Fusco, tried to call witnesses who were to testify that Sundae was not in town at the time of the beating. Kistler, who had become suspicious of the ready availability of such witnesses at previous incidents, refused to hear them. He bound Sundae over to the county grand jury with a bond of $500. After the hearing an indignant crowd gathered on the steps of the courthouse. Sheriff Thomas arrived to clear the crowd, but ended up by taking some of the leaders, including Jim Jennings, back into the courtroom to talk with Kistler. "This is a fine way to act," Jennings told Kistler, "after last night's meeting when you agreed to give us fair treatment." A repentant Kistler offered to recall Fusco and hear the witnesses, but Fusco refused and questioned his ability to get a fair trial.[28] The following day, in apparent retaliation for the fact that no Klan members had been arrested for the Mineral Ridge riot, Tony Nigro, one of the Circle leaders arrested for his participation in the riot, swore out warrants for five Klan members, including Joseph and Louis Rummell, owners of the Rummell pool hall and Klan rendezvous, as the real instigators.[29]

Meanwhile, a frustrated Mahoning County Klan had scheduled a mass rally at Idora Park on Friday, 9 August. Colonel C. A. Gunder, who was returning from his assignment in Massachusetts to address his former followers, offered to lead the crowd of 10,000 on a parade through Niles. "We treated the antis up in Massachusetts different," he noted, "than you treated that gang of thugs up in Niles. We filled them full of salt. You're a fine lot for letting a bunch of Wops scare you out." Amid Gunder's calls for action, the audience offered support: "You lead and we'll follow."[30] The ineptitude of the Niles Police Department finally had caused the Klan to consider extralegal means of enforcing the law.

The possibility of outside interference provoked a reassessment by all sides and a call to Sheriff Thomas to mediate. "The citizens of Niles," commented Thomas, "are not the kind of people who will allow their religious opinions to lead them into civil war." He lamented the presence of outside influences and openly supported legislation to limit demonstrations or parades reliant on outsiders.[31]

By Monday, 11 August, Thomas had produced an agreement to stop the burning of all symbols in Niles and the surrounding township and to drop the warrants on both sides. Thomas was pleased with the results and praised the signers of the truce as sincere and willing "to do all in their power to prevent any further trouble." Kistler also banned Klan parades for the next thirty days.[32]

In response the exalted cyclops in both Mahoning and Trumbull counties issued carefully worded statements calculated to reduce tensions. Web Lentz denied that his Klan subscribed "to any such doctrine as preached by Col. Gunder at Idora Park and as reported by the press." Dr. B. A. Hart insisted that "such methods are not our methods. We stand by the authorities and by the law. We believe in obeying the law and that is one of the principles of the order. The true Klansman is one who stands by the law and does not advocate violations of it." Hart, as well as Lentz, was obviously trying to serve as a model to rival ethnic groups; both were overlooking the Protestant tinge to American laws as a cause of disobedience.[33]

Peace prevailed in Niles for the next two months. The only incident was a burglary at the Rummell sporting goods store—an adjunct of the pool hall—of twenty-two revolvers and rounds of ammunition on 8 September. Although the robbers were not caught, local citizens worried that it foreshadowed more trouble between the opposing forces. Eventually trouble did come, but not until the middle of October, when the mayor and city council agreed to grant the Klan a permit to parade.[34]

No one knows for sure why he did it, but Harvey Kistler granted the Klan a permit to march in Niles on 1 November. It would appear that Klan members had decided to prove that they had a backbone, that they were not going to allow, as Gunder put it, a "bunch of Wops scare you out." It was also rather obvious that Osborne was trying to revive Klan fortunes. He was well aware of the Klan riot in Carnegie, Pennsylvania, the previous summer, and of Hiram Evans's advice to Grand Dragon Sam Rich to hold more marches because the riot had spurred a growth in Klan membership.[35] For Kistler the Klan desire to march was defensible; simply put, it was their constitutional right. There was no basis, however, for believing that the right would go unchallenged. Harvey Kistler was taking a chance, and he knew it.

Except for Vincent Lapolla, the Klan-dominated city council supported Kistler's decision. They too knew the potential dangers of such a march, but felt that all that was needed was greater backbone from the safety forces than was exhibited in the previous occurrences. Councilman Elmer Jones naïvely advised the police simply to keep an eye on the troublemakers and arrest them if they started anything. Lapolla forewarned that the wearing of masks was an irritant and offered a resolution to ban masks, but the other councilmen voted it down. [36]

The possibility of a violent confrontation did not serve the Klan cause well. It alienated moderate elements whose support the Klan was seeking. A group of Niles citizens identifying themselves as the Constitutional Defense League and claiming to represent American citizens of all faiths appeared before public officials to beg them to stop the parade. The league representatives had canvassed Niles civic clubs and merchants, who were fearful for their businesses and of the notoriety that would befall Niles if a riot ensued. The officials refused to reconsider. The following evening a flaming circle appeared in front of Central High School. [37]

The Circle's counterstrategy was to hold its own parade, a tristate function, on the same day. Their circulars invited "all eligibles," and, in an oblique reference to potential violence, advised participants to "avoid bringing the women and children." Amidst estimates that ten thousand Circlers might show up to confront twenty-five thousand Klan members, Kistler warned the Flaming Circle that he had given them no permit. In a conciliatory tone, he offered them a permit for another day.

Realizing the potentially explosive nature of the situation and the overwhelming numbers involved, Kistler nervously began to cast around for additional safety forces. He appealed to both Sheriff Thomas and Kedgwin Powell, chief of the Youngstown police force, for aid. Powell suggested a conference between the opposing sides, which took place on 28 October. The Klan, under the orders of Grand Dragon Clyde Osborne, offered to remove its masks to placate some of the opponents; but for a militant segment of the anti-Klan forces, the real issue was whether they could march at all. With no compromise possible, the meeting broke up. [38]

The following day about 2:00 A.M., Harvey Kistler's house blew up. His wife had been unaware of the threats made against her husband when they retired at 10:30 the evening before. She slept, but he was restless. At 1:20 he heard a car slow down in front of his house. The sound of rattling tools led him to think that the car possibly had a flat tire. Another car joined the first, and they both proceeded to pass slowly in front of the Kistler home several times. Kistler never rose to check; fifteen minutes later his porch exploded, his windows shattered, and he fell out of bed unharmed. The bombing only intensified his resolve to permit the march.[39]

The problem of providing adequate police protection remained. Sheriff Thomas was searching for more deputies, and Powell had finally promised assistance from Youngstown. Attorney Nathan Kaufman, of Youngstown, filed for an injunction against using municipal police forces outside the city limits, which forced Powell to back off. Chief Round then telegraphed the governor about the bombing in the hope of securing state assistance, but Donahey, who had political ties to the Irish Democratic community in Youngstown through Joseph Heffernan, cautiously sent special investigators instead of the national guard. Round, Thomas, and their men were all that stood between the opposing forces, but the willingness of the individual officer to enforce the law was in serious doubt.[40]

Meanwhile, Clyde Osborne unilaterally issued orders to the Klan. Apparently in an effort to placate Klan opponents, the orders forbade Klan members to wear masks or to bear firearms during the parade. They were also forbidden to direct traffic or to undertake any police functions. Finally, Osborne commanded that "no Klansmen shall resent remarks from the sidelines or take action against any denominations excepting in actual self-defence."[41] If followed, such orders would also make the Klan appear as the offended party and perhaps result in a groundswell of votes in the following Tuesday's election.

On 30 October the chamber of commerce made one last effort to settle the matter peacefully when it called a conference open to all concerned citizens for 4:00 P.M. at the McKinley Memorial. An estimated three hundred to five hundred citizens in attendance chose Walter F. McQueen, prominent local lawyer, as the permanent chairman.[42] In order to facilitate the business of the meeting, McQueen appointed a committee of six citizens to come up with some resolutions. The committee included John McDermott, former state senator; Samuel Brown, the general manager of the Niles Republic Iron and Steel Company; John Hosack, the manager of the Mahoning Valley Steel Company; John Sharkey, an official of the Empire Mill; and Joseph Pallante. The majority of the committee did not want the parade but recommended that, in light of Kistler's failure to call it off, all citizens should cooperate with Sheriff Thomas to achieve a peaceful event.[43]

The only dissident was John McDermott, who filed a minority report requesting Kistler to cancel the parade. Speaking twice on behalf of his resolution, McDermott reminisced about former years when English, Welsh, Irish, and Italians lived together peaceably in Niles. "After the trouble at the Klan parade in the spring," he lamented, "there have been many enmities. Men, long friends, have ceased to speak to one another." Another outbreak would cement those hatreds, rather than heal the wounds. "For the protection of lives and property and for the good name of Niles," he called on the mayor to revoke the parade permit. After defeating an attempt to table the McDermott resolution, the remaining citizens passed the resolution to ban the parade by a 5-to-1 margin. A committee was named to communicate the resolution to Mayor Kistler.[44]

Kistler refused to grant their request. He deplored the potential notoriety that might accrue to the city of Niles, but stood firmly on the grounds of the Klan's constitutional right to parade. "Let us be law abiding and broad-minded," Kistler pleaded, "and be willing to extend constitutional rights and prerogatives to every group of whatever race, color or creed."[45]

The city bustled with excitement and tension. Newspaper reporters from the region, as well as from New York, crowded into Niles hotels in anticipation of a scoop. Businessmen began to board up their storefronts; some even sought riot insurance. Many were prepared to leave town for the day.[46]

At this point Sheriff Thomas made one final effort to secure the aid of the governor. Donahey responded that sending troops prior to trouble was "without precedent in Ohio." According to Donahey, both Thomas and Kistler had the time and the power to deputize enough officers to control the situation. "In any event," he warned, "I will hold you and the mayor strictly accountable." Considering that Donahey had received the endorsement of the Klan in the gubernatorial election, it would have been politically difficult for him to send in troops four days before the election to end the parade.[47]

Halloween night, the evening before the parade, had more than its share of pranksters. Knights of the Flaming Circle were out in force, checking on strangers and locally known Klan members. Some fights occurred, and Klan members with weapons were rousted off to the police station. Sheriff Thomas sent deputies to aid the beleaguered nineman Niles force, but the situation was reaching a point of no control.[48]

Frank McDermott, son of the former state senator, had been in Erie, Pennsylvania, working for his father's construction company for much of the day. A boxer and football player for Jennings A. C., he had returned that evening with his fellow workers "Dude" Murphy and "Shine" Jennings (Leo, the third Jennings son). Around midnight they had eaten in the City Restaurant before joining some other Circlers. The word around 3:00 A.M. was that the Klan was gathering at Rummell's pool hall, so they headed along Main Street toward the bridge across the Mahoning River.[49]

Rummell's pool hall was halfway up the hill from the river. As McDermott and his friends reached the crest, they could see an auto pulling up in front of the pool hall. The group fired their guns at the auto. McDermott, in a fit of bravado, ran to the auto and hopped on the running board. Inside were Rex and Willard Dunn, brothers who had armed themselves and had headed into Niles after being awakened by the noise of a distant explosion. Under a hail of bullets and stung by at least one, Rex Dunn turned and fired three times at McDermott, wounding him near the ear and in the shoulder. Stunned, McDermott held on as the car sped away, finally falling into the road several hundred feet away. Rex Dunn was later arrested and charged with shooting with intent to kill.[50]

Meanwhile, Colonel Watkins was headed to Niles to post bond for three Klan members turned in by the Circlers for carrying concealed weapons. He was recognized, and several hundred men gathered in front of the police station. After posting bond, Watkins left hurriedly in his sidecar motorcycle and headed toward Girard. An estimated twelve cars took off in pursuit. The high-speed chase cut off Watkins, who returned to Niles and ran inside the jail. Amid cries of "Lynch Watkins!" and "He's afraid to come out!," Sheriff Thomas provided an armed escort for Watkins to Girard. Watkins's escape marked the end of the evening's activities, but Circlers hardly slept as they laid plans for the next day's blockade.[51]

The center of preparations was Jennings Hall. The leaders of the Flaming Circle were the Jennings brothers and Tony Nigro. Only twenty-five at the time, Nigro was picked because of his reputation as a fearless combatant. On occasion he had marched into Klan meetings, ordered them to disperse, and pulled a gun to enforce his command. The Jenningses, in their early thirties, were no less belligerent; they had assembled an arsenal of weaponry, including machine guns. Their stable of boxers, including Dude Murphy, was ready to assist.[52]

The Circle plan was simple—stop all Klan members coming through Niles on their way to the Klan field, located on Deforest Road north of the city. The fact that there were only two routes through the city made it easy to control the traffic. Coming from the east, cars would have to travel on Robbins Avenue past the almost finished Italian Catholic church, Our Lady of Mount Carmel; travelers from the south would drive along Main Street. Both routes eventually passed the General Electric Glass Works at the corner of Main and Federal. Blockades were established at the Glass Works field and in front of Mt. Carmel Church. In case Klan members did push past the blockades and attempt to march through the East Side, there were machine guns placed across the corners of Mason and Wood streets, the site of Jennings's pool hall. The rallying cry became, "They shall not pass."[53]

The Circlers also prepared to protect the nuns at St. Stephen's Church. Rumors abounded that the Klan intended to march on the convent of the Sisters of Humility of Mary to molest them. Shine Jennings accepted the assignment of taking a cadre of men to surround the convent. They sat there and waited for an attack that never came.[54]

The morning dawned clear and crisp. Our Lady of Mount Carmel held a crowded 6:30 mass for 1,700 members of the Italian community. They were united in their support for one another and in their willingness to die while resisting the Klan.[55] By mid-morning Circlers had positioned themselves at the blockade points.

Meanwhile, the mayor had left his office. No one seemed to know his whereabouts. It was rumored that he had taken off for Warren the night before. Left to defend Niles were Chief Round, his nine-man force, and Sheriff Thomas with twenty-five special deputies, a barely adequate force in the midst of an armed camp.

On Robbins Avenue, Circlers armed with guns and knives had begun to stop all automobiles. If Klan robes were found, they were seized and sometimes torn apart, sometimes mounted on a nearby pole or tree, and sometimes taken to a nearby house. Beatings usually accompanied the search; the stronger the resistance, the more violent the beating. Klan members were then told to turn their cars around and leave. Peter Greco, a laborer for the Thomas Steel Company, led the Circle brigade. He was assisted by forty or fifty men and many women, who carried away the confiscated robes and guns.[56]

G. E. Victor, of Farrell, Pennsylvania, an auto trimmer, left his home about 1:30 in the company of Harvey Brauchle; they proceeded

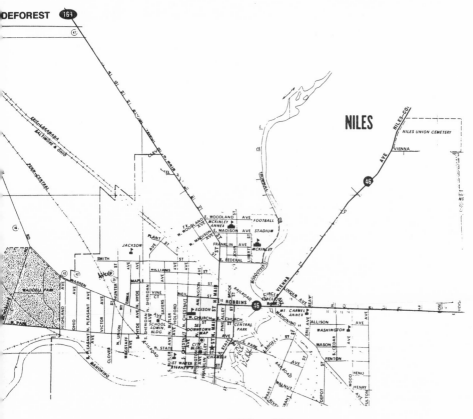

Street map of Niles, Ohio

to the Niles Klan site via the cities of Sharon and Hubbard. Circlers stopped them on Robbins Avenue. Victor's response is uncertain, but four men pulled him from the auto amid shouts, curses, and cries of "Me shoot, me shoot." Grabbing his arms, they pummeled his face while one of the assailants reached from behind to plunge a six-inch knife into Victor's chest through the left lung and near the heart. They released him, but, instead of falling, he staggered across the street. He asked his friend for a drink of water before getting back into the car. As they began to pull away, the Circlers opened fire at the tires and flattened them. One of the bullets glanced off Brauchle's forehead. Brauchle then walked his friend to a doctor in Niles, who refused treatment. An ambulance was finally called, and Victor was taken to Warren City Hospital, where he remained until Thanksgiving.

At the hospital attendants pumped blood from Victor's lung. The next day, according to Victor, a man who identified himself as the Reverend Matthews, of Struthers, visited and offered him some candy; but his nurse, Miss Ernest, would not allow Victor to eat it. Later the candy was found to contain a dose of arsenic that would have killed the disabled man. After leaving the hospital at Thanksgiving, Victor recuperated at home. His wounds healed, but he was permanently disabled.[57]

The scene at Main and Federal, now identified by the Circlers as the "deadline," was even more tumultuous than the one at Robbins and Linden. More than one hundred fifty Circlers stood ready to withstand any Klan onslaught. Many lay in wait in the Glass Works field, and others stood watch on the embankments running alongside the railroad tracks. The determination of the Circlers to protect their way of life was evident in the attitude of one elderly lady, whose three sons were standing guard at the intersection. She told a *Vindicator* reporter that her sons will "never go back on their tradition and their God. They'll go to hell first. And if they are killed, Daddy and I are still here and we'll carry on."[58]

For much of the morning, Klan members from north of Niles had been gathering at the field. Byron Filkins, a staff photographer for the *Cleveland News-Leader*, who had arrived in Niles during the morning, decided to examine the Klan encampment. There he was welcomed by W. H. Kline, the Klan manager, and given permission to take all the pictures he wanted. Filkins estimated that about one thousand Klan members were there picnicking. Others were in a hastily constructed cafeteria eating food and drinking coffee prepared by some Kamelias.

Filkins noticed a broad range of participants. "Some of them," he asserted, "looked like prosperous businessmen. Others looked quite the reverse and you could see a few here and there who'd look much better for a shave." Most of them were also armed. "They had rifles, shotguns, bluesteel automatics, 32's, 22's and those who didn't have guns had clubs." The main sport for the moment was comparing weapons; "Isn't this a dandy?" was the most common way of asserting one's manhood and readiness for battle.[59]

Although Clyde Osborne had forbidden the carrying of weapons in the parade, it was evident that the sweep of events and the inevitability of conflict had overridden his orders. In a test of mettle, the Klan did not intend to march unarmed. Many Klan members belonged to the Ohio State Police, started by Colonel Watkins, and wore white ribbons designating them as "Special Police." Mayor Harvey Kistler had formalized their quasi-military status that morning. At 10:00 A.M. he had sworn in about one hundred fifty young men between the ages of twenty-one and thirty-five to serve as an advance guard to clear the streets. The Klan had finally succeeded in blurring the line between itself and the municipal police forces.[60]

Another reporter, Arthur Lynch, of the *Youngstown Vindicator*, had settled himself at Main and Federal, where he was accorded the "courtesy of the camp." An unidentified anti-Klan leader told him, "We'll fight it out till the last man drops." Lynch was there about 12:30 when the first major incident occurred. He saw a Ford truck with a wooden gun mount on the back coming south on Main Street. A machine gun opened fire, as a siren sounded and the members of the crowd gasped, "They're coming." For the next twenty seconds, a hail of bullets from both sides drove Lynch into a nearby gas station for cover. The driver gave up and headed back. According to Lynch, several wounded men had to nurse their wounds at backyard pumps. Within moments a second reddish-tan touring car, also armed and firing, came within two hundred feet of the "deadline." As Circle guns began to fire, "the driver of the car halted, wheeled about, and also disappeared in a rain of lead." Someone told Lynch that the cars were full of Klan policemen hired to blaze a path for the marchers. Lynch was the only eyewitness to provide an account of the machine gun incident.[61]

About the same time Paul Barkhurst, George Skaggs, and W. E. Hillman were driving from Rummell's pool hall out to the Klan field. Barkhurst had been among the young men sworn in by Mayor Kistler as special police. As the car crossed the railroad tracks and neared the "deadline," Circlers rushed out to stop it. It is unclear as to which side fired first, but it was evident that Barkhurst and Skaggs were more accurate. Three Circlers fell, Dominic Perone with a foot wound, Albert Davis with a minor back wound, and Joseph Mohan with a bullet lodged in the back of his head after passing through his mouth. The green Willys-Knight auto scurried past the distraught Circlers and sped along North Main Street toward the Klan field as shots splattered around and through the car.[62]

A state of frenzy prevailed at the deadline. As a result of the mêlée, one older Italian woman was unconscious for an hour. With a meat cleaver still in hand, she awoke in a nearby house with an assertion, "Me fight, too!" Sheriff Thomas had thought to send a doctor and three nurses from Warren City Hospital to aid the wounded. Unfortunately their arrival in white uniforms was seen as an advancing guard of the Klan; the crowd harassed them for several minutes before realizing its mistake. Nurse Mary Hoffman later commented to a reporter that "it wasn't the first time I ever faced gunfire. . . . But I'll admit I never faced a more formidable lot than that mob today." They were able to set up an emergency first aid post at a gas station across the street from the Glass Works, but most of the Circlers preferred to take care of their own wounded in nearby homes.[63]

Policemen and deputy sheriffs were receiving numerous calls by this time, all seeking immediate relief. Many policemen, intimidated by the rioters, took off their badges or simply stood at a distance to avoid any trouble. Accompanied by Lt. Col. Wade Christy, of the Ohio National Guard, who had been sent by the governor as an observer earlier in the week, Thomas roved the streets trying unsuccessfully to calm participants. About 1:30 P.M. he and Chief Round answered a call to Federal Street between Main and Vienna streets, close to Mosquito Creek. There a group of twenty-five Klan "police" were marching toward a crowd of Circlers, who were yelling and screaming in Italian. Thomas and Round arrested the special police but left behind the armed Circlers. At headquarters the young men, most of whom were from Toledo, were disarmed and placed on bond.[64] Thus ended the Klan's attempt to use a police force of its own making. Although the Klan viewed these men as legitimate officers, the Circlers did not. Whether Thomas's actions were based on sympathies with the Circlers, as concluded by the Klan, or a strategy devised to avoid bloodshed, was not clear.

Other Circlers, including Marty Flask and his uncle, Joe Jennings, had gathered at the corner of Federal and Vienna to monitor vehicles coming down Vienna Road. Joe had been driving back and forth dispensing arms from the trunk of his car. Police had appeared several times at the corner to move these men away, but they would return when the police left. It was the misfortune of Ralph Games, who lived a short distance away on Vienna Road, and his cousin, Russell Brock, to drive past this corner in the early afternoon. Supposedly buying cigars in Niles, they were accosted and ordered out of the car. Brock responded, "You got a lot of nerve. I will go as I goddamned please." To which Joseph Jennings retorted, "Let's kill him!" Jennings tore off Brock's glasses and thrashed him. Flask joined in, but Brock managed to tear away and run between some houses. Flask fired five or six errant shots at the fleeing Klansman. They also pummeled Games before he managed to drive his car away.[65]

Unable to deal with the overwhelming size and physical intimidation of the Circlers, Sheriff Thomas decided to try conciliation. Along with former state senator McDermott, he called the crowd into the Glass Works park to ask for a twenty-minute truce. An unidentified leader of the Flaming Circle responded, "We are standing on our rights as American citizens to defend ourselves against a mob of armed yeggs imported here at the instance of the KKK to shoot down our residents. They shall not pass here." "Boys, let me talk," Thomas persisted. "This is a damned serious situation. Give me a little time and I'll fix things all right. Put your guns away and give me a chance." The crowd responded with a cheer and yells—"Attaboy, Brickey" (Thomas's nickname) and "We're with you, Brickey!" A possible breakthrough seemed at hand for Thomas.[66]

But at the very moment that Thomas and McDermott were speaking in the park, another car was speeding past the "deadline." Shots were fired, possibly from both sides, but the car broke through the railroad gates that the Circlers had put down and proceeded south on Main. Inside the car were Ellsworth Kaiser, from Youngstown, and Melvin C. Cope, from Sebring, both Klan special police sworn in by Kistler and ordered into Niles. Although bullets struck the car, they were able to proceed to their rendezvous at the Allison Hotel on Park Avenue. Four of the Circlers—Leo Davis, John Desmond, William "Boots" McCauley, and Dude Murphy—jumped into a green Oldsmobile and gave chase. They caught up with the Klansmen on Park Avenue, surrounded the car, and captured them. Neither Kaiser nor Cope offered resistance, primarily because they saw several deputy sheriffs nearby. To their surprise they were put into the green car accompanied by one of the deputy sheriffs and taken back to the Glass Works field.

The car rolled over the curb, across the pavement, and down an incline to the field. A solo voice bragged, "We got 'em," followed by the crowd's antiphon, "Let's lynch them!" As Kaiser stepped timidly out of the auto, Dude Murphy or Leo Davis shot him in the back; he fell to the ground. Someone then kicked him in the face and intoned, "That's the way to fix them." Cope was more fortunate: he was merely beaten. Someone cried, "Get those damned stiffs out of here before the troops get here," and the two men were carried over to the sidewalk. Holloway's Ambulance picked up Cope, and a deputy sheriff helped Kaiser to Doctor Elder's, on Robbins Avenue, but he refused treatment. Some friends finally brought Kaiser to the Warren City Hospital. The bullet remained in his shoulder as a souvenir of the riot.[67]

Thomas's policy of assuagement had failed. Further escalation was in the air, as the crowd turned its attention to the railroad depot. Throughout the day streetcars were stopped, riders searched, robes

The anti-Klan forces gathered in the field in front of the General Electric Glass Works factory at the corner of Main and Federal. Klan marchers had to pass this point to enter downtown Niles.

taken, and beatings administered. But now word came through that a train filled with Klan members was on its way into Niles. Earlier in the morning a young Irish woman named Catherine Ritter happened to be at the Erie Depot, where she overheard two railroad agents discussing the scheduled arrival in the afternoon of a special train with carloads of Klan members, who were to disembark at the depot and march to the Klan field. She hastily informed Msgr. James McDonough, of St. Stephen's Church, who in turn informed Msgr. Joseph Trainor, of St. Columba's Church in Youngstown. Trainor was the chaplain of the Ohio National Guard Unit from Youngstown.[68]

No one knows how the information filtered down, but Carmine De-Cristofaro, a six-foot, 200-pound giant who played football for the Jennings Athletic Club, gathered at least fifty Circlers around the depot. They were armed with "guns of all sizes, knives, clubs and even homemade bombs." About 2:30 the train slowly chugged into view, its iron carriages full of 1,200 unsuspecting and untested Klansmen, chanting "Onward, Christian Soldiers." As they pulled into the station, the head of the Klansmen, former army captain Jack Curley, of Massillon, used to the conditions of battle, made an instantaneous decision—"It's no place for us. We go right back." The Circlers had outmaneuvered the retreating Christian soldiers.[69]

Amid a swirl of events rapidly twirling out of control, Sheriff Thomas marched onto the Glass Works field to order the crowd to "put your guns away and stay off the street. Stay in the field over there and keep quiet." The crowd retreated as Thomas strode down the middle of the street. At that moment two motor lorries of the Ohio National Guard arrived from Warren with machine guns mounted and ready to fire. The Circlers cheered—"Here are the troops, we've won!" They realized that martial law would preclude the Klan parade. Their task accomplished, many now dropped their guns and fled.[70]

Meanwhile, the governor had sent a telegram declaring martial law. An Associated Press staff man had gotten wind of it at the *Tribune Chronicle* office while talking to Columbus. With the mayor out of town, the telegram was given to the sheriff, who intrepidly proceeded north to the Klan field. Catcalls and jeers greeted the sheriff, who was now seen as any ally of the Flaming Circle. Many viewed his arrest of the special police as interference with duly constituted authority; some called him "yellowback" and "un-American citizen." The sheriff mounted an improvised platform and read the governor's telegram declaring martial law. As he left the platform, someone leveled a rifle at him; others drew their guns ready to shoot.[71]

The sheriff quickwittedly asked to see Colonel Watkins. The colonel remembered his own predicament of the previous night and ordered a guard to escort Thomas from the field. "Queer, isn't it?" Thomas mused. "Last night when the antis chased you, I served as the guard that escorted you safely out of Niles. Now you're guarding me!"[72]

The sheriff left the crowd angry and severely divided. The earlier arrest of twenty-five special police dispatched into Niles had reduced the young men's enthusiasm for patrol, but the Klan leaders had regrouped and were planning to march as the sheriff entered the field. An argument between Watkins and Dr. B. A. Hart over who should

In 1925, one year after the riot, the Jennings A.C. football team won the Mahoning Valley championship. Jim Jennings coached, Joe Jennings, Jr., was

lead the parade had created a delay. The governor's orders opened another rift, as Watkins decided to obey; the Klan manager and organizer of the parade, W. H. Kline, said, "If I had my way we'd parade, troops or no troops." The fact that the order came from proper authorities, however, convinced most of the Anglo-Saxon Klan members that their duty lay in obedience. In their minds legitimate authority had settled the issue.[73] Only a few hundred Klan members remained at the field during the night.

The Knights of the Flaming Circle had won. Their neutralization of the police force and employment of physical intimidation was a successful gambit. The fact that the governor would inevitably dispatch troops if things were getting out of hand made their task all the easier. The availability of a stable of boxers from the Jennings Athletic Club combined with the experience of many of these men with breaking the law gave the Circlers an advantage. The public image of the Klan as an organ of prejudice, rather than of law enforcement, had drawn together the Italian community. Assisted by the Irish, it had successfully defied the Klan.[74]

the mascot, and many of the players had been key participants in the riot.

For the remainder of the day, the troops patrolled the city with rifles and fixed bayonets. In the evening national guard units from Canton, Berea, Akron, and Cleveland continued to arrive, and set up machine gun nests around the city. Ironically, one of the Klan members, a major in the Akron National Guard, was called back to Akron and then returned to Niles as an enforcer of martial law. By the time Major General Benson Hough arrived, around midnight, the city and surrounding areas were peaceful. Only soldiers walked the parade route.[75]

8

The Judgment

We're the boys from Niles, Ohio,
We don't give a good god-damned,
We're the boys from Niles, Ohio,
We licked the Ku Klux Klan.
　　　　—Song of the Knights of the Flaming Circle

With the riot over, attention now turned to the question of who or what had caused it. Klan members believed that their constitutional right to parade guaranteed that the public would view them as an innocent party. Their arms, they claimed, were legitimately employed because Kistler had sworn them in as deputies. They overlooked, however, the widespread opinion that their religious prejudices had provoked opposition and that they were more the aggressor than the aggrieved.

Clyde Osborne had not been in the city on Saturday, but he hastened to interpret the riot as caused by a "few 100 infuriated outsiders largely of foreign birth" who "attempted to show that mob rule was greater than that of the state." Alarmed that the rights of free citizens to march had been violated, he downplayed religious differences. Instead he suggested that "the responsibility rested with the confessed enemies of the republic, with the hidden forces of sovietism and anarchy which acknowledges (sic) no God."[1] This statement was reminiscent of the steel owners' charges during the 1919 strike.

Osborne's observation was a desperate attempt to gather support for the Klan. He could not believe that other religions opposed the pietists' crusade; after all, vice laws were for everyone. Hoping to maintain a society dominated by pietistic values, Osborne blamed godless forces for the riot, a foe that might serve to reunite the fragmented Klan.

The *Citizen*, however, was more specific in its identification of the enemy. Now edited by the vitriolic Paul Morris, it blamed Irish and Italian Catholics, particularly the foreign-born element, for the riot.

140

According to the *Citizen*, Niles was a city of gang rule, rowdyism, and gambling, and the "ruffians in Niles won't get away with it."[2]

It was Sheriff Thomas, however, who drew the harshest attacks from Klan leaders. In a statement issued to local newspapers the day of the riot, Exalted Cyclops B. A. Hart and Klan manager W. H. Kline chastised the sheriff for his failure at the conference of 27 October to assure Klan marchers of his protection. Mayor Kistler, on the other hand, fulfilled his duties in the Klan's mind not only by permitting the parade but also by swearing in one hundred fifty special deputies in spite of Thomas's assertions that most men were unwilling to serve. In a short, Klan-sponsored pamphlet entitled *The Truth about the Niles Riot*, an unidentified eyewitness suggested that "the sheriff could have prevented most of the shooting that went on if he had sincerely tried to do so." Instead he had arrested the special police, which, "of course, gave courage to the cowardly Flaming Circle band and they got bolder than ever, knowing the sheriff had played into their hands and would arrest state police so they felt that they had undisputed authority then." According to the eyewitness, the Klan was ready to march, and its advance guard would have taken care of the "law violators," but again Thomas had blocked their efforts by calling in the state militia. Another eyewitness cited the response of the Flaming Circle—"We're with you, Brickey!"—when the sheriff called them to a conference on the Glass Works field as further indication of his collusion with the lawless elements.[3]

In a statement issued on Monday, Sheriff Thomas made no apology. He contended that he "did all in my power to preserve peace and order."[4] The sheriff received encouragement from influential supporters, such as Major General Benson Hough, who judged Thomas's actions impartial. Colonel Connelly contended that Thomas's work had "prevented a pitched battle and the almost certain 'deadly massacre' that would have resulted from a clash of the two large forces." The *Warren Tribune Chronicle* printed a supportive front-page editorial that denied the rumor that the governor had summoned Thomas to Columbus to face impeachment charges. "Called in when the Klan mayor of Niles confessed he could not handle the situation," the editor asserted, "Sheriff Thomas did all that any man could do." According to the *Tribune Chronicle*, visiting reporters from a dozen newspapers had also congratulated Thomas. Their response to critics of Thomas's failure to confront and break up the crowd at Main and Federal was a question: "How could any sheriff with 30 men or even with 200 men have marched into that crowd of wild, crazy-to-shoot men to disarm them?"[5]

Thomas's defense did not wash with most of the voting citizenry: he lost the election by more than 6,000 votes. The next day the *Tribune Chronicle* described the defeat as ironic, since Thomas had compiled "one of the best records of law enforcement in the history of the county." In his two years in office, Thomas had been responsible for 3,040 arrests and $100,000 in fines, twice the expense of his office. Moreover, he had collected 75 percent of those fines, the highest percentage ever. Most importantly, according to the *Tribune Chronicle*, "both the sheriff and his deputies have worked diligently during the two years past and have aided greatly in bringing the foreign element of the county into closer touch with the law of the land and have been instrumental in bringing them to the realization that playing the part of the law-abiding citizen is much better than being a bootlegger and on the outs with the law all the time."[6] The Klan and Thomas had parted company not over the issue of vice law enforcement but over the wisdom of provoking a violent confrontation with East Siders.

While the voters were assessing Thomas's performance, Colonel L. S. Connelly appointed a military review board to gather evidence regarding individual responsibility for the riot. More than two hundred witnesses appeared before the panel, headed by Lt. Col. Wade Christy; their testimony was recorded and forwarded to the county prosecutor, Harvey Burgess. Many of the witnesses were quite willing to describe the day's events, but too intimidated to identify participants in the violence. The possibility of placing blame was at best muddied when the report was delivered.[7] Klan opponents, it seemed, might once again escape legal retribution.

Within Niles there was no question as to who the rioters were, and some citizens, determined to see that they were punished, formed a Citizens Committee for the Enforcement of Law and Order to gather funds for prosecution.[8] On 18 November the governor ordered the incumbent county prosecutor, Burgess, to conduct a probe into the riot.[9] After Clyde Osborne complained to the governor about Burgess's hostility toward the Klan, Donahey appointed the newly elected County Prosecutor Wick W. Pierson to assist Burgess.[10] The grand jury sat for ten days and heard 257 witnesses, some of whom changed their affidavits in testimony before the grand jury. Its report, issued on 4 December, led to 104 indictments of men from both sides. In its assessment of official responsibility, the grand jury did not agree with Sheriff Thomas's handling of the pre-riot situation, but now was "fully convinced that he did all in his power to preserve order and to avoid bloodshed with the limited means at his hands on that day." Mayor Kistler and Chief of Police Round, however, were less fortunate; the grand jury recommended their removal and "a thorough reorganization of the police department of that city."[11]

Within the week more than five hundred citizens of Niles met at the Methodist church to protest the attack on Kistler. The citizens adopted a petition that labeled the grand jury censure of Kistler unjust. "Mayor Kistler," the petition asserted, "did all in his power to prevent trouble during the disorders of November 1st, with the means at hand." George Swegan and John Rose circulated the petition in the factories and mills. Eventually, the Reverend Ketchum took 2,800 signatures to Columbus for Donahey's consideration.[12]

The grand jury also recommended that the state pass a constabulary law similar to those of other states and rescind all laws that permitted civilians to act with police power. The recommendation referred to the Klan members who had carried guns during the riot as members of the Ohio State Police, which they had joined after paying $17.50 to Colonel Watkins. In what appears to have been another of his attempts to profit by Americans' penchant for joining fraternal societies, Watkins had created the organization after stealing a yellowed charter given by the state to a horse-thief protection society organized in Kinsman, Ohio, about 1900. After the Civil War the state had authorized such bodies within townships "to proceed to any part of Ohio without warrants to make arrests for horse thievery or other felonies and to detain offenders until a warrant has been obtained." The statute, however, did not permit the carrying of arms.[13] In mid-December David Scott, of the Western Reserve Intelligence Bureau, tracked down several organizers who had worked with Watkins, as well as the original charter and a roster of 600 members in the home of a Salem, Ohio, woman. He also discovered how Watkins had acquired the charter. Some Kinsmanites had invited the colonel to a dinner of the Pennsylvania and Ohio Police, where they regaled him with stories of their origins. He was invited to join, but the colonel had better use for the charter: it mysteriously disappeared.[14]

In testimony before the grand jury, Osborne would deny any connection between the Klan and the Ohio State Police. If such an organization existed within the Klan, Osborne speculated, it had been organized by outsiders without the knowledge of Klan officials. Some members, he admitted, had sought his legal opinion regarding the powers of such police; and he had informed them that they had no more authority than an ordinary citizen, and no right to bear arms. In short, Osborne contended that he had done everything in his power to discourage the OSP.

It was true that the OSP was organized by an outsider, Colonel Watkins, who could not officially belong to the Klan because of his foreign birth; but it was also true that Watkins had played such a prominent role in the development of the valley Klan that Osborne must have been aware of the use of the OSP as guards at Klan activities. Indeed, a well-publicized incident had occurred in August 1924, involving the OSP in East Youngstown. Twenty-five men, including Ellsworth Kaiser, were found roaming the streets of East Youngstown and conducting raids. In light of the fact that Osborne had helped Watkins to secure a charter in September for the Ohio Police Intelligence Service, it would appear that his denials were self-serving. [15]

Colonel Watkins's trouble with the OSP was but one loose thread in the unraveling of his clothing. A man of many suits—lecturer, minister, army officer, newspaper editor, and raconteur—Watkins was a mystery to many of his friends. He never allowed photographers to take a picture (nowhere does his face appear in the newspapers of that time). He also had no known address, although friends often dropped him off in front of the Tod House, a downtown hotel. Investigations precipitated by the riot began to focus on these irregularities and to demand answers regarding Watkins's background.

Efforts to discover his living quarters uncovered a Mr. Montague, who was also short and stocky, with gray hair, bushy mustache, and a British accent. Mr. Montague lived at the Albany Hotel, on Front Street, with a woman identified as his niece. As stories began to circulate of Watkins's other affairs—supposedly, he had proposed marriage to a Youngstown woman he had met at a Klan rally in Canfield—friends began to admit that "the Colonel liked the ladies." Always in the company of good-looking women, Watkins wined and dined in the best restaurants, and he often gave parties for selected guests. There were also unconfirmed suspicions that the colonel had a wife in Canada.

Once Watkins's veracity was challenged, all of his background invited investigation. Watkins had occasionally worn a British army uniform; he even claimed to have been with General Allenby during World War I. He also wore a medal from the British Red Cross and an emblem from the Veterans of the Canadian Expeditionary Force on his lapel. One of his friends finally wrote letters to Canadian and British army officials to check on the war record of Watkins, only to find out that he had none.

The combination of revelations regarding Watkins's war record and love life prompted his friends to seek his departure. They concocted a story that immigration officials were on his trail. Watkins did not appear in the pulpit of the Girard Baptist Church on Sunday, 7 December. His "niece," Mrs. Montague, withdrew his money, collected his clothing, and also left town. Initial reports from his personal secretary identified health problems as the immediate cause of his departure, and Little Rock as his destination, where he was to serve as the Grand Rider of the Order of Crusaders. His friends, however, had escorted him to Salem, Ohio, to put him on a train to New York.

Although Watkins had been exposed as a charlatan, it was evident that his wiles engendered little hostility. He was indeed a charming rogue capable of beguiling large or small crowds. He was a very bright, well-traveled man who could speak Yiddish to a Jewish merchant or discuss the Syrian landscape with such familiarity that an immigrant woman was brought to tears. Watkins boasted of his earlier ties to Youngstown and of his marriage to a local woman. Mary Dyer, his sister-in-law, corroborated the marriage, but it was his vivid description of Youngstown forty years earlier that fascinated many local residents. The *Telegram* commented on his encyclopedic grasp of medical and religious subjects, his continuous smile and willing handshake—all the makings of a successful salesman, a weaver of spells, a charlatan.[16]

Watkins's actual destination was Worcester, Massachusetts, where he rejoined Colonel Gunder. A *Vindicator* reporter caught up with him in New York to ask the obvious questions. The colonel denied that he had left under the threat of possible arrest and pleaded ill health as the cause of his unexpected departure. Watkins told the reporter that her newspaper had barely avoided libel in its coverage and that he would return to answer all charges. He never did.[17]

Watkins's departure did little to reduce the frictions between the rival ethnic factions. When the Klan held a New Year's Eve dance at the Knights of Pythias Hall, a burst of gunfire, at least fifteen or twenty shots, hit an electric cross mounted on top of the building. One stray bullet lodged without serious damage in a guard's stomach. The anti-Klan elements had acted on the belief that the cross constituted a violation of a truce that forbade burnings of respective symbols by either side. Kistler disagreed: "If the fiery cross is the emblem of the KKK, then the Klan has as much right to exhibit it at its headquarters or meeting place as any other organization has to display its emblem." The next day, however, the cross was gone; no one knew who had taken it.[18] After further meetings both sides agreed that the Klan could restore and light the cross at future meetings.[19]

The new truce did not bring an end to confrontations between such embittered foes. Encouraged by their success in halting the Klan parade, the anti-Klan forces were intent on intimidating their opponents. Late on the night of 28 January, someone fired thirty shots into the back wall of the Knights of Pythias Hall, followed by a midnight beating in early February of three men outside Rummell's pool hall.

At times the fighting involved well-known members of the opposing camps. In February, Carmine DeChristofaro, who had prepared the reception for the incoming Klan train on the day of the riot, fought Ted Croft, a member of the Ohio State Police. DeCristofaro drubbed Croft and disfigured his face. Both men were arrested, DeCristofaro for being drunk and fighting and Croft for assault with intent to kill or wound because he was carrying a gun. A month later Dude Murphy accosted Fred Henderson, a member of the OSP, and ordered him off the street. Murphy knocked Henderson down, and, when police officers arrived, resisted arrest. Although Chief Round denied that the fight was related to the Klan, there was little possibility that each man's loyalties had not contributed to the spat.[20]

These hostilities served as a backdrop for the court trials, which took place during February, March, and April 1925. Most of the men tried were charged with rioting, carrying a concealed weapon, or assault with intent to kill. Although there were rumors of dead bodies dumped into Mosquito Creek near Federal Street, no one was charged with murder. "I did not believe the story," commented Colonel Connelly, "but dragged the creek to satisfy those who told the story." All persons injured in the major incidents from the Klan side were accounted for, and the Circlers who were taken to a doctor or hospital as well. It was assumed that many of the injured Circlers had received care in nearby homes.[21]

The shooting of Frank McDermott was the first case brought to trial. The key to the trial was the dispute over who had fired the first shot. Rex Dunn claimed self-defense for firing three shots at McDermott as he came alongside his car the night before the riot. McDermott, however, claimed that he and a friend, Shine Jennings, were innocently walking along the curbside near Rummell's pool hall when the Dunn car drew alongside and the driver began firing. The newly elected county prosecutor, Wick Pierson, presented six witnesses to corroborate McDermott's testimony, including his brother, a cousin, and some workers from his father's construction company. The defense attorney,

Jay Buchwalter, had twenty-five to thirty witnesses available, but most of them were in Rummell's pool hall at the outbreak of the incident. Faced with a lack of neutral witnesses, the jury found Dunn guilty of assault, rather than shooting with intent to kill, fined him $200, and sentenced him to the workhouse for six months. Years later McDermott admitted that he had lied about the incident.[22]

The Klan fared better in the trial of Peter Greco for carrying a concealed weapon. This time the Klan produced numerous witnesses to testify before Judge J. S. Thomas, of Portsmouth, Ohio. Carl Rettig, a former secretary of the chamber of commerce, and Elmer Jones, a city councilman, charged that Greco had stuck a gun in their car as they passed the intersection; patrolman Thomas Reese testified that he had confiscated a .38 caliber gun from Greco. The defense argued that Greco had participated in the blockade only after the mayor's departure from town and the shooting of his cousin, Dominic Parone. He had taken Klan guns only as a measure of protection. In his summation prosecutor Harvey Burgess presented the issue as one of southern Italian culture and its variance from American laws and customs. "But because he may have obtained ideas from his ancestors or from his foreign birth," Burgess advised the jury not to try "to mold the laws of this country to his frame of mind." The jury took two ballots to convict Greco.[23]

In the third trial the Klan hoped to secure a severe punishment for Joseph Jennings, a recognized leader of the Flaming Circle and the man they considered responsible for the riot. Jennings faced a charge of assault with intent to kill Russell Brock at the corner of Federal and Vienna. William Llewellyn, who was driving past the intersection, testified that Jennings, whom he had known for twenty years, had hit Brock, a statement corroborated by a nearby resident, George Swift. Another witness, a sixteen-year-old woman named Leona Dray, portrayed Jennings as a leader of the rioters; she had seen him driving back and forth in a Studebaker sedan near her home, taking weapons out of his trunk, and giving them to the Circlers.[24]

Jennings's attorney did not deny that he had struck Brock, but constructed his defense on the claim that Jennings was acting on behalf of the Niles police department! One of the officers, John Jones, testified that he had seen Jennings at Linden and Robbins and asked him for help in restoring order. "I'll do everything I can," Jennings had allegedly responded. Jennings then proceeded to Vienna and Federal, where he claimed to have been diverting cars from the trouble at Main and Federal when Brock and Games approached. Another officer,

William Mullen (fired earlier from the police force for intoxication on duty), praised Jennings for giving him a ride to one of the trouble spots. The most startling development was the testimony of police chief Round, who came forth as a character witness for Jennings. In spite of having conducted raids on the Mason Street speakeasy and gambling den, Round contended that Jennings had a good reputation in Niles. The ties of the police department to the East Side were never more apparent.

The prosecutors countered Jennings's claim of impartial assistance with the testimony of Ward Stephenson, who had driven past the corner in question several times. He had heard Jennings say, "Don't let any cars get through." In summation, Pierson contended that Brock and Games had the right to travel on the streets of Niles and to carry their robes with them. Jennings, in Burgess's supporting argument, could not claim self-defense, the prosecutor asserted, because he was the aggressor. After eight ballots the jury pronounced Jennings guilty of assault with intent to kill; he was initially sentenced to 1–15 years in the Ohio Penitentiary.[25] The Klan rejoiced at the verdict.

The first Klansman to be tried was Paul Barkhurst, from Girard, for carrying a concealed weapon. Barkhurst had been in the Willys-Knight car when it shot its way past the crowd at Federal and Main. Barkhurst's attorney contended that he was acting as a member of the special police sworn in by Mayor Kistler at the Klan field between 10:00 and 11:00 A.M. If Kistler had acted in an official capacity, he argued, Barkhurst had the right to carry a gun.

It is apparent that Kistler's action had blurred the line between the Klan as a fraternal organization that supported law enforcement and the Niles police force as the actual enforcing body. In Kistler's mind there may indeed have been no distinction, but to many others, including the defense, he was not attempting to quell the riot but to arm one side. According to Harvey Burgess, assistant prosecuting attorney, "Mayor Kistler was not the acting mayor of Niles on the day of the rioting. He was out on the Klan field attempting to arm his own mob." Judge Thomas instructed the jury that Kistler did have the right to appoint special police, but only if a riot was occurring in Niles; the fact that Kistler had left Niles the day before could lead to questions about his knowledge of conditions in the city. Thomas left it to the jury to decide whether Kistler had acted appropriately. The jury decided that Kistler had no power to appoint the special police. They did, however, recommend clemency for Barkhurst.[26]

Once the verdict was in, Barkhurst's accomplice, George Skaggs, of Waynesburg, Ohio, pleaded guilty to carrying a concealed weapon. While praising Skaggs for pleading guilty, Judge Thomas criticized Kistler for "trying to serve two masters on November 1st. "The mayor," Thomas asserted, "was trying to serve the United States Constitution and the constitution of the State of Ohio, and second an organization entrenched upon American free soil attempting to dictate the policies of the US government." In Thompson's mind, "the men that are really responsible for the Niles trouble, the men higher up, placed themselves beyond all possible danger. They are the ones who should suffer and not the men who did their bidding. If there had been murder in Niles on that day," he concluded, "the blood most certainly would have been on their hands."[27] As a result, both Barkhurst and Skaggs were fined $50 instead of the usual $300.

The fact that each of the first three trials had ended in a verdict of guilty opened the gates to plea bargaining for reduced charges. Clyde Osborne had already begun working behind the scenes with his brother-in-law, Sam Mango, an Italian-American lawyer from Niles, to have those charged on both sides to plead guilty, throw themselves on the mercy of the court, and receive suspended sentences in return.[28] Within the next few days, thirty-eight men, including Marty Flask, Dude Murphy, Jim Jennings, and Tony Nigro pleaded guilty to reduced charges such as rioting, assault and battery, and carrying concealed weapons. The judge reduced the $300 fines to $50 for everyone except Marty Flask for his part in the Brock incident and Dude Murphy for the attack on Kaiser and Cope. In a statement to these men that both the *Tribune Chronicle* and the *Vindicator* cited as improper, Judge Thomas sympathized with their right to resent an organization that was by hearsay in support of religious discrimination. He advised them, however, to live peaceably and to let the Klan parade if it wished; eventually, it would wear out of its own accord.[29]

In spite of Joseph Jennings's self-proclaimed role in the riot—for the week following the riot he had ridden around town in his auto with a Klan robe on the front grillwork—the judge continued his lenient policy. Since he had not killed anyone, and since "people in this part speak well of Mr. Jennings," the judge suspended Jennings's sentence of one year in the Ohio Penitentiary. At the beginning of the trials, Thomas believed that Jennings was the leading conspirator, but he now viewed him as only one of many. Jennings's lawyer, Oscar Diser, of Youngstown, congratulated Thomas for his discretion and his contribution in defusing an explosive situation in Niles.[30]

The final case to come before Judge Thomas involved the twenty-five deputized Klan members arrested by Sheriff Thomas near Federal Street. They had jointly decided to plead not guilty, but to forgo a jury trial and any testimony. Judge Thomas ruled Kistler's appointments illegal on the basis that the Mayor's departure from town the preceding day had taken him outside his jurisdiction when swearing in the estimated one hundred fifty men. All twenty-five men were fined the customary $300 with $250 suspended.[31]

Thus ended the Niles riot cases. In spite of the violence of the day, few of the individuals involved suffered severe penalties. Only Rex Dunn, Dude Murphy, and Marty Flask were to spend time in the Canton workhouse, whereas the rest paid minimum fines totaling some $3,000. Only one of those injured, George E. Victor, was permanently disabled. Victor would eventually sue the county commissioners for failing to provide protection and win a $5,000 judgment. Ironically, one of the commissioners was Joseph Rummell.[32]

On one level the riot had pitted lawbreakers against law enforcers. The leaders of the Flaming Circle, Joe and Jim Jennings and Tony Nigro, were well known for their illegal activities. Many of the rioters, such as Marty Flask, Dude Murphy, Frank McDermott, and Leo Davis, were associated with the Jennings Athletic Club, on Mason Street. The Klan represented much more to them than a threat to their religion: it threatened their business, their livelihood. The Klan was putting pressure on local politicians and police departments to crack down on vice offenders; it had managed to place men with a stricter commitment to enforcement in the mayor's office and on city council.

The police department and its chief, however, remained independent of the Klan because they were under civil service and proof of malfeasance was required. The ties between the Niles police force and the Jennings brothers were apparent in the testimony of John Jones and Chief Round on behalf of Joe Jennings. The fact that members of the police force accepted payoffs—usually $10 per week—was well known among the bootleggers. And yet there were crackdowns, arrests, and fines, many times just to make the police or mayor look good, but always within the limit of what the bootleggers and gamblers could afford.[33] The problem with the Klan was that it favored a total shutdown; it offered no living space. Thus, the Klan provoked a violent response from people who felt they were being backed into a corner.

The broader issue involved here was that of law and order and how to accomplish it. The riot was a frustrating indication to the Klan that it could not achieve perfect enforcement. Not only did the Klan not

THE JUDGMENT   151

march in Niles—in spite of its constitutional right to do so—but the perpetrators were treated lightly by the courts. Judge Thomas, apparently chosen in the hopes that an outsider might be more objective, was lenient in an effort to reduce tension. Klan efforts to establish its own police force as a means of sidestepping the regular police were not effective and only provoked widespread public opposition. Despite the foibles of the Niles police, the public was less willing to place that power in the hands of what was seen as a prejudiced, narrow organization.

On a second level, the riot resulted from a clash of cultures. Pietistic Protestants of Welsh and German origins had dominated the valley in the late nineteenth century and had created a society that reflected their mores. As Christians they believed in control of one's appetites and pious Sunday observance. In order to foster the practice of Christianity in children, they advocated the reading of the Bible in the classroom and lessons on character development in the curriculum. Government, they believed, should be run honestly and efficiently and support Christian morality through appropriate legislation and strict enforcement. Such attitudes often brought pietists into conflict with members of their own ethnic background, but it was the Italian community that provided the strongest opposition. With a culture that permitted enjoyment of the senses, albeit in moderation, that placed family loyalty above the individual, and that viewed the strictures of government with a jaundiced eye, the Italian community reacted violently to what it considered to be an affront to its honor and an attack on its religion.[34]

On Christmas Day, 1924, Father Santoro celebrated the first mass at Our Lady of Mount Carmel Church; it was also the occasion of his Silver Jubilee in the priesthood. The church was full, the congregation much larger than the handful Santoro had found in Niles in 1914. The Italian community celebrated its survival and growth on that day. In the year of construction, numerous parishioners had donated money; some donated bricks. The church survives today as a reminder of their presence.[35]

9

The Residue

Ah, could my anguish but be measured
And my calamity laid with it in the scales,
They would now outweigh the sands of the sea.

—Job 6:2–3

The Klan base of support had eroded. Once capable of generating a parade with 50,000 participants, the Klan marched no more in the Mahoning Valley. Although political candidates had eagerly sought its endorsement in 1923, the Klan now ceased to endorse candidates publicly. When Web Lentz resigned as exalted cyclops in February 1925 to work with Clyde Osborne, only 193 members gathered to elect the Reverend Leroy Myers, of the Struthers Presbyterian Church, as his successor. Members of his church were so upset with Klan activities that they asked Myers to leave. Although the Mahoning Presbytery permitted him to stay, the dissension threatened to create a split within the church. Meanwhile, the Klan newspaper, the *Citizen*, continued to report on Klan happenings in the valley, but changed its name to the *Ohio Citizen* in the spring of 1925, with more coverage of the Klan in Akron. It folded by the end of 1925.[1]

Similar patterns developed in nearby Trumbull County. Dr. B. A. Hart, who consented to serve in November 1925 as grand titan, was unable to get anyone to fill his post as exalted cyclops. Dr. Don M. Kent, a Girard dentist, was at one point identified by the *Tribune Chronicle* as Hart's successor, but later denied that he was serving in an official capacity. In December, Hart announced that the charter was now inoperative pending a reorganization of the county Klan.[2]

The decline of the Klan locally was apparent on the state level as well. Klan gubernatorial candidate Joseph Sieber, of Akron, lost in the Republican primary in August 1924. Because his victorious opponent, Harry Davis, former mayor of Cleveland, was a wet, the Klan had to switch its endorsement to the Democrat, Vic Donahey. Mahoning

152

County Klan members were favorable because Donahey had removed former police chief James Watkins and suspended Mayor William Reese.[3] Although the reelection of Donahey represented a dry, rather than Klan, victory, Osborne took credit. He boasted that the Klan was in sight of controlling the state legislature.[4]

Osborne had overestimated the extent of Klan influence. Eventually he announced that the Klan was supporting three bills: (1) to ban intermarriage of the white and black races, (2) to require a public school education in order to receive a teaching certificate, and (3) to require Bible-reading in the public schools.[5] Neither of the first two bills received any consideration. Only the Buchanan Bible Bill, with provisions for mandatory daily readings and memorization of the Ten Commandments by the fourth grade, secured passage. Governor Donahey, however, established his independence by vetoing the bill, thereby marking the limits of Klan power.[6]

There were many factors that affected the decline of the Klan in the Mahoning Valley, but the riot and the embarrassing disappearance of Watkins were pivotal points. Factionalism and the failure to eradicate bootlegging and gambling had taken a relatively minor toll through the primaries of August 1924. Even the publication and sale of the stolen Klan list had not discouraged the majority of Klan members. But now there was sufficient evidence of the corruption of Klan kleagles and lecturers sent by the national headquarters. Watkins's departure with whatever funds he had in the bank and his fraudulent war record exposed the charlatanry and greed so prevalent among kleagles. Even Osborne was to later admit the troubles he faced when taking over as grand dragon. He categorized many kleagles as mercenary or "honest without a business sense" and others as "plain crooks."[7] The revelations regarding former Grand Goblin D. C. Stephenson—his rape of Madge Oberholtzer in the spring of 1925 and the sensational trial that followed in nearby Indiana—confirmed suspicions about the Klan leadership. Finally, the opposition of Italian and Irish Catholics had intimidated the usually nonviolent Klan members, most of whom were not prepared to withstand physical assaults or to support an organization that would put them in such danger.

As the number of Klan members declined, the most intolerant elements gained control. Paul Morris plastered the pages of the *Citizen* with paranoid articles. In an article entitled "Roman Octopus Crushing Ohio Public Schools," Morris charged that Roman Catholic teachers were infiltrating public schools, bringing in priests for substitute work, placing pictures of the Virgin on the walls, and introducing prayer begun with the sign of the cross. For Morris the world was two-sided. On the side of evil were "Rome, atheists, the extreme Continental Sunday, followers of the petty political bosses, defenders of corruptionist methods in politics, and their campaign followers which includes, of course, the so-called liberal element, the ex-saloon keeper, the gambler, the scarlet woman and the bootlegger; on the side of good, the Junior Order of American Mechanics, the Knights of Malta, the Masons, Odd Fellows, the Knights of Pythias, evangelical Protestants and civic groups promoting righteousness." The causes of this division were the immigrants who "have failed to adjust themselves to American law, language, social customs and moral principles. They have rather sought the principle of bringing here and maintaining the Old World social, moral and political ideals that are often contrary to everything American." In lauding the "spiritual unity, the moral strength, the racial harmony and the religious homogeneity of our national life" that existed prior to the arrival of the immigrants, Morris projected a self-assured nativism that could not conceive of tolerating variant customs.[8]

Underlying Morris's nativism was a belief in genetic determinency that precluded any possibility of living together in peace. When Dr. Isidor Philo, rabbi of the Rodof Sholem congregation, spoke of America as a melting pot, Morris countered that the superiority of America was based on its Nordic and Protestant stock. The culmination of Morris's thinking appeared in a May editorial entitled "To Your Guns!" Calling on his fellow Klan members to fight the entrenched enemy, Morris bragged that "Americans have never surrendered to a foreign foe and we will not now bow in humble submission to the Roman Catholic-Jew Menace." "Drop not the Fiery Cross," Morris continued, "but 'Carry On' over vale and hill, till pagan Roman Catholicism is expelled from our fair and free American life forever."[9]

Morris's battle cries gathered no troops, aroused no citizenry. In fact, the cries came from a sense of desperation, as the numbers engaged in Morris's crusade dwindled. By August, Morris was carping at three prominent Youngstown lawyers, former subscribers to the Citizen, for refusal to renew their subscriptions. Their sarcastic refusal prompted Morris to question their gentlemanliness, but it was clear that his call for the Klan to wake up and fight fell on deaf ears.[10] The more Morris appealed, the less attention he drew. And so it would seem that only a minority of militantly anti-Catholic or anti-Jewish members remained. Those who had left or were leaving did not share

Morris's desire to do battle with other religions. The Niles riot had lessened their appetite for such conflict.

What many Klan members had shared was a desire to "clean up" the valley and a penchant for law enforcement. A nativist bias had colored their perceptions and made it seem all the more urgent to accomplish their goals. Although the Klan no longer appeared to be the organization to lead the crusade, the quest for pietist law and order and honest government remained a dominant issue in the valley's politics. Ironically, the term of Scheible's successor, Joseph Heffernan, demonstrated that an Irish Catholic could share the reformer's goals.

The grandson of four Irish immigrants, Heffernan had been born in Youngstown in 1887 to a puddler and his wife. After passing the bar examination in 1915, he worked as a reporter for the *Vindicator* until he enlisted in the army during World War I. Only in his early thirties after the war, Heffernan returned to enter local politics. Having become Democratic county chairman in 1922, he directed the local campaign to elect Vic Donahey as governor, out of which developed a political friendship that paid off in Heffernan's appointment to an unexpired term as Youngstown's municipal court judge in 1923. Heffernan parlayed this opportunity into a successful bid to become Youngstown's first Catholic mayor in 1927.[11]

Some might interpret Heffernan's victory as a change of direction for the city of Youngstown. In later years Heffernan would typify his success as a foreshadowing of the New Deal—as the formation of a coalition similar to that of Franklin Roosevelt. After all, he had defeated the Republican finance director Arthur Williams, heir-apparent to Charles Scheible and former Klan member, in the 1927 mayoral election. In that campaign Heffernan had concentrated upon the ethnic communities by appearing at Polish and Hungarian churches and speaking in a foreign tongue at Romanian, Italian, and German halls. The immigrant wards (the second and third) rewarded him with a strong majority.[12]

Deeper analysis of the election results, however, would suggest that Heffernan's victory did not portend the formation of a Roosevelt coalition. In the election of 1927, a second Republican candidate, Frank Vogan, drew more than 5,200 votes. Thus, Heffernan was in reality a minority victor with only 39.2 percent of the total vote. Although Heffernan's knowledge of history was extensive, his interpretation of his own situation drew a stronger parallel than actually existed in Youngstown. It was, in the final analysis, a split in the Republican party between Klan and non-Klan that ensured his victory. The failure of Al Smith or FDR to carry the city in 1928 or 1932 would lend added credence to the conclusion that the New Deal coalition had not yet crystallized in Youngstown.[13]

It would appear, however, that reform elements, many of whom had not voted for Heffernan, received an unexpected carbon copy of the Scheible administration. As Heffernan assumed office, it seemed appropriate, considering his base of support, that he would have rejected the political aims of the reformers to become a boss, for no machine existed in Youngstown at that time. The closest thing to a boss, Edmund Moore, had died in 1925; and even when he was alive, the Democrats won few elections. The rapid growth in immigrant population interested in jobs and social mobility and the burgeoning of city contracts and services had primed Youngstown for the advent of a boss, but Heffernan was too much a reformer to employ inept political supporters. For Heffernan, government was "scientific. Just as much so as medicine or metallurgy." He lamented the fact that "we have run our cities too much with taxi drivers and others untrained in high posts. It is time," he asserted, "we viewed city government as an exacting science and elected people who will run our affairs on a scientific basis."[14]

Heffernan also echoed the reformers in his struggle to enforce the vice laws. Limited by a police force that was understaffed, underpaid, and corruptible, Heffernan provided additional training classes to upgrade skills and rotated beats to limit contacts between corrupt police officers and vice establishments. He also created vice squads because he could exert greater control over their pay, evaluations, and firing. Frustrated by the failure of these actions to secure a total shutdown of vice operations, Heffernan later called in the county sheriff to conduct unannounced raids.[15]

For Heffernan the greatest frustration and disappointment, though, was his discovery that some of his supporters were corrupt. Two Irish brothers, John and Thomas Farrell, who had emigrated from Philadelphia, had been key figures in the Heffernan campaign.[16] After the election the Farrells had organized the Hickory Club, consisting of the Heffernan circle, to meet daily for lunch in the Ohio Hotel; but within a few months Heffernan and his cabinet ceased attending the luncheons.[17] The undisclosed reason for the break, according to Heffernan, was the expectation of the Farrells that the mayor would accept payoffs. Apparently John Farrell had repeatedly chided Heffernan for not accepting the $50,000 of graft available yearly. Unable to convince the mayor, Farrell tried to place Heffernan in compromising situations: one evening he tucked a sizable sum of money in the mayor's pocket at an inappropriate moment for its refusal, but the mayor had an aide take the money back the next day. When numerous arguments and entreaties (and even bribes) failed, Farrell had Heffernan's background combed to uncover flaws that he was sure existed in every man. Nothing ever was found.[18]

Unfortunately for Heffernan, his crusade was running against the political tides, especially in regard to Prohibition, yet his ardor did not slacken. Although it is possible to suggest that Heffernan's efforts at enforcement were politically motivated (especially since he was a minority winner), no evidence exists of a lack of sincerity on his part. As a third-generation immigrant, Heffernan had adopted the mores of the dominant culture. His assimilation was not so much a political ploy as a reflection of his Irish Catholic background. As indicated by Irish historian Lawrence McCaffrey, Anglo-Protestant influence on Irish Catholicism had made many of its followers "more law and order conscious and puritanical than Latin Catholics."[19]

Despite the political continuity that Heffernan provided, he never felt accepted by the voters. In 1931 he left city hall in despair, never again to hold a major elected office.[20] Because of the charter Heffernan was not permitted to run again, but he believed that his administration had failed because, "First, I was a Catholic who had unexpectedly won the election; secondly, I refused to be a grafter." Caught between the remaining members of the Ku Klux Klan and the criminals and grafters, Heffernan complained privately to the rest of Youngstown's citizens. "Too indifferent to ask why, too craven to help, you stand by and see your mayor manhandled and the government he represents again wrecked." Heffernan's bitterness was unhealable.[21]

Heffernan would grouse years later about becoming mayor "at what some might regard as the worst period in our history, when America was in the midst of a moral transition and a religious unsettlement." He condemned the welcoming of racketeers, the development of "the obvious sexualized dance," and financial irresponsibility as a triumvirate "so woven together that they reveal a composite character which historians will inevitably note as they study our post-war years and try to determine the cause of our greatness, or decline." Familiar with the works of J. Gresley Machen, the noted fundamentalist theologian, Heffernan bemoaned the postwar questioning of Christian beliefs and the conflict between "scientific advancement and the tenets of Christian theology."[22] Although Heffernan gave no indication that he interpreted the Bible literally, he was a prime example of the fact that Irish Catholicism was equally as capable as pietistic Protestantism of producing a strain of moral perfectionism ill-equipped psychologically to deal with an imperfect world.

Conclusion

ome local studies do not extend beyond the border. They reveal
the uniqueness of the community, but tell us little about broader
relationships. It is particularly important with a nationwide organization such as the Klan not only to study the effects of the locale
on its success but also to uncover how the local Klan fits into a national mosaic. Local variation must not become local exceptionalism.

This study of the Ku Klux Klan covers only a small segment of that
organization's activities during the 1920s. Yet it is an important study
because of its quantitative description of Klan members, its challenge
of the standard interpretation that all Klansmen were fundamentalists,
and its contribution as an intensive local study to the recent school of
thought that views the Klan as more an adapter to local conditions
than a unified nationwide movement. There is little doubt that nationally the Klan was a hydra-headed monster that espoused white supremacy, anti-Catholicism, anti-Semitism, fraternalism, nativism, and a
return to moral order. The drawing power of each issue, however, depended on the local community and the skill of the kleagle in recognizing the key issues.

Thus, the initial fears of Youngstown residents, black and white
alike, that white supremacy was the key plank in the Klan platform
alerted kleagles to downplay that issue. Although the flood of southern
blacks into Youngstown in the late 1910s had doubled the black population, the migration did not frighten the white community as much as
the appearance of the Klan did the black community. Thus, except for
a funeral cortege in honor of a Klan policeman killed by a black thief,
the Klan did not take direct action against black residents, nor did it

159

try to bring southern racial mores to Youngstown. Indeed, no laws came before the council or the school board that directly concerned racial issues. Only on the state level was a bill presented to ban intermarriage, and it received little consideration. Nor were there beatings or other forms of intimidation of black citizens during the Klan years in Youngstown.[1]

This is not to suggest that prejudices did not exist or were not acted upon in the areas of employment and housing, traditional targets in northern cities. However, the presence of the Klan did not change the structure of racial relations in Youngstown, nor did its presence lead to confrontations. Instead, the Klan had to deny discriminatory objectives in order to succeed in the election of 1923.[2]

In the Mahoning Valley, Klan growth resulted instead from a too rapid infusion of other cultures into a fast-changing industrial society. As indicated by the work of Kenneth Jackson, the Klan was most successful in cities that were changing the fastest.[3] The new immigrants from southern and eastern Europe brought customs and mores that seemed strange and even immoral to the Welsh and German populations of Youngstown. Questions regarding the loyalty of these predominately Catholic immigrants to American institutions because of their allegiance to the pope were common, as well as complaints about Catholic unity, about parochial schools as segregated institutions, and about the allegedly unfair depiction of Protestant ministers in films. The response of the northern European population was to join the Ku Klux Klan to defend its values, a response best typified as religious nativism.

Similar conditions existed in other communities that supported the Klan, but the Mahoning Valley Klan differed in its appeal to moderates. Whereas anti-Catholicism was blatant in Chicago, Klan leaders within Youngstown, such as Charles Scheible, Colonel Evan Watkins, and Clyde Osborne, downplayed the Klan's religious and ethnic biases.[4] Of course, they were still attempting to impose a pietistic moral order on Youngstown. It was this moderate group that carried the Klan to its electoral victories.

Many of these moderates eventually shared the experience of O. P. Harmon, a Klansman from Toledo. He believed initially that the Klan charter sought to promulgate the "affairs of the white, Protestant American . . . and was not a group to condemn, blast, nor attack the various ethnic, racial or religious groups." He observed, however, that greedy kleagles too readily admitted overly bitter and prejudiced elements and alienated members "who were honestly proud of a semi-religious group to back up Protestantism with a semi-militant party, against any possible attack, verbal or otherwise." Harmon was to relinquish his membership "long before the organization died."[5]

The other group, headed by Paul Morris, prevailed after moderates such as Harmon left. Morris hated Catholics and immigrants; he viewed them as an intractable challenge to Protestant America. Dredging forth the old myths that Catholics were plotting to take over America, Morris hoped to use the Klan to launch a war. His language and rhetoric suggested that Morris could no longer tolerate the existence of a pluralistic society. The inability of less tolerant elements to sustain the Klan once moderate elements left would suggest that most old-stock Americans were supportive of religious freedom and nonviolence but ambivalent about the new immigrants and their values. Where the Klan recognized and played upon this ambivalence without resorting to overt and combative forms of prejudice, it was successful in attracting a much broader spectrum of followers. It was the Klan's ability to appeal to moderates that explains its successes in the Mahoning Valley.

The Mahoning Valley was but one variation in the Klan pattern; indeed, no historian can adequately explain the Klan nationally without examining local conditions. It is equally important, however, for Klan historians to generalize from local conditions regarding the national implications of the Klan. Although it is quite evident that the Klan appealed on a variety of levels, but most especially to religious nativism, this study would suggest the need to reexamine the strength of the pietistic moral crusade as a contributor to Klan growth nationally. It is becoming increasingly apparent in the studies of Alexander, Gerlach, Goldberg, and Loucks that the Protestant effort to impose a conservative moral code did influence the rise of the Klan.

More than fifty years ago, Emerson Loucks completed his study of the Pennsylvania Klan, which benefited from the availability of participants less than ten years removed from their involvement. Loucks found that the Klan tried to impose a "national culture" of Protestantism on groups challenging the mores "which the fathers had built up." Klan members visualized it as a law enforcement agency to purge personal immorality; some parents even wrote letters to the Klan to request assistance in straightening out wayward children. Because members also emphasized "the more personal aspects of evil whether it was found in public officials or in their neighbors," the local klaverns often focused on the rousting out of weak or corrupt public officials.[6]

Distant from Pennsylvania and inhabited by fewer immigrants, Colorado was the home of an especially strong Klan. Robert Goldberg's study of five Colorado cities found that law and order, resentment of ethnics, fraternalism, and reform of local government were the key issues that contributed to the rise of the Klan. Although Goldberg is correct in asserting that Klan growth in each city depended on local grievances and the ability of the kleagle to adapt the Klan platform, it is important to note that several of the Klans—Denver's and Pueblo's in particular—focused on law enforcement. "The Klan's most effective draw," according to Goldberg, "was its pledge to clean up Denver and rid the city of its criminal element." In Pueblo the Klan linked a breakdown in law and order, as well as morality, to the foreign element, and typified itself as "an 'instrument of justice,' able to succeed where law enforcement officials had failed." Unfortunately Goldberg was unable to track the religious affiliations of most Klan members, but he did identify the Methodists, Baptists, and Disciples of Christ as most associated with Klan activity in Denver. Thus, pietist concern with moral observance seems to have played an important part in the successes of the Colorado Klan.[7]

In recent studies of the Utah and El Paso Klans, Larry Gerlach and Shawn Lay have discovered that the ability of opponents to mimic the Klan's focus on morality and vice-law enforcement limited the Klan's appeal and its success politically. In Utah, Gerlach uncovered a multivariate level of causation of Klan activity, but he readily admits that "mobilization for war against crime and immorality was perhaps the principle common denominator among Klansmen in the Beehive State." According to Gerlach, "the majority of Klansmen were motivated by the sincere desire to defend and to disseminate traditional middle class WASP religious and political values." Most telling, however, is his conclusion that the Klan did not fare well in Utah because of the Mormon church's ability to supervise its communicants' personal conduct. Thus, the Klan was unable to feed on corrupt local conditions as it did in Pennsylvania and Ohio. "With little to rail and rally against or fester or feed upon," Gerlach notes, "the Invisible Empire languished."[8]

In El Paso, Shawn Lay has studied an Anglo-American border city dependent on Mexican labor. According to Lay, the Klan fed upon the tensions created by an influx of thousands of Anglos from "the racially intolerant South" between 1910 and 1920. Klan growth also depended on religious revivals, which swelled the ranks of the local Protestant churches, and the advent of woman suffrage. The key issues, though, were moral order and law enforcement, with attention focused on the Mexican community as the prime offender. Unlike Youngstown, the El Paso Klan won control only of the school board because its opponents wisely ran a business progressive for mayor. His shrewd promise of a tolerant, yet efficient, government and strict enforcement of the vice laws attracted the support of many residents fearful that "a Klan-run municipal government would disrupt the community's social and business relations." The Klan lost the election and declined rapidly thereafter.[9]

The most important indicator, though, of the strength of moral reform and law enforcement as significant Klan issues occurred in Charles Alexander's study of the Klan in the Southwest. Although the immigrant and black populations were small, the Klan flourished there. According to Alexander, a "passion for reform" and a desire to impose conservative moral values on any offenders provoked an extralegal response by Klan members. Thus, the Klan grew in spite of the smallness of the non-Anglo-Saxon population. Recent studies of Tillamook, Oregon, and Macon, Georgia, with low immigrant and black populations, draw similar conclusions.[10]

Historians must be cautious, however, in assuming that nativism did not exist in areas without a significant mixture of immigrants or blacks. Frank Bohn, a sociologist who investigated the Klan in Marion County, Ohio, in 1923, talked to a kleagle there whose main fear was that Catholics and Jews would come to dominate America. "If our 100% Americans are properly organized," asserted this local farmer, "we can speedily control the country politically." Such fears existed in spite of the fact that there were only 954 foreign-born residents and 239 blacks out of a population of 42,000 in Marion County. Unfortunately, Bohn did not conduct a thorough study of issues raised by the Klan in the election of its candidate, the Reverend Harold Buckey, of the Disciples of Christ, as mayor in 1923. More work needs to be done on this correlation not only in Marion but also nationally.[11]

Besides suggesting a need to reexamine the contribution of moral issues to the rise of the Klan, this study also raises questions about the Jackson thesis. A composite portrait of Klan members in Youngstown corroborates the conclusions of Robert Goldberg and Charles Alexander about Klan membership. Although blue-collar workers predominated on Klan rolls, the majority of members did not belong to the low-achieving, low-status segment of the population described by Kenneth Jackson as resenting the competition of the new immigrants for jobs and housing. Admittedly, such motivation may have attracted some members, as well as fraternalism, greed, and political ambition; but it was the clash between the cultures of rival ethnic groups and the concern over the link between conflicting mores and the status of the United States as a democratic and Christian society that attracted the most active members.

This study poses a further challenge to the prevailing interpretation that suggests a strong link between fundamentalism and the Klan. Though there is no doubt that some Klan members were fundamentalists, a confusion over the distinction between doctrinal beliefs and moral principles has led many historians to conclude erroneously that the Klan was exclusively a fundamentalist organization. In reality, the pietistic sects were more united in their support of a conservative Protestant moral code than of fundamentalism. The Methodists, as the largest contributor to Klan rosters, did not accept fundamentalist dogma, but were among the more conservative Protestant sects morally. Ironically, they were also liberal politically in their espousal of the Social Gospel. An analysis of the Methodists and their theology, as well as that of Presbyterians, Baptists, and Disciples, should lead historians to a reevaluation of the tie between the Klan and fundamentalism.[12]

Further evaluation is also needed of the role of women in the Klan. Historians have not ignored the participation of women in Klan auxiliaries, but they have not usually commented on its significance. Admittedly, the lack of documents poses a problem for studying not only the Klan at large but also the role of women in the Klan. Mahoning Valley newspapers commented briefly on the involvement of many women in Klan activities. They played a traditionally supportive role by preparing food and drinks for the numerous rallies and picnics and by marching in the parades.[13] But they did extend their role politically by making parlor visits during the Scheible campaign and voting in the Klan primary during the spring of 1924. Whether they voted at other Klan rallies is not clear.[14]

Women's history in the early 1920s provides a context for interpreting their participation in the Klan. The recent passage of the woman suffrage amendment meant that women could now exert political power. Though some historians have been skeptical about the level of women's participation in the political process in the 1920s, the fact that more than 43 percent of the voters in the Youngstown election of 1923 were female suggests that there was a link between the Klan's crusade for moral order and the granting of woman suffrage.[15] After all, the major argument behind the suffrage crusade had been the contention that women's sense of morality would cause the cleansing of urban politics. Harriet Ritter's assertion that Youngstown "may need a woman mayor on moral grounds" represented a logical development of the suffrage argument. Her participation in the Federation of Women's Clubs and the role played by that organization in the efforts to bring a home rule charter to Youngstown prepared the way for the Klan. [16] Admittedly, this evidence is more suggestive than conclusive, but further investigation of other Klans should substantiate its validity.

Although this study of the Mahoning Valley has focused on Protestant moral reform coupled with a law enforcement campaign as the prime cause of Klan political successes, there is no doubt that concerns, fears, and prejudices regarding Catholics were among the major causes of support for such a campaign. Moderates expressed dissatisfaction with Catholics' refusal to send their children to public school or with their nonobservance of vice and blue laws. Intolerant factions listened avidly to the tales of an escaped nun while worrying about the infiltration of priests and nuns into the public schools. The shared belief that Catholic moral practices violated the mores that had made America a prominent and democratic country sparked efforts to keep Catholics from teaching in public schools or from holding political office. Pietistic Protestants were trying to maintain control of school and government—institutions that were important mainstays of pietistic Christianity.

Such tactics frightened Catholic communities and set back the process of assimilation. Catholics and Protestants who had worked together, lived in the same neighborhood, or even been friends separated in an atmosphere of hostility that took years to heal. Though the Klan had made a realistic assessment of the moral attitudes of Catholics, its efforts to coerce Catholic immigrants into obedience and to unite WASPs in that effort backfired. It was not possible for moderates to institute such a campaign without unleashing hostility and immoderation and without uniting its opponents.

In the final analysis, the Mahoning Valley Klan represented yet another effort of pietistic Protestants to impose their values on American society. Threatened by the influx of immigrants with decidedly different values, they joined the Ku Klux Klan to defend their way of life. Ironically, it was the moral corruption of its leaders that damaged the Klan the most. White Anglo-Saxon Protestant members of the Klan had failed to heed the biblical injunction to remove the specks from their own eyes.

Appendix A
Occupation Listings

1. Professional—
High Nonmanual

Architects
Artists
Chemists
Clergymen
College professors
Dentists
Designers
Lawyers
Engineers
Musicians
Physicians
Teachers
Nurses

2. Proprietors, Managers, and Officials—*Middle Nonmanual*

Farmers
Wholesale and retail dealers
Building contractors
Manufacturers
Postmasters
Bankers
Undertakers
Officials and inspectors, government
Conductors, steam railroad
Garage owners
Managers
Officials
Superintendents
Restaurant and hotel keepers

3. Clerks and Kindred Workers—*Low Nonmanual*

Baggagemen and freight agents
Ticket and station agents
Clerks
Mail carriers
Radio operators
Inspectors
Insurance and real estate agents
Salesmen
Professional apprentices
Lodge officials
Dental assistants
Credit men
Bookkeepers
Accountants
Stenographers

4. Skilled Workers and Foremen— *High Manual*

Blacksmiths
Boilermakers
Cabinetmakers
Electricians
Stationary engineers
Puddlers
Jewelers
Machinists
Millwrights
Molders
Painters
Plumbers
Rollers
Tailors
Locomotive engineers
Locomotive firemen
Foremen
Firemen
Policemen

5. Semiskilled Workers—*Middle Manual*

Apprentices, building and hand trades
Apprentices, manufacturing
Polishers
Oilers
Operatives, manufacturing
Chauffeurs
Truck drivers
Linemen
Delivery men
Guards
Ushers
Barbers

6. Unskilled Workers—*Low Manual*

Factory laborers
Furnace men
Heaters
Coal mine operatives
Longshoremen
Garage laborers
Servants
Janitors

Appendix B
Population Composition

TABLE B-1
Warren

	1880	1910	1920
% of foreign-born residents	15.7	12.2	17.3
% of foreign-born and native white with foreign-born parents	NA	32.6	37.9
% of foreign-born from southern and eastern Europe	0	NA	60.8
% of blacks	3.2	0.6	2.6
Total Population	4,428	1,081	27,050

SOURCES: U.S. Bureau of the Census, *Tenth Census of the United States, 1880,* Table 6, 423, and Table 9, 454; *Thirteenth Census of the United States, 1910,* Table 1, 384, and Table 3, 421; *Fourteenth Census of the United States, 1920,* Table X, 785; *Abstract of the 12th Census,* Tables 81 and 82, 103–8.

TABLE B-2

Niles

	1910	1920
% of foreign-born residents	29.9	24.9
% of foreign-born and native white with foreign-born parents	65.8	59.2
% of foreign-born from southern and eastern Europe	NA	63.1
% of blacks	0.0	0.1
Total Population	8,361	13,080

SOURCES: U.S. Bureau of the Census, *Thirteenth Census of the United States, 1910*, Table 1, 384, and Table 4, 424; *Fourteenth Census of the United States, 1920*, Table X, 788.

TABLE B-3
Girard

	1910	*1920*
% of foreign-born residents	28.0	22.8
% of foreign-born and native white with foreign-born parents	63.5	53.6
% of foreign-born from southern and eastern Europe	NA	NA
% of blacks	0.3	0.37
Total Population	3,736	6,556

SOURCES: U.S. Bureau of the Census, *Thirteenth Census of the United States, 1910*, Table 1, 384, and Table 4, 423; *Fourteenth Census of the United States, 1920*, Table II, 790.

TABLE B-4
Struthers

	1910	1920
% of foreign-born residents	31.3	25.1
% of foreign-born and native white with foreign-born parents	62.7	60.8
% of foreign-born from southern and eastern Europe	NA	NA
% of blacks	1.2	4.2
Total Population	3,370	5,847

SOURCES: U.S. Bureau of the Census, *Thirteenth Census of the United States, 1910*, Table 1, 378, and Table 4, 424; *Fourteenth Census of the United States, 1920*, Table II, 792.

TABLE B-5
East Youngstown

	1910	*1920*
% of foreign-born residents	77.8	50.9
% of foreign-born and native white with foreign-born parents	3.3	90.6
% of foreign-born from southern and eastern Europe	NA	96.7
% of blacks	0.04	5.3
Total Population	4,972	11,237

SOURCES: U.S. Bureau of the Census, *Thirteenth Census of the United States, 1910*, Table 1, 378, and Table 4, 423; *Fourteenth Census of the United States, 1920*, Table X, 787.

Notes

INTRODUCTION

1. David M. Chalmers, *Hooded Americanism: The History of the Ku Klux Klan*, 2d ed. (New York, 1981).

2. Charles C. Alexander, *The Ku Klux Klan in the Southwest* (Lexington, 1966).

3. Robert A. Goldberg, *Hooded Empire: The Ku Klux Klan in Colorado* (Urbana, Ill., 1981).

4. Robert K. Murray, *Red Scare: A Study of National Hysteria, 1919–1920* (New York, 1964), 90–92, 264–65; Kenneth T. Jackson, *The Ku Klux Klan in the City, 1915–1930* (New York, 1967), 10–11; Alexander, *Klan in the Southwest*, 11–19; John Higham, *Strangers in the Land: Patterns of American Nativism, 1860–1925* (New York, 1966), chaps. 9 and 10. Goldberg suggests that local conditions, rather than the war or Red Scare, caused the rise of the Klan (Goldberg, *Hooded Empire*, 164–66). It should also be noted that, while Higham coined the term, "Tribal Twenties," he did suggest very strongly that Klan prejudices built upon a base already very evident in the Progressive Era.

5. Richard Jensen, *The Winning of the Midwest: Social and Political Conflict, 1888–1896* (Chicago, 1971), 58–88. Equally as important as Jensen's work is that of Paul Kleppner, *The Cross of Culture: A Social Analysis of Midwestern Politics, 1850–1900* (New York, 1970) and *The Third Electoral System, 1853–1892: Parties, Voters, and Political Cultures* (Chapel Hill, 1979). Edward Banfield and James Q. Wilson also note the ethnic influence on politics in *City Politics* (Cambridge, 1967), 38–44.

6. Clifford S. Griffin, *Their Brothers' Keepers: Moral Stewardship in the United States, 1800–1865* (New Brunswick, N.J., 1960), ix–xv.

7. Sidney E. Mead, "American Protestantism since the Civil War: From Denominationalism to Americanism," *The Journal of Religion* 36 (January 1956): 2–3. In *Righteous Empire: The Protestant Experience in America* (New York, 1970), Martin Marty contends that evangelicals established a Protestant culture within American society (see chaps. 7–9). He does not, however, distinguish between pietists and liturgicals. In his later work, *Pilgrims in Their Own Land: 500 Years of Religion in*

America (New York, 1984), Marty does note that Lutherans were not evangelistic (p. 170) and that they opposed prohibition (pp. 367–69, 377).

8. Norman H. Clarke, *Deliver Us From Evil: An Interpretation of American Prohibition* (New York, 1976), 68–117. See also Jack S. Blocker, Jr., *Retreat from Reform: The Prohibition Movement in the United States, 1890–1913* (Westport, 1976).

9. Aileen Kraditor, *The Ideas of the Woman Suffrage Movement, 1890–1920* (Garden City, 1965), chap. 3.

10. Mead, "American Protestantism since the Civil War," 2–3; Jensen, *Winning of the Midwest*, 58–88.

11. Higham, *Strangers in the Land*, 80–87, 101–12, 128–29, 162–64, 189–93, 202–3.

12. John Buenker, *Urban Liberalism and Progressive Reform* (New York, 1973), 163–97. Also see Clarke, *Deliver Us*, 89–117.

13. Clarke, *Deliver Us*, 121–22; Peter H. Odegaard, *Pressure Politics: The Story of the Anti-Saloon League* (New York, 1966), 48–60. K. Austin Kerr has suggested that the Anti-Saloon League was a part of the organizational revolution that accompanied the reform movements of the Progressive Era. He focuses on the idea that the League represented a phase in the development of government-business relations similar to the attacks on the trusts and the effort to have the government regulate them. He also sees it as part of a wellspring of idealism, evangelism, and moralism that arose prior to the world war. See Kerr, *Organized for Prohibition: A New History of the Anti-Saloon League* (New Haven, 1985), 1–11.

14. Jackson, *Klan in the City*, 240–42.

15. It is noteworthy that the Interchurch World Movement in its study of the 1919 steel strike praised the impartiality of both papers in reporting the strike (Interchurch World Movement, *Public Opinion and the Steel Strike* [New York, 1921], 156–58).

CHAPTER ONE

1. *Youngstown Vindicator*, 8, 13 September 1921.

2. Alexander, *Klan in the Southwest*, 1–5, 115–18; Chalmers, *Hooded Americanism*, 8–30; Jackson, *Klan in the City*, 6. John Moffatt Mecklin in his work *The Ku Klux Klan: A Study of the American Mind* (New York, 1924), 20, contends that "its official documents indicate in perfectly clear language that the Klan originally, no matter what it became in later practice, was a purely fraternal and patriotic organization . . . one of hundreds of similar secret societies in this country."

3. Stanley Frost, *The Challenge of the Klan* (New York, 1924), 57, 61. See also Mecklin, *The Ku Klux Klan*, 127–28.

4. Frost, *Challenge of the Klan*, 57–58.

5. Alexander, *Klan in the Southwest*, 5–6.

6. Chalmers, *Hooded Americanism*, 32.

7. Alexander, *Klan in the Southwest*, 7.

8. *Vindicator*, 23 May 1922.

9. Alexander, *Klan in the Southwest*, 8; Chalmers, *Hooded Americanism*, 32.

10. Henry Fry, *The Modern Ku Klux Klan* (Boston, 1922), 2–3.

11. Ibid., 12–15; 4; 24–30.

12. Chalmers, *Hooded Americanism*, 39–48, 59–65.

13. Alexander, *Klan in the Southwest*, vi–viii, 18–19, 29–35.

14. Chalmers, *Hooded Americanism*, 36; Jackson, *Klan in the City*, 12–13.

15. Chalmers *Hooded Americanism*, 35–38; Alexander, *Klan in the Southwest*, 9–10; Jackson, *Klan in the City*, 11–12.

16. Alexander, *Klan in the Southwest*, 9–10; Chalmers, *Hooded Americanism*, 32, 100–102.

17. Alexander, *Klan in the Southwest*, 41, 80; Chalmers, *Hooded Americanism*, 41.

18. Chalmers, *Hooded Americanism*, 42.

19. Alexander, *Klan in the Southwest*, 79–80, 109–10; Chalmers, *Hooded Americanism*, 101–2.

20. Jackson, *Klan in the City*, 13–16; Chalmers, *Hooded Americanism*, 101–4.

21. Alexander, *Klan in the Southwest*, 79–81; Frost, *Challenge of the Klan*, 17–34.

22. Chalmers, *Hooded Americanism*, 105–8.

23. Alexander, *Klan in the Southwest*, 19, chap. 2.

24. Goldberg, *Hooded Empire*, 166–74.

25. Norman Weaver, "The Knights of the Ku Klux Klan in Wisconsin, Indiana, Ohio, and Michigan" (Ph.D. diss., University of Wisconsin, 1954), 225–26; Chalmers, *Hooded Americanism*, 175–76. The Weaver dissertation must be used cautiously by the historian of the Ohio Klan: it contains numerous inaccuracies.

26. Chalmers, *Hooded Americanism*, 162–63.

27. Ibid., 165.

28. F. Mark Cates, "The Ku Klux Klan in Indiana Politics, 1920–1925" (Ph.D. diss., Indiana University, 1970), 38. Embry B. Howson interviewed an Ohio Klan lecturer who claimed that more than one-half of the Klan lecturers were ministers. Howson, "The Ku Klux Klan in Ohio After World War I" (Master's thesis, Ohio State University, 1951), 23–24.

29. Oliver S. Baketel, ed., *The Methodist Yearbook* (Cincinnati, 1924), 181.

30. United Presbyterian Church of North America, *Minutes of the 60th General Assembly of the United Presbyterian Church of North America* (Pittsburgh, 1918), 446; *Minutes of the 62nd General Assembly of the United Presbyterian Church of North America*, pp. 22–23; Presbyterian Church of the United States of America, *Minutes of the General Assembly of the Presbyterian Church of the United States of America: 1920* (Philadelphia, 1920), 392; *Minutes of the General Assembly of the Presbyterian Church of the United States of America: 1922*, 62–63, 182–84.

31. Northern Baptist Convention, *Thirteenth Annual of the Northern Baptist Convention: 1920* (American Baptist Publication Society, 1920), 243–45; *Fourteenth Annual of the Northern Baptist Convention: 1921*, 296–98.

32. *Thirteenth Annual*, 249–52.

33. Disciples of Christ, *Yearbook and Annual Reports: Organizations of the Disciples of Christ* (St. Louis, 1924), 285; Henry K. Shaw, *Buckeye Disciples: A History of the Disciples of Christ in Ohio* (St. Louis, 1957), 4–20.

34. The Protestant Episcopal Church did not indicate any support for moral legislation nationally; see the *Annual Report of the Presiding Bishop and Council* (Domestic and Foreign Missionary Society of the Protestant Episcopal Church in the United States of America) for the years 1918–25. E. Clifford Nelson, ed., *The Lutherans in North America* (Philadelphia, 1975), 355–56; Kleppner, *Cross of Culture*, 153–63; Willard D. Allbeck, *A Century of Lutherans in Ohio* (Yellow Springs, Ohio, 1966), 252–56.

35. Buenker, *Urban Liberalism*, 198–239; Peter Filene, "An Obituary for the 'Progressive Movement,' " *American Quarterly* 22 (1970): 20–34.

36. Robert H. Wiebe, *Search for Order* (New York, 1967).

37. Charles N. Glaab and A. Theodore Brown, *A History of Urban America* (New York, 1967), 201–27.

38. Hoyt L. Warner, *Progressivism in Ohio, 1890–1917* (Columbus, 1964), 10–18; Odegaard, *Pressure Politics*, 1–5, 9, 39–48. In his article "The Ku Klux Klan in the Middle West" (*World's Work* 46 [August 1923]: 363), Robert L. Duffus suggests that there was a link between Klan members and "the same portions of our population that followed Mr. Roosevelt's train in his great days, and which have contributed many a progessive measure to the national programme" (363).

39. Odegaard, *Pressure Politics*, 15–22; *Minutes of the 62nd General Assembly of the United Presbyterian Church of North America: 1920*, 22.

CHAPTER TWO

1. Goldberg, *Hooded Empire*, 168–74, 179–80. See also Emerson H. Loucks, *The Ku Klux Klan in Pennsylvania: A Study in Nativism* (Harrisburg, 1936), 31–33, for evidence that Pennsylvania kleagles tailored their messages to local conditions.

2. Joseph G. Butler, Jr., *History of Youngstown and Mahoning Valley Ohio* (Chicago, 1921), 1:118–25.

3. Ibid., 180–85.

4. Ibid., 200–202.

5. Ibid., 690–96.

6. Ibid., 707–10.

7. Ibid., 700–706.

8. Ibid., 60–87.

9. Ibid., 75–78, 311–13.

10. *Youngstown Telegram*, 4 April 1896. At that time the *Telegram* was the Republican newspaper.

11. Butler, *History of Youngstown*, 706–10; U.S. Bureau of the Census, *Fourteenth Census of the United States Taken in the Year 1920: Population*, 3:767–810 (see tables 10 and 12).

12. Butler, *History of Youngstown*, 86, 530–32; *Vindicator*, 1 January 1916; David Brody, *Labor in Crisis: The Steel Strike of 1919* (Philadelphia, 1965), 164, 174; David Brody, *Steelworkers in America: The Nonunion Era* (Cambridge, 1960), 239–42, 252, 262; William Z. Foster, *The Great Steel Strike* (New York, 1920), 176–77.

13. Brody, *Steelworkers in America*, 255; *Vindicator*, 25, 30 January 1921; 19 April, 24 May 1924; 15 March 1925; 3 June 1931; 2 May 1941. *Fourteenth Census*, 3:784–88. A local chapter of the NAACP does not appear until June 1942; see the *Vindicator*, 8 June 1942.

14. Butler, *History of Youngstown*, 703–6.

15. Ibid., 83–86.

16. *Ohio Worker*, January, February 1919; August, October 1920.

17. Ibid., September 1920; May, September 1922; June 1925. The Baptists did not indicate similar tendencies at their state conventions, but the Ohio Baptist Association, located in southern Ohio, and the Akron Baptist Association passed resolutions at their conventions supporting Prohibition. The Ohio Baptist Association resolution asked that "all temperance legislation and all law enforcement tending to suppress crime and to establish a higher standard of moral living be encouraged and sup-

ported." See the *Minutes of the Ohio Baptist Association* (n.p., 1921), unpaged; *Minutes of the Akron Baptist Association* (n.p., 1920), 9; *Proceedings of the 96th Annual Meeting of the Ohio Baptist Convention* (n.p., 1921).

18. *Minutes of the East Ohio Conference of the Methodist Episcopal Church* (West Methodist Book Concern Press, 1910), 300; *Minutes of the Northeast Ohio Conference of the Methodist Episcopal Church* (Cleveland, 1921), 267.

19. *Yearbook of the Ohio Annual Conferences of the Methodist Episcopal Church: 1921* (Cincinnati, 1921), 194–95.

20. *Minutes of the Synod of Ohio of the Presbyterian Church of the United States of America: 1922* (Cincinnati, 1922), 48–49; *Minutes of the Synod of Ohio: 1921*, 51; *Minutes of the Synod of Ohio: 1920*, 17; *Minutes of the First Synod of the West: 1921* (n.p., 1921), 28–30.

21. Four of the eleven Lutheran churches in Youngstown (Bethelem, Grace, Honterus, and St. Luke's) belonged to the United Lutheran Church in America. There was also a Swedish Lutheran Church and a Swedish Mission (Nelson, *Lutherans in North America*, 348–56); *Minutes of the Synod of Ohio, United Lutheran Church of America* (Columbus, 1921), 144; *Proceedings of the 83rd Annual Convention of the East Ohio Synod of the General Synod of the Evangelical Lutheran Church* (Pittsburgh, 1918), 41.

22. *Minutes of the Eastern District, Joint Synod of Ohio and Other States* (Columbus, 1917), 17. I examined the minutes of the Joint Synod from 1917 through 1925. See also the *Journal of the Annual Convention of the Protestant Episcopal Church in the Diocese of Ohio* (Cleveland, 1918), 43; *Journal of the Diocese of Ohio, 1919*, 43; see also the *Journal* from 1920 to 1925.

23. *Vindicator*, 4 October 1921; 15 November 1923; 16 February 1923.

24. *The Federal Churches Monthly Bulletin*, 1 January 1923. In 1926 the leading Protestant denominations (non-black) were the Methodists (7,635), Presbyterians (6,929), Lutherans (6,034), Disciples of Christ (3,531) and Baptists (2,915). U.S. Bureau of the Census, *Religious Bodies: 1926*, 1:375–76.

25. *Vindicator*, 21 December 1922.

26. Kraditor, *Ideas of the Woman Suffrage Movement*, chap. 3. The number of women in the federation expanded from approximately 4,000 in 1922 to 5,800 in 1923 and 6,100 in 1924 as the crusade intensified. See the *Official Registry and Directory of Women's Clubs in America, 1922–26*. See also J. Stanley Lemons, *The Woman Citizen: Social Feminism in the 1920s* (Urbana, Ill., 1975), chap. 4, "The Lady and the Tiger." Of particular note was the campaign of the Franklin County Woman Suffrage Association, in conjunction with the WCTU, YWCA, YMCA, and the Federation of Churches, to clean up vice and corruption in Columbus, Ohio. In 1919 they ousted George Karb from the mayor's office, a position he had held for sixteen years (Lemons, 92–93).

27. The concern about increasing crime did correspond to an increase in the commission of felonies. During the years from 1901 to 1910, the average of felonies per year was 137; from 1911 to 1920 it was 407 and from 1921 to 1930, 417.9. The increase became apparent in 1914 and continued thereafter. Since the percentage increase of felonies was significantly larger than the rate of population increase in the teens, but not in the twenties, it would appear that the law enforcement campaign did have the desired effect. 1900, 99; 1901, 106; 1902, 85; 1903, 111; 1904, 100; 1905, 96; 1906, 129; 1907, 171; 1908, 169; 1909, 197; 1910, 195; 1911, 208; 1912, 205; 1913, 296; 1914, 333; 1915, 360; 1916, 588; 1917, 633; 1918, 541; 1919, 646; 1920,

362; 1921, 499; 1922, 356; 1923, 362; 1924, 358; 1925, 428; 1926, 444; 1927, 527; 1928, 420; 1929, 502; 1930, 421. These figures were gathered from the Mahoning County *Criminal Docket*, vols. 5–25.

28. *Vindicator*, 5 May 1921.

29. Howard C. Aley, *A Heritage to Share: The Bicentennial History of Youngstown, Mahoning County, Ohio* (Youngstown, 1975), 245–46.

30. Ibid., 240; *Vindicator*, 18 October 1921; 1, 3, 5 November 1921.

31. Aley, *A Heritage to Share*, 238. Oles gave his salary to charity.

32. *Vindicator*, 9 November 1921.

33. Ibid., 14 December 1921.

34. Ibid., 8 November 1921; Aley, *Heritage to Share*, 238.

35. *Vindicator*, 7, 23, 25, 26, 29, 30 January 1922; *Telegram*, 23, 25, 26, 28 January 1922.

36. Oles's intentions had created other embarrassments. Suspicious of vagrants and their connection to the number of robberies in Youngstown, Oles ordered the rounding up of people without visible means of support. The police dragnet landed 124 persons, but without evidence of any wrongdoing, they had to be released. *Vindicator*, 9 January, 7, 28–30 June 1922.

37. Ibid., 1 July 1922. Interest in the development of a new charter predated Ritter's call for change. The previous year city council had approved submission of a choice between the city manager and federal forms to the voters during the August primary of 1922. The voters rejected both plans. Doris L. Dunwoody, "Building a City" (Master's thesis, Youngstown State University, 1971), 53–56.

38. *Vindicator*, 1 July 1922.

39. *Telegram*, 3 July 1922.

40. *Vindicator*, 5 July, 8 November 1922; *Telegram*, 8 November 1922.

41. Dunwoody, "Building a City," 60–61. The final form of the proposed charter appeared in both newspapers on 14 March 1923.

42. Ibid., 62; *Telegram*, 16 May 1923.

43. *Vindicator*, 5 June 1923.

44. *Federal Churches Monthly Bulletin*, 3 April 1923.

45. Ibid., 1 January, 3 April 1923; May 1924 (day not on masthead).

46. Ibid., 1 January 1923.

47. Ibid.

48. Ibid., 10 May 1923.

49. C. Glen Anderson, *One Hundred Years of Church History: The Story of First Baptist Church* (Youngstown, n.d.), 1–3.

50. *Vindicator*, 26 November 1922. Archibald was a fundamentalist who attacked church heretics and ministers who expected freedom to preach modernist views from the pulpit. He commented, "I say to the bottom of the bottomless pit with such heresy." See the *Vindicator*, 5 February 1923.

51. Ibid., 27, 28 November 1922; *Telegram*, 27, 28 November 1922; *Dawn*, 16 December 1922, 10.

52. *Vindicator*, 28 November 1922.

53. *Vindicator*, 29 November 1922.

54. Ibid., 28 November 1922; *Telegram*, 28 November 1922.

55. *Vindicator*, 2, 4 December 1922; *Telegram*, 2, 4 December 1922.

56. *Vindicator*, 3 December 1922.

57. Ibid., 24 June, 28 November 1922.

58. Ibid., 5 December 1922; *Telegram*, 5 December 1922.
59. *Vindicator*, 2 March 1923.
60. Ibid., 3 March 1923.
61. Ibid., 21 December 1922; *Telegram*, 21 December 1922.
62. *Vindicator*, 27, 29 December 1922; 9, 18 January 1923; *Telegram*, 30 December 1922.
63. *Vindicator*, 16 February 1923.
64. Youngstown *Citizen*, 16 August 1923.
65. *Vindicator*, 10, 11, 27 July 1923.
66. Ibid., 7 August 1923.
67. Ibid., 30 July, 11 August 1923.
68. Ibid., 11, 16, 23 August 1923.
69. Ibid., 24 August 1923.
70. Ibid., 27 August 1923.
71. Ibid., 26, 28 August 1923.
72. Ibid., 28 August 1923. James Watkins would later be indicted in New Jersey as a codefendant with noted criminal Nicky Arnstein for fraud. See *Tribune Chronicle*, 18 October 1924.
73. *Vindicator*, 29 August 1923.
74. See the earlier *Citizen*'s masthead; also *Citizen*, 19 July, 9 August 1922.
75. Ibid., 3 June, 12 August 1922.
76. Ibid., 17 June 1922; 25 January, 15, 29 March 1923; 10 November 1922; 1 February 1923.
77. Ibid., 8, 29 July 1922; 2, 16 August 1923.
78. Ibid., 25 August, 8, 15, 22 September 1923. Although D. Webster Brown continued to serve as editor throughout this transition, there is no available source to explain his conversion to support for the Klan.
79. *Vindicator*, 13 July 1923. Stanley Frost notes that Hiram Evans commented about the relationship between Klan and Anti-Saloon League tactics in an interview with the journalist. See Frost, *Challenge of the Klan*, 90.

CHAPTER THREE

1. *Vindicator*, 15 October 1923.
2. *Tribune Chronicle*, 6, 20 April; 7, 9 May 1923.
3. *Vindicator*, 1, 2 September 1923.
4. Ibid., 2 October 1923.
5. Ibid., 6, 8 October 1923; *Telegram*, 8 October 1924.
6. *Vindicator*, 6, 11 October 1923; *Telegram*, 11 October 1923.
7. *Vindicator*, 5, 12 October 1923; *Telegram*, 5 October 1923.
8. *Vindicator*, 1, 4 October 1923; *Telegram*, 5 October 1923. The fifth candidate, George Snyder, assumed the role of neutrality. In his speeches Snyder placed himself above either faction—Klan or anti-Klan—at one point calling for "peace," no further newspaper reports, and an emphasis on the fitness of the candidates for office. Snyder cited his experiences as a reporter and city editor for the *Vindicator*, and endorsed law enforcement and prohibition—indeed, he had "signed the pledge when he was a boy" (*Vindicator*, 13 October 1923).
9. *Vindicator*, editorial, 23 October 1923.

10. Ibid., 5 September, 31 October 1923; *Telegram*, 31 October 1923.
11. *Vindicator*, 31 October, 3 November 1923.
12. Ibid., 23, 30 October 1923; *Telegram*, 24 October 1923.
13. *Vindicator*, 30 October 1923; *Telegram*, 2 November 1923.
14. *Vindicator*, 11, 30 October 1923; *Telegram*, 19 October 1923.
15. *Vindicator*, 13 October, 3 November 1923; *Telegram*, 13, 18 October 1923.
16. *Vindicator*, 3 November 1923.
17. *Vindicator*, 19, 26 October, 2 November 1923; *Telegram*, 19 October 1923.
18. *Telegram*, 2 November 1923.
19. *Vindicator*, 19 October, 2 November 1923; the background of these men was traced through Butler's *History of Youngstown* in the 2d and 3d volumes of biography.
20. *Vindicator*, 15 October 1923.
21. Ibid., 16, 19 October 1923; *Telegram*, 19 October 1923.
22. *Vindicator*, 20 October 1923 (a reference to Jack Walton, governor of Oklahoma, a Klan opponent). Copies of the *Citizen* that printed these statements were not available, and, to my knowledge, may have been lost forever.
23. *Vindicator*, 30 October, 3 November 1923; *Telegram*, 19, 31 October 1923.
24. *Vindicator*, 17 October 1923.
25. Ibid., 8 May, 8 October 1923.
26. *Telegram*, 2 November 1923.
27. *Vindicator*, 11 December 1924; *Telegram*, 10, 11 December 1924.
28. *Vindicator*, 10 December 1924; *Tribune Chronicle*, 11 December 1924.
29. *Vindicator*, 24 October 1923; *Telegram*, 24 October 1923. Many of these points correspond to the general goals of urban reformers listed in Banfield and Wilson, *City Politics*, 138–42.
30. *Telegram*, 3 November 1923.
31. Ibid., 31 October 1923; *Vindicator*, 31 October 1923.
32. *Vindicator*, 22 October 1923.
33. Ibid., 30 October 1923.
34. Ibid., 22 October 1923; *Telegram*, 22 October 1923.
35. *Vindicator*, 30 October, 2, 3 November 1923.
36. Ibid., 1 October 1923.
37. Ibid.
38. *Telegram*, 3 November 1923. Journalist Stanley Frost quoted a New York physician who complained that politicians "cater to the German vote, the Catholic vote, the Jewish vote, the Italian vote, the bootleg vote, the vice vote, and sometimes even to the violently criminal vote. What the Klan intends to do," he added, "is to make them pay some attention to the American vote, the Protestant Christian vote and the decent, God-fearing law-abiding vote" (see Frost, *Challenge of the Klan*, 92).
39. *Vindicator*, 8 January, 25 October 1923.
40. Ibid., 26, 27, 29 October 1923; *Telegram*, 26, 27, 29 October 1923. It was quite common for the Klan to have a special organization so that prominent figures could deny Klan membership. See interview with Clyde Osborne in Howson, "The Ku Klux Klan in Ohio," 23–24.
41. *Vindicator*, 3 November 1923.
42. Ibid., 5 November 1923.
43. Ibid., 23 October, 1 November 1923.
44. *Telegram*, 30, 31 October 1923; *Vindicator*, 30, 31 October 1923.
45. *Vindicator*, 28 October 1923.
46. Ibid., 3 November 1923; *Telegram*, 3 November 1923.

47. *Vindicator,* 21 October, 5 November 1923.

48. The Klan Council winners were: Frank B. Jones, Third Ward; W. L. Buchanan, Fourth Ward; George H. Roberts, Fifth Ward; John Rothwell, Sixth Ward; and Owen James, Seventh Ward. W. R. Lentz was the eventual winner in the Second Ward. Klan school board winners were George Hopkins, L. U. Hulin, E. G. Perkins and Charles Stillson (*Vindicator,* 7 November 1923, 7 January 1924; *Telegram,* 7 November 1923). Disgruntled incumbents tried to pass a resolution requesting Charles Scheible to ask the Klan for the $600,000 to take the city out of debt, but Council President Robert Backus ruled the resolution out of order (*Dawn,* 24 December 1923, 17; *Niles Evening Register,* 20 November 1923).

49. *Vindicator,* 3 November 1923.

50. *Telegram,* 30 October 1923.

51. *Vindicator,* 9 November 1923. Klan leaders had approached the mayor in mid-October about a parade permit for the Saturday after the election. Reese denied the permit, but the ordinance regulating such parades did not give him any power to refuse permission; it did allow the police chief to designate the streets. Reese's denial gave the Klan an opportunity to appear as the offended party in its demand for its constitutional rights (*Vindicator,* 17, 19 October 1923; *Telegram,* 18 October 1924).

52. *Vindicator,* 11 November 1923; *Telegram,* 9 November 1923.

53. *Vindicator,* 12 November 1923.

CHAPTER FOUR

1. *Tribune Chronicle,* 27, 28 September, 3, 5, 8 October 1923; *Vindicator,* 7 October 1923.

2. Butler, *History of Youngstown,* 403–22.

3. Ibid., 430, 434.

4. Ibid., 430–32, 465.

5. Ibid., 434–37.

6. Ibid., 434.

7. *Tribune Chronicle,* 20, 22 November 1922.

8. Ibid., 22 November 1922.

9. Ibid., 2 February 1923.

10. Ibid., 12, 13 December 1922; *Telegram,* 11, 12 December 1922.

11. *Tribune Chronicle,* 20, 25 January 1923.

12. Ibid., 22, 25 November 1922.

13. Ibid., 23 November 1922; 6 January 1923.

14. Ibid., 6 April 1923.

15. Ibid., 7, 9 May 1923. On Monday, 7 May, Watkins held another meeting of 100 percent Americans.

16. Ibid., 14 May 1923.

17. Ibid., 15 May 1923.

18. Ibid.

19. Ibid., 8 May 1923.

20. Ibid., 7, 10, 15 August 1923.

21. Ibid., 25 January, 4 April, 4 May 1923.

22. Ibid., 16 August 1923.

23. Ibid., 31 October 1923.

24. Ibid., 3 November 1923.
25. Ibid., 27 October, 1, 3 November 1923. Unfortunately the newspaper did not include a list of members.
26. Ibid., 24 October 1923.
27. Ibid., 5 November 1923.
28. Ibid., 7 November 1923; *Vindicator*, 8 November 1923.
29. *Tribune Chronicle*, 7 November 1923.
30. Ibid., 12 November 1923.
31. Butler, *History of Youngstown*, 471–78.
32. Ibid., 478–80.
33. Ibid., 487–92. The *Niles Evening Register* estimated that there were 4,000 Irish, 3,500 Italians, 3,000 Welsh and 2,000 English-Canadian residents in Niles. More than 60 percent of the Irish and Italian residents owned homes. The newspaper described the Welsh as regular churchgoers and the least criminal of the ethnic groups (3 February 1923, 3).
34. I interviewed many residents of Niles who remembered the sign but did not recall its history. The black population in 1920 was .1 percent of all Niles citizens (*Fourteenth Census*, 3:784–88).
35. Gina Buccino, "Niles Remembers Bagnoli," *Sunday Tribune Magazine*, 14 December 1980, 12–16; *Evening Register*, 3 February 1923, 3.
36. Humbert S. Nelli, *From Immigrants to Ethnics: The Italian Americans* (New York, 1983), 19–35; Luigi Barzini, *The Italians* (New York, 1964), 234–51; Lucianno J. Iorizzo and Salvatore Mondello, *The Italian-Americans* (New York, 1971), 38–46. According to Nelli, most Italian immigrants came from the *Mezzogiorno*, the area south of Rome. Nelli and Barzini ascribe these qualities to the inhabitants in general, although many of their examples focus on the provinces of Calabria and Sicily. Although most of the Niles Italians came from Campania, the ones that I interviewed—not a representative sample—shared in these attitudes.
37. *Niles Daily Times*, 11 January 1941.
38. Interview with Martha Pallante, 6 May 1984.
39. Interview with Rita Jennings Gregory by Steven Papalas, Youngstown State University Oral History Program, 19 August 1982.
40. Interview with Joseph Jennings, Jr., by Steven Papalas, Youngstown State University Oral History Program, 20 August 1982.
41. *Tribune Chronicle*, 26 January 1923; *Niles Daily News*, 30 January 1923.
42. *Niles Daily News*, 6 January 1923.
43. Ibid., 26 January 1923.
44. Ibid., 5, 8 March 1923.
45. Interview with John C. Crow by Steven Papalas, Youngstown State University Oral History Program, 21 June 1982.
46. *Niles Evening Register*, 10, 17 March 1923.
47. *Niles Daily News*, 12 March 1923; *Niles Evening Register*, 17 March 1923.
48. *Niles Evening Register*, 20 March 1923.
49. Ibid., 8 February 1923.
50. Ibid., 8 February, 3 May, 13 June 1923; *Niles Daily News*, 2 March, 13, 14 June 1923. In March the governor removed Herman H. Vogt, of Massillon.
51. *Niles Evening Register*, 3 May, 8 June 1923.
52. *Niles Daily News*, 14 June 1923.
53. *Tribune Chronicle*, 15 June 1923.

54. *Niles Evening Register,* 14 June 1923.
55. *Niles Daily News,* 18 June 1923.
56. *Niles Daily News,* 9 June 1923.
57. *Niles Evening Register,* 17 March 1923; *Niles Daily News,* 5, 17 April 1923; *Tribune Chronicle,* 20 April 1923.
58. *Niles Daily News,* 26 April 1923; *Niles Evening Register,* 26 April 1923; *Tribune Chronicle,* 26 April 1923.
59. *Niles Evening Register,* 2, 18 June 1923.
60. *Niles Evening Register,* 19 May 1923.
61. Ibid., 16 August 1923.
62. Interview with Karl Kistler by Steven Papalas, Youngstown State University Oral History Program, 24 February 1923.
63. *Tribune Chronicle,* 10 September 1923.
64. *Niles Evening Register,* 7 November 1923.
65. Butler, *History of Youngstown,* 502–4.
66. Ibid., 506; *Vindicator,* 6, 7 October 1922; 15 February 1923.
67. *Citizen,* 10 June 1922.
68. Interview with Nicola Criscone by William D. Jenkins, Youngstown State University Oral History Program, 10 May 1985.
69. *Citizen,* 2, 9 August 1923.
70. *Vindicator,* 7 November 1923.
71. Butler, *History of Youngstown,* 494–500.
72. *Vindicator,* 7 November, 24 December 1923; *Citizen,* 12 February 1925.
73. Butler, *History of Youngstown,* 528–29.
74. Ibid., 530–32; *Vindicator,* 1, 2, 3 January 1916.
75. Butler, *History of Youngstown,* 531.
76. Ibid., 532–38; *Youngstown City Directory* (Akron, 1924), 1248.
77. *Vindicator,* 10 November 1923.
78. *Telegram,* 8 November 1923.
79. *Vindicator,* 9 November 1923.

CHAPTER FIVE

1. *Vindicator,* 1 October 1923, 1 April 1924; *Telegram,* 1 October 1923; *Is Your Neighbor a Kluxer?* (Chicago, 1924).
2. Jackson, *Klan in the City,* 102–7, 115–17.
3. *Vindicator,* 10 December 1922, 10 September 1923; *Telegram,* 18 October 1923.
4. Fry, *Modern Ku Klux Klan,* 17.
5. Frost, *Challenge of the Klan,* 2.
6. Frederick Lewis Allen, *Only Yesterday: An Informal History of the Nineteen Twenties* (New York, 1929), 56; Robert S. and Helen M. Lynd, *Middletown* (New York, 1929), 482; Alexander, *Klan in the Southwest,* 18. In an article, "Ancestry and End of the Ku Klux Klan," *Worlds Work* 46 (September 1923): 527–36. Robert L. Duffus described a delegation from Chicago to the Valparaiso, Indiana, Klan rally in May 1923 as "of an inferior type." "Certainly, they were not the 'average American citizens, home owners, voters, and folk relied upon in the communities from which they came'

which one Klan paper described them as being. Most of them could be classified as belonging to the less successful strata of the 'white collar' class" (528).

7. Jackson, *Klan in the City*, 241–42.

8. Ibid., 244.

9. Goldberg, *Hooded Empire*, 174; Larry R. Gerlach, *Blazing Crosses in Zion: The Ku Klux Klan in Utah* (Logan, Utah, 1982).

10. Goldberg, *Hooded Empire*, Table V, 46.

11. Ibid., 178.

12. *Vindicator*, 1 October, 26 November 1923, 19 May 1924. The *Vindicator* claimed that 17,000 members voted in the Klan primary held in May 1924.

13. Jackson, *Klan in the City*, 239.

14. *Youngstown City Directory* (Akron, 1923); *Is Your Neighbor a Kluxer?*; see also Jackson, *Klan in the City*, 116.

15. *Fourteenth Census*, 3: 344, 535.

16. Alba M. Edwards, *A Socio-Economic Grouping of the Gainful Workers of the United States: 1930* (Washington, 1938), Table 1, 3–6.

17. *Fourteenth Census*, 4: 1297–99. I subtracted figures for the ten-to-seventeen-year-old age group for the final graph figure, since Klan members were at least eighteen. The random sample consists of 288 Klan members whose data I cross-checked in the *City Directory*, local newspapers, church records, county title bureaus, and obituaries. I could find occupations for only 269 members of the sample.

18. Ibid., 3: 1286–87.

19. Jackson, *Klan in the City*, 244–45. See also chaps. 3, 4, 8, and 10.

20. U.S. Bureau of the Census, *Fifteenth Census of the United States Taken in the Year 1930*, 3: 536. I have used the 1930 census because the wards were redrawn in 1923 after passage of the home rule charter and reduced from nine to seven.

21. I have used the *Youngstown City Directory* for 1924 to examine names of residents on ward streets as a means of determining ethnic residence.

22. I talked to twenty-nine former Klan members by telephone. Most were reluctant to discuss their involvement. I uncovered these members by using the phone book and comparing names to the list.

23. James Q. Wilson, *Political Organizations* (New York, 1973), 64.

24. Ibid., 62.

25. Examples of such churches include the Brownlee Woods United Presbyterian, South United Presbyterian, Evergreen United Presbyterian, and Indianola Methodist Episcopal.

26. *Vindicator*, 8 October 1923, 24 April 1931; *Citizen*, 6 November 1924.

27. Wilson, *Political Organizations*, 32–36.

28. Howson, "The Ku Klux Klan in Ohio," 70.

29. *Citizen*, 30 October 1924. John Moffatt Mecklin issued a questionnaire regarding Klan motivation. From several hundred responses, he concluded that anti-Catholicism took precedence over all other motivations—not, however, to deny religious freedom but to protect it against alleged Roman Catholic treason (Mecklin, *The Ku Klux Klan*, 28, 157–59).

30. *Citizen*, 14, 21 June, 19 July 1924; *Vindicator*, 15 July, 19 August, 1 September, 7 October, 3, 10, 11 November 1923.

31. Wilson, *Political Organizations*, 34–36.

32. Non-pietistic Lutherans constituted 5.1 percent and Episcopalians 2 percent. I attempted to see how many Klansmen in the random sample from chapter 5 belonged

to a Protestant church. Unfortunately, some churches no longer existed, some kept poor records, and some refused to open their records at all. I was able to look at the records of 31 Protestant churches out of 71 that existed in 1926. In light of the missing records, and since many citizens of Protestant background or heritage identified with the crusade, it is safe to conclude that much more than 33 percent of the Klan sample belonged to a Protestant church. Moreover, this survey also revealed that pietistic churches—Methodists (261), Presbyterians (191), Disciples of Christ (138), Lutherans (63), and Baptists (69)—attracted the most participants. Non-pietistic churches provided only 7 + percent. By 1926 Youngstown had 134 churches and 89,963 members out of a total population approaching 170,000. See U.S. Bureau of the Census, *Religious Bodies: 1926*, 1: 356.

33. Jensen, *Winning of the Midwest*, 67, 80–85; Kleppner, *Cross of Culture*, 148, 153–58; Nelson, ed., *Lutherans in North America*, 348–52, 356. The ULC churches were Bethelem (the oldest in Youngstown, with nineteen members), Grace Evangelical (twenty members), Honterus (unwilling to open records), and St. Luke's (seventeen members).

34. The Joint Synod churches were Martin Luther (twenty-three members), St. Paul's (seven members), Trinity (six members), and Woodland Avenue Evangelical (no records); Butler, *History of Youngstown*, 73–75, 317; Nelson, ed., *Lutherans in North America*, 396–400; *Telegram*, 28 August 1927, 20 March, and 15 May 1918; *Vindicator*, 19, 20 March 1920.

35. *Vindicator*, 2 October, 11 November 1923; *Telegram*, 9 November 1923.

36. George M. Marsden, *Fundamentalism and American Culture: The Shaping of Twentieth Century Evangelism, 1870–1925* (New York, 1980), 117–18.

37. Robert Moats Miller, "The Ku Klux Klan," *Change and Continuity in Twentieth Century America: The 1920s*, ed. John Braeman, Robert H. Bremner, and David Brody (Columbus, 1968), 223.

38. Ernest R. Sandeen, *The Roots of Fundamentalism: British and American Millenarianism, 1800–1930* (Chicago, 1970), ix–x. Sandeen contends that fundamentalism was a doctrinal controversy not much affected by social or psychological considerations. Marsden tends to accept Sandeen, but suggests that there were these influences.

39. Stewart G. Cole, *The History of Fundamentalism* (Westport, Conn., 1971), 188–207.

40. Marsden, *Fundamentalism and Culture*, 148.

41. Nelson Hodges Hart, "The True and the False: The Worlds of an Emerging Evangelical Protestant Fundamentalism in America, 1890–1920" (Ph.D. diss., Michigan State University, 1976), 218.

42. Marsden, *Fundamentalism and Culture*, 128, 162–63.

43. Cole, *History of Fundamentalism*, 163–92.

44. Norman F. Furniss, *The Fundamentalism Controversy, 1918–31* (New Haven, 1954), 149–51. Martin Marty distinguishes between evangelicals, who supported personal salvation and strict moral codes, and social gospelers. He does admit that both supported Prohibition, however. See *Pilgrims in Their Own Land*, 375–76. He sees only a generalized anti-Catholicism and anti-Semitism as causes of Protestant entry into the Klan (390–97).

45. Winfred E. Garrison and Alfred T. DeGroot, *The Disciples of Christ: A History* (St. Louis, 1948), 424; *The Ohio Work*, June 1922, 4; July 1924, 4; Shaw, *Buckeye Disciples*, 351. One can also find acceptance of a social gospel message at the national

conventions of both Presbyterian denominations; indeed, they even endorsed the Dyer Anti-Lynching Bill. See the *Minutes of the General Assembly of the Presbyterian Church of the United States of America: 1920*, 392, and the *Minutes of the General Assembly of the United Presbyterian Church of North America: 1922*, 563. The Northern Baptist Convention of 1923 endorsed the social principles of the Federated Council of the Churches of Christ in America (see page 247).

46. Paul Boyer, *Urban Masses and Moral Order, 1820–1920* (Cambridge, 1978), 195.

47. *Vindicator*, 15, 22 January 1923. The Reverend William Hudnut, of the First Presbyterian Church, also supported Blue Law enforcement strongly at the same time that he roundly condemned the Klan (see the *Vindicator*, 12 March, 25 October, and 5 November 1923). Robert Moats Miller, "A Note On the Relationship between the Protestant Churches and the Revived Ku Klux Klan," *Journal of Southern History* 22 (August 1956): 355–68. In this article Miller contends that newspapers of the major denominations condemned the Klan, sometimes indirectly. On the other hand, I have been able to find only one instance (Lutheran) where a national assembly or regional convention warned its members about societies "which operate in secret for the supposed purpose of supplementing the work of law enforcement." Though it admitted that such societies were often based on good principles, the report deplored the negative attitudes created toward government and enforcement agencies. See *Minutes of the Synod of Ohio: 1923*, 119.

48. Sociologists who have studied rioting have contended that such clashes usually result from scarce resources and/or value differences. See Gary T. Marx, ed., *Racial Conflict: Tension and Change in American Society* (Boston, 1971), 2.

49. The reader can pick up this pattern in local publications, such as the *Citizen*, regional publications, such as the *Dial* from Chicago, or the national Klan paper entitled the *Kourier*.

CHAPTER SIX

1. *Vindicator*, 12 November 1923.

2. Ibid., 28, 30 November 1923.

3. Ibid., 3 December 1923; *Telegram*, 30 November 1923.

4. *Vindicator*, 28 November 1923; *Telegram*, 28 November 1923.

5. *Vindicator*, 9 December 1923.

6. Ibid., 14 December 1923; *Telegram*, 15 December 1923.

7. John Struthers Stewart, *A History of Northeast Ohio*, 2 vols. (Indianapolis, 1935), 2: 543–44.

8. *Vindicator*, 28 November, 1, 27 December 1923.

9. Ibid., 1 January 1924.

10. Ibid., 12 January 1924; *Telegram*, 12 January 1924.

11. *Vindicator*, 2 January 1924.

12. Ibid., 21 January, 3, 6, 7, 10 March 1924; *Telegram*, 3, 4, 5, 6, 7, 8, 10 March 1924.

13. *Vindicator*, 11 March 1924.

14. Ibid., 10, 11 March 1924.

15. Ibid., 14 March, 1 May 1924; *Telegram*, 14 March 1924.

16. *Vindicator*, 13, 21, 22 May 1924.

17. *Tribune Chronicle*, 10 January, 31 May, 7 June 1924.

18. *Vindicator*, 10 February 1924.

19. Ibid., 15 November 1923; *Telegram*, 15 November 1923.

20. *Vindicator*, 1 January 1924.

21. Ibid., 21 November 1923; 31 July, 26 September 1924; 24 January 1926; *Telegram*, 21 November 1923.

22. *Vindicator*, 15 November 1923; 10, 11 January 1924.

23. Ibid., 15, 17, 20, 21 November 1923; 13 May, 3, 4 June, 13, 22 August, 6, 12 November 1924.

24. Though no direct evidence of police corruption surfaced under the Scheible administration, the next mayor, Joseph Heffernan, was told by a police captain that he was foolish not to accept the graft available. In nearby Niles the conditions covered in this paragraph were detailed in the famous bootlegger-policemen hearings of 1927 and 1931 (see chap. 7). See also William D. Jenkins, "Moral Reform after the Klan: Joseph Heffernan as Mayor of Youngstown, 1928–31," *The Old Northwest: A Journal of Regional Life and Letters* 9 (Summer 1983): 148–51.

25. *Vindicator*, 26 August, 22 September, 23, 26 December 1924.

26. Ibid., 9 September 1924; 8 March, 8 July 1925.

27. Ibid., 15 September, 5, 13 October, 1 December 1925.

28. Ibid., 18 January 1926.

29. Ibid., 27 December 1925; 20 January 1926.

30. Ibid., 8, 9 March, 9 April, 26 May 1926. An additional indicator of the Klan's decline was the appointment of a manager, F. M. Cox, to direct the Klan.

31. Ibid., 2 December 1925; 1 March 1926.

32. *Tribune Chronicle*, 16 January, 4 June, 20 August 1924; 23 February, 19 May 1925.

33. Ibid., 2, 4 November 1925.

34. *Vindicator*, 27 December 1923; 1 January 1924.

35. *Citizen*, 19 March 1925.

36. *Vindicator*, 26 November, 1 December 1923; *Telegram*, 26 November, 1 December 1923.

37. *Vindicator*, 3 December 1923.

38. Ibid., 4 December 1923; *Telegram*, 4 December 1923.

39. *Vindicator*, 11 May 1924.

40. Ibid., 8, 10 December 1923; *Telegram*, 8, 11 December 1923.

41. *Vindicator*, 18 May, 12 July 1924; *Citizen*, 2, 16 August 1924. The candidates selected were Griff Jones and Albert Cooper (brother of the Nineteenth District's congressional representative, John Cooper) for county commissioners; Samuel Evanson for state senate; and George Roberts, Irene Leonard (leader of the Kamelias), and Charles Westover for state representative. Adam Stone received the endorsement for county sheriff and James Hartwell for county prosecutor. Overlooking the fact that Mrs. C. J. Ott was already a female representative from the area, Leonard said that she was running because "women should have representation in our legislature." Her goals as a representative included "laws protecting pure womanhood . . . the open Bible in the schools instruction for our boys and girls in the book of books."

42. *Vindicator*, 13 August 1924.

43. Ibid.

44. Ibid., 13, 14 August 1924; *Telegram*, 13 August 1924.

45. *Vindicator*, 5, 6 September 1924; *Citizen*, 30 August 1924.

46. *Citizen*, 9 October 1924; *Vindicator*, 5 November 1924.

47. *Citizen*, 19 July 1924.

48. *Vindicator*, 6, 14 September 1924.

49. Ibid., 16 July 1924; *Citizen*, 19, 26 July 1924.

50. *Citizen*, 23 August 1924.

51. Ibid., 6, 13 September, 9 October 1924.

52. *Vindicator*, 27, 30, 31 December 1923; *Telegram*, 27 November 1923.

53. *Vindicator*, 7, 8 April 1924. Warren passed a similar ordinance on firearms on 18 April 1924 (*Warren Tribune Chronicle*, 19 April 1924).

54. *Vindicator*, 21, 22, 25 March, 3 April 1924.

55. Frank Jones and William Buchanan allied with Harry Payne, Charles Scheible, and Clyde Osborne to propose moderation; Owen James, George Robertson, John Rothwell, and Web Lentz wanted all aliens banned from owning businesses. *Telegram*, 4, 5 April 1924; *Vindicator*, 4, 5 April 1924.

56. *Vindicator*, 6 May 1924.

57. Ibid., 5 December 1922.

58. Ibid.

59. Youngstown Board of Education, *Minute Book No. 8*, 3 December 1923, 1766.

60. *Vindicator*, 1 February, 20 September 1925.

61. Ibid., 22 January 1924; Youngstown Board of Education, *Minute Book No. 8*, 21 January 1924, 1803; *Minute Book No. 9*, 16 March 1925, 2133–34; 20 April 1925, 2162–64.

62. On 11 June 1923 there was a fire that caused $40,000 damage to Our Lady of Mount Carmel, an Italian nationality church in Youngstown. Rumor had it that the Ku Klux Klan was responsible; it was claimed that the pastor, Fr. Victor Franco, had seen a Klansman in full regalia prior to the fire. In a *Vindicator* report on the following day, Fr. Franco denied such a story and claimed that he saw a man in a light suit only (*Vindicator*, 12 June 1923). Though it is true that a Klansman might still have set the fire, such activity does not fit the general pattern of Klan activities.

63. *Vindicator*, 3 November 1923.

64. Ibid., 18 April 1924; *Citizen*, 12 July 1924.

65. *Vindicator*, 12 July, 6 August, 6 November 1924; *Citizen*, 20 November 1924.

66. *Citizen*, 13 November, 11 December 1924; 22 January 1925.

67. Ibid., 15 October 1925.

68. *Vindicator*, 26 October, 4 November 1925.

69. Lawrence J. McCaffrey, *The Irish Diaspora in America* (Bloomington, 1976), 30–58, 108–11.

70. *Vindicator*, 5 September, 31 October 1923; *Telegram*, 31 October 1923; Jackson, *Klan in the City*, 102–7. Patrick Corbett, George Meyer, and Michael Cannon were the young men involved (*Citizen*, 21 June 1924). Patrick H. O'Donnell, president of the AUL, had come to Youngstown in January 1923 to speak at the Moose Temple. He promised the audience that "a complete list of the Youngstown members of the Klan will be obtained and the names will be published" (*Vindicator*, 7 January 1923).

71. Ronald E. Marec, "The Fiery Cross: A History of the Ku Klux Klan in Ohio, 1920–1930" (Master's thesis, Kent State University, 1967), 122–32; *Tribune Chronicle*, 24, 28 June 1924; *Vindicator*, 21, 25, 28, 29 June 1924.

72. *Telegram*, 28 July, 26 August 1924.

73. *Vindicator*, 28 June 1924.

74. Ibid., 29 June 1924.

CHAPTER SEVEN

1. Lewis Coser, in *The Functions of Social Conflict* (New York, 1956), notes that conflict with other groups contributes to the establishment and reaffirmation of the identity of the group and maintains its boundaries against the surrounding "social world" (p. 38).

2. *Niles Evening Register*, 10 March 1924.

3. Ibid., 19 February, 4 April 1923.

4. Ibid., 22 January 1924.

5. Interview with Lee E. Hewitt by Steven Papalas, Youngstown State University Oral History Program, 14 December 1983.

6. Ibid.

7. *Niles Evening Register*, 8 March 1923.

8. In 1927 two bootleggers accused three policeman—including Lt. Gilbert—of accepting bribes. Their testimony before the Civil Service Commission led to the dismissal of the officers. According to the *Daily News*, the three policemen had an excellent record in the pursuit of Prohibition violators. The bootleggers faced no charges. The successes of 1927 prompted the Jenningses in 1931 to adopt the same tactic. The admissions of Jim Jennings and Marty Flask that they had bribed seven officers for the past five years created a public furor, but backfired on them when the county decided to prosecute the confessed bootleggers. They were found guilty and sentenced to prison. *Vindicator*, 7, 8 January; 18 February; 2, 3, 4 March 1927; *Niles Daily Times*, 3, 4, 7 February; 2, 3, 5 March 1927; 9, 23 February 1928; 26, 30 October; 1, 3, 4, 12, 13, 22 November 1930; 3, 11 March; 18 June; 22 July 1931; *Tribune Chronicle*, 2 November; 8 December 1930.

9. *Tribune Chronicle*, 27 March, 6 May 1924; *Niles Daily Times*, 4 August 1925.

10. *Tribune Chronicle*, 17 April 1924.

11. Ibid., 10 May 1924; *Vindicator*, 10 May 1924.

12. *Vindicator*, 10 May 1924.

13. Again see Coser, *Functions of Conflict*, 33–38. The in-group attack on vice had already caused bootleggers and gamblers to unify as a deviant group. In attacking the Italians and their religion, the Klan pushed the entire Italian community together when it would have been better served by isolating vice law violators.

14. *Tribune Chronicle*, 19, 21 June 1924.

15. *Vindicator*, 18, 20, 21 June 1924; *Tribune Chronicle*, 21 June 1924.

16. *Vindicator*, 22 June 1924; *Tribune Chronicle*, 23 June 1924; *Citizen*, 28 June 1924.

17. *Vindicator*, 23, 24 June 1924. The chief witness, Thomas "Butch" Lewis, contended that he had thought the warrants were actually drawn against Chief Round for allowing the anti-Klan forces to be armed! Patrick Fusco immediately filed a damage suit for $50,000 against Kistler, Round, and Lewis that charged defamation of character. According to Fusco, he was not even near the scene of the riot, and most of the other men were out of town.

18. *Vindicator*, 25, 26 June 1924; *Tribune Chronicle*, 25, 26 June 1924.

19. *Citizen*, 28 June 1924.

20. *Vindicator*, 24 June 1924; *Tribune Chronicle*, 24 June 1924.

21. *Steubenville Herald Star*, 27 September 1923; *Vindicator*, 27 September 1923.

22. *Vindicator*, 28 June 1924; *Tribune Chronicle*, 28 June 1924.

23. *Citizen*, 26 July 1924; *Tribune Chronicle*, 19, 21 July 1924; *Telegram*, 19, 21 July 1924.

24. *Tribune Chronicle*, 4 August 1924; *Vindicator*, 5 August 1924; *Telegram*, 5 August 1924.

25. *Tribune Chronicle*, 4 August 1924; *Vindicator*, 4 August 1924.

26. *Vindicator*, 5 August 1924; *Telegram*, 5 August 1924; *Tribune Chronicle*, 5 August 1924.

27. *Vindicator*, 6 August 1924; *Tribune Chronicle*, 6 August 1924.

28. *Vindicator*, 7 August 1924; *Tribune Chronicle*, 7, 8 August 1924.

29. *Vindicator*, 7, 8 August 1924; *Tribune Chronicle*, 9 August 1924; *Telegram*, 8 August 1924.

30. *Vindicator*, 9 August 1924; *Tribune Chronicle*, 9 August 1924.

31. *Vindicator*, 10 August 1924.

32. Ibid., 10, 11 August 1924; *Tribune Chronicle*, 11 August 1924.

33. *Tribune Chronicle*, 11 August 1924.

34. *Vindicator*, 8 September 1924.

35. Chalmers, *Hooded Americanism*, 238-39.

36. *Tribune Chronicle*, 17, 20 October 1924; *Telegram*, 16 October 1924.

37. *Tribune Chronicle*, 23, 24 October 1924; *Niles Daily Times*, 23 October 1924.

38. *Niles Daily Times*, 29 October 1924; *Vindicator*, 27, 28, 29 October 1924; *Tribune Chronicle*, 27, 28 October 1924.

39. *Tribune Chronicle*, 29 October 1924; *Niles Daily Times*, 29 October 1924.

40. *Telegram*, 27, 28, 29 October 1924; *Tribune Chronicle*, 28 October 1924; *Vindicator*, 28, 29 October 1924.

41. *Vindicator*, 29 October 1924.

42. *Niles Daily Times*, 30, 31 October 1924; *Tribune Chronicle*, 31 October 1924.

43. *Tribune Chronicle*, 31 October 1924; *Vindicator*, 31 October 1924.

44. *Tribune Chronicle*, 31 October 1924.

45. Ibid., 30 October 1924; *Vindicator*, 29, 31 October 1924; *Telegram*, 31 October 1924; *Niles Daily Times*, 31 October 1924.

46. *Vindicator*, 31 October 1924; *Telegram*, 31 October 1924; *Tribune Chronicle*, 30 October 1924.

47. *Vindicator*, 30, 31 October 1924; *Niles Daily Times*, 31 October 1924.

48. *Tribune Chronicle*, 1 November 1924.

49. Interview with Frank McDermott by Steven Papalas, Youngstown State University Oral History Program, 18 December 1982; *Tribune Chronicle*, 31 October 1924; *Niles Daily Times*, 6 February 1925.

50. *Niles Daily Times*, 6 February 1925; *Vindicator*, 1 November 1924; *Tribune Chronicle*, 31 October 1924.

51. *Telegram*, 1 November 1924; *Vindicator*, 1 November 1924.

52. Interview with Anthony Nigro (son), 19 October 1985; interview with Pasqual Ruberto by William D. Jenkins, Youngstown State University Oral History Program, 9 January 1985.

53. Ruberto interview.

54. Rita Jennings Gregory interview.

55. Weaver, "The Knights of the Ku Klux Klan," 252.

56. *Transcript of Evidence Taken by Military Investigation Board Appointed by General Orders No. 7*, Ohio National Guard, 3 November 1924, R. L. McCorkle, 12-18; Dr. John B. Claypool, 4-5; Elmer Jones, 20-21, 25; Carl Reddy (Rettig), 256-58.

57. *The Truth About the Niles Riot* (Niles, 1924), 7–8; petition filed in G. E. Victor case, no. 23034, Trumbull County Courthouse.

58. *Vindicator*, 1 November 1924; ONG transcript, Arthur Lynch, 97–98; Arthur Davis, 61–63; David Ague, 84–85.

59. *Cleveland News-Leader*, 2 November 1924.

60. *Niles Daily Times*, 21 March 1925.

61. *Vindicator*, 1 November 1924.

62. *Tribune Chronicle*, 1, 3 November 1924; 21 March 1925; *Niles Daily Times*, 21 March 1924; ONG transcript, Arthur Davis, 61–62; Dave Thomas, 73–74; David John Crooks, 321–22; Patrick N. Fusco, 346–47; H. C. Harmon, 357.

63. *Vindicator*, 2 November 1924.

64. *Tribune Chronicle*, 3 November 1924; *Telegram*, 1 November 1924; ONG transcript, John H. Rose, 146–52; Weaver, "The Knights of the Ku Klux Klan," 259–62.

65. *Tribune Chronicle*, 19 March 1925; *Niles Daily Times*, 19 March 1925; ONG transcript, W. G. Llewellyn, 111; Archie L. Cramer, 171–73; Harry Bradbury, 213; Mrs. Dray, 221–22.

66. *Tribune Chronicle*, 3 November 1924; *Vindicator*, 2, 3 November 1924.

67. *Vindicator*, 2 November 1924; *Truth*, 8–9; *Tribune Chronicle*, 3 November 1924; ONG transcript, Dr. J. M. Elder, 37–38; F. M. Woodward, 49–52; W. M. Woodworth, 53–56; Arthur Davis, 61–62; James Copeland, 65–67; Dave Thomas, 73–74; George Alexander, 209–10; E. E. Cope, 387–91; Russel Near, 252.

68. Interview with Catherine Ritter.

69. *Vindicator*, 2 November 1924; letter from Robert DeCristofaro, Jr., 23 December 1982.

70. *News-Leader*, 2 November 1924; *Tribune Chronicle*, 3 November 1924.

71. *Tribune Chronicle*, 3 November 1924; *Truth*, 19. A Captain Voorsanger accompanied Sheriff Thomas. When Thomas entered the tent, according to Voorsanger, "one of the men told me they were going to get the sheriff's resignation and then kill him because they blamed him for the trouble they had with their parade." Voorsanger threatened a bloody massacre when the troops arrived unless Thomas was released. Some of the men then told him to back up the car to the tent in order to avoid any potshots (*Cleveland Plain Dealer*, 2 November 1924).

72. *Tribune Chronicle*, 3 November 1924.

73. *Truth*, 20; *Tribune Chronicle*, 3 November 1924. Dr. Hart, however, was not convinced until he received a copy of the governor's proclamation. Colonel Connelly antagonized the Klan members by sending Chaplain Joseph Trainer, from St. Columba's Church, to deliver the proclamation. Connelly also refused to provide an escort for Klan members (*Truth*, 10; *Tribune Chronicle*, 3 November 1924; *Vindicator*, 1 November 1924).

74. *Tribune Chronicle*, 3 November 1924; *Vindicator*, 2 November 1924.

75. *Tribune Chronicle*, 3, 4 November 1924; *News-Leader*, 2 November 1924.

CHAPTER EIGHT

1. *Tribune Chronicle*, 3 November 1924; *Vindicator*, 2 November 1924.

2. *Citizen*, 6, 13 November 1924.

3. *Truth*, 12–16, 18.

4. *Tribune Chronicle*, 3 November 1924; *Vindicator*, 3 November 1924.

5. *Tribune Chronicle*, 3 November 1924; *Telegram*, 5 November 1924.

6. *Tribune Chronicle*, 13 December 1924.

7. ONG transcript; *Niles Daily Times*, 14 November 1924.

8. *Niles Daily Times*, 10, 13 November 1924.

9. *Vindicator*, 18 November 1924; *Tribune Chronicle*, 18 November 1924.

10. *Telegram*, 19, 20 November 1924; *Niles Daily Times*, 18, 19, 20 November 1924.

11. *Telegram*, 3, 4 December 1924; *Niles Daily Times*, 5, 6 December 1924; *Tribune Chronicle*, 5 December 1924; *Plain Dealer*, 6 December 1924. Unfortunately, the transcript of the grand jury hearing was lost in a fire.

12. *Tribune Chronicle*, 8, 9 December 1924; *Niles Daily Times*, 8, 10 December 1924.

13. *Tribune Chronicle*, 13 November 1924; *Vindicator*, 13 November 1924; *Telegram*, 13 November 1924.

14. *Vindicator*, 17 December 1924; *Tribune Chronicle*, 18 December 1924; *Telegram*, 17 December 1924.

15. *Telegram*, 16 August, 3 December 1924; *Vindicator*, 16 August 1924. Watkins told the *Telegram* that he viewed the OPIS as a new state police organization that had the power to "aid in the detection of crime and the enforcement of all laws" (*Telegram*, 12 September 1924; *Vindicator*, 12 September 1924).

16. *Vindicator*, 8, 10, 11, 12 December 1924; *Telegram*, 10, 11, 12 December 1924; *Tribune Chronicle*, 12 December 1924. Colonel Wade Christy checked through regular army channels regarding Watkins's claim to have been with Gen. Allenby as head of an intelligence unit (S-2). He learned that Watkins had been with Allenby, but in a noncombatant unit, not as head of S-2 (Norman B. Weaver, "Knights of the Ku Klux Klan in Wisconsin, Indiana, Ohio and Michigan," 243).

17. In 1935 Colonel Watkins died after spending his remaining years as a circuit lecturer on the Holy Land (*Telegram*, 10 April 1935; *Vindicator*, 18 December 1924).

18. *Tribune Chronicle*, 1, 2 January 1925.

19. Ibid., 23 January 1925.

20. Ibid., 29 January, 2, 9 February, 9 March 1925.

21. *Telegram*, 4 November 1924; *Tribune Chronicle*, 4 November 1924. The court trial proceedings were also lost in a fire.

22. I have checked newspaper accounts to compile lists of the wounded and then searched through the death records for both Mahoning and Trumbull counties. No evidence exists to support the charge of unaccounted death.

23. *Niles Daily Times*, 6, 7, 9 February 1925; *Tribune Chronicle*, 6, 7, 9 February 1925; *Telegram*, 10 February 1925; McDermott interview.

24. *Niles Daily Times*, 17, 18 March 1925; *Tribune Chronicle*, 17, 18 March 1925; *Telegram*, 18 March 1925.

25. *Niles Daily Times*, 19 March 1925; *Tribune Chronicle*, 19, 20 March 1925.

26. *Niles Daily Times*, 19, 20 March 1925; *Tribune Chronicle*, 19, 20 March 1925.

27. *Niles Daily Times*, 21, 23 March 1925; *Tribune Chronicle*, 21, 23 March 1925.

28. *Tribune Chronicle*, 24 March 1925; *Niles Daily Times*, 23 March 1925.

29. *Telegram*, 12 March 1925.

30. *Niles Daily Times*, 24, 25 March 1925; *Vindicator*, 25 March 1925; *Tribune Chronicle*, 25 March 1925.

31. *Niles Daily Times*, 27 March 1925; *Tribune Chronicle*, 27 March 1925; Rita Jennings Gregory interview.

32. *Niles Daily Times*, 30 March, 1 April 1925; *Tribune Chronicle*, 1 April 1925.

33. Petition filed in G. E. Victor case, no. 23034, Trumbull County Courthouse. Robert L. Daugherty has mistakenly contended that no blame was ever fixed for the riot in "Problems in Peacekeeping: The 1924 Niles Riot," *Ohio History* 85 (Autumn 1976): 292.

34. See footnote 8 in chap. 7.

35. Marx, ed., *Racial Conflict*, 2. Sociologists have argued that riots usually result from a clash over values or scarce resources. In the case of Niles, we have a clash of values rather than scarce resources.

36. *Niles Daily Times*, 11 January 1941.

CHAPTER NINE

1. *Vindicator*, 12 February 1925; *Citizen*, 12 February, 23 April 1925.

2. *Tribune Chronicle*, 5 November, 17 December 1925.

3. *Vindicator*, 20 October 1924; Marec, "The Fiery Cross," 133–37.

4. *Vindicator*, 10 November 1924.

5. Ibid., 6 February 1925; *Tribune Chronicle*, 6 February 1925.

6. Marec, "Fiery Cross," 137, 149–54.

7. *Vindicator*, 24 August 1925; Howson, "The Ku Klux Klan in Ohio," 93–107.

8. *Citizen*, 22 January, 7 May 1925; 19, 26 March 1925.

9. Ibid., 26 February, 14 May 1925.

10. Ibid., 6 August 1925.

11. Interview with Joseph L. Heffernan by Hugh G. Earnhart, Youngstown State University Oral History Program, 2 May 1974, 1–13.

12. *Vindicator*, 16, 18, 31 October, 2, 9 November 1927; Heffernan interview, 21–22.

13. *Vindicator*, 9 November 1927.

14. Heffernan interview, 12–20, 23; untitled story, Joseph L. Heffernan Papers, Youngstown State University, 9–11; *Vindicator*, 3 January 1928. See the *Telegram*, 25 April 1930, for statement by Heffernan that no machine existed in Youngstown.

15. Jenkins, "Moral Reform after the Klan," 149–53.

16. *Telegram*, 21 December 1931.

17. *Telegram*, 18 May, 13, 18 June 1928; *Vindicator*, 13 June 1928.

18. Heffernan Papers, untitled story, 11–21. Unable to entrap, Heffernan's enemies also tried to manufacture a case. Matteo Parisi, who lived in Philadelphia, brought suit against Heffernan for allegedly accepting the defense of his brother, Anthony, in a murder trial several years earlier, and then failing to appear. Although Heffernan was also supposedly liable for working as an attorney while serving as municipal judge, the case offered little more than harrassment value, and was later dropped (*Vindicator*, 20, 21 May, 4, 5, 12 June, 24 December 1929).

19. McCaffrey, *Irish Diaspora*, 76.

20. In the 1930s Heffernan was elected to the post of Democratic state central committeeman. His connections with Donahey, then a senator, brought him an appointment as an attorney for the FCC. In 1936 he served as an assistant to the attorney general of the state of Ohio, Herbert S. Duffy (Heffernan interview, 70–71).

21. Joseph L. Heffernan, untitled paper in author's possession, 2–3.

22. Joseph L. Heffernan, "Our Moral Transition," unpublished paper, ca. 1938, 1, 12–13.

CONCLUSION

1. *Vindicator,* 8 September 1921; 22 October 1923; 29, 30 March, 2 April 1924. After Scheible's election as mayor, black households began to purchase guns through the mail; the local postmaster contended that more than one thousand guns had been purchased. In late March 1924 an incident occurred in which a black robber shot and killed a white policeman who belonged to the Klan. The Ku Klux Klan attended the wake and funeral in robes and served as a cortege. His minister, the Reverend M. M. Amundsen, of Central Christian Church, praised the slain policeman as a "martyr to the cause of law and order." Local black leaders complained to the authorities and to the *Vindicator* that no one had attended to the wounds of the black man—he had been beaten into submission by another officer. Indeed, they had dragged him from the police van by his heels into the station, and the man had died from a fractured skull.

2. Ibid., 9 November 1927. Instead, the Klan activities served to unite the black community. In 1927 William S. Vaughn was elected the first black councilman from the Third Ward. With seven candidates running, he managed to win with only 25 percent of the vote. Jerry Sullivan, an Irish Catholic, won the Second Ward seat.

3. Jackson, *Klan in the City,* 241.

4. The *Dawn,* a Chicago Klan newspaper, printed numerous articles on the Catholic menace. See especially the issues of 6 November 1922, 25 November 1922, 30 December 1922, 13 January 1923, 10 February 1923, 10 March 1923, 24 March 1923, and 1 December 1923. In the 12 May 1923 issue, there was an editorial entitled, "Do Roman Catholics Want Civil War?" which made the following charge: "The tactics that have made Rome synonomous with infamy and the Roman Church an enemy of America's best traditions are being employed in Chicago today."

5. Marec, "The Fiery Cross," 44–45.

6. Loucks, *Klan in Pennsylvania,* vi, 36, 40–44, 105.

7. Goldberg, *Hooded Empire,* 19, 47, 62.

8. Gerlach, *Blazing Crosses,* 139, 141, 150–51.

9. Shawn Lay, *War, Revolution, and the Ku Klux Klan: A Study of Intolerance in a Border City* (El Paso, 1985), 14–15, 31–32, 48, 77–78, 81–103, 105, 113–15, 121, 123–26, 140, 155–59. The number of articles on the Klan in historical journals is less than thirty-five. Some of them deal indirectly with the Klan; others vary in the extensiveness of their research. The following articles provide further evidence of the importance of the enforcement of moral order in the rise of the Klan: Robert A. Goldberg, "The Ku Klux Klan in Madison, 1922–27," *Wisconsin Magazine of History* 63 (Autumn 1974): 31–44; Blaine A. Brownell, "Birmingham, Alabama: New South City in the 1920s," *Journal of Southern History* 38 (February 1972): 20–48; and Frank Granger, "Reaction to Change: The Ku Klux Klan in Shreveport, 1920–1929," *North Louisiana Historical Association Journal* 9 (1978): 219–27. Although not a documented history, Paul M. Angle's *Bloody Williamson: A Chapter in American Lawlessness* (New York, 1952) portrays a bloody struggle between pietist Protestants and Italian immigrants over bootlegging. Williamson County, in Illinois, was a hotbed of pietist revivalism, and its followers were willing to engage in extralegal enforcement of

the law. Numerous violent confrontations followed until the community finally tired of the bloodshed. See especially 134–205.

10. Alexander, *Klan in the Southwest*, chap. 2; Roger Hux, "The Ku Klux Klan in Macon, 1919–25," *Georgia Historical Quarterly* 62 (Summer 1978): 155–68; William Toll, "Progress and Piety: The Ku Klux Klan in Tillamook, Oregon," *Pacific Northwest Quarterly* 69 (April 1978): 75–85.

11. Frank Bohn, "Ku Klux Klan Interpreted," *American Journal of Sociology* 30 (January 1925): 387–90. A recent dissertation on the state of Indiana has suggested that no such tie existed there. With a small immigrant and black population, the Indiana Klan supposedly focused on white Protestant values and the building of community. Leonard Joseph Moore, "White Protestant Nationalism in the 1920s: The Ku Klux Klan in Indiana" (Ph.D. diss., University of California, 1985). Moore sees any connection between ethnic conflict and the rise of the Klan as superficial at best.

12. See chapter 5 for a fuller explanation.

13. *Citizen*, 26 July 1924; *Tribune Chronicle*, 6, 8 October 1923; *Telegram*, 9 November 1923.

14. *Vindicator*, 17 October 1923, 18 May 1924; *Telegram*, 11 October 1923.

15. *Vindicator*, 21 October 1923. For an evaluation of female voting patterns in the early twenties, see William H. Chafe, *The American Woman: Her Changing Social, Economic, and Political Roles, 1920–1970* (New York, 1972), 29–34.

16. June Sochen, *Herstory: A Record of the American Woman's Past*, 2d ed. (Sherman Oaks, Calif., 1981), 151–52; Lois W. Banner, *Women in Modern America: A Brief History*, 2d ed. (New York, 1984), 43; Kraditor, *Ideas of Woman Suffrage Movement*, chap. 3.

Bibliography

PRIMARY SOURCES

Baketel, Oliver S., ed. *The Methodist Yearbook*. Cincinnati: Methodist Book
   Concern, 1924.
Cleveland News-Leader, 1924.
Cleveland Plain Dealer, November 1924.
Dawn, 1922–24.
Disciples of Christ. *Yearbook and Annual Reports: Origins of the Disciples of
   Christ*. St. Louis: United Christian Missionary Society, 1918–25.
———. *The Ohio Worker,* 1917–25.
Federal Churches Monthly Bulletin, 1922–25.
Fry, Henry. *The Modern Ku Klux Klan*. Boston: Small, Maynard and Co.,
   1922.
General Synod of the Evangelical Lutheran Church. *Proceedings of the 83rd
   Annual Convention*. Pittsburgh: Lutheran Publication Society, 1918.
Is Your Neighbor a Kluxer? Chicago: Tolerance Publishing Company, 1924.
Joint Synod of Ohio and Other States. *Minutes of the Eastern District*. Colum-
   bus: Lutheran Book Concern, 1917–25.
Methodist Episcopal Church. *Minutes of the East Ohio Conference*. N.p.: West
   Methodist Book Concern, 1909–11.
———. *Minutes of the Northeast Ohio Conference*. Cleveland: Evangelical
   Press, 1919–23.
———. *Yearbook of the Ohio Annual Conference*. Cincinnati: Methodist Book
   Concern, 1918–27.
Niles Daily News. 1923.
Niles Daily Times. 1924–25.
Niles Evening Register. 1923–24.

Northern Baptist Convention. *Annual of the Northern Baptist Convention.* N.p.: American Baptist Publication Society, 1918–25.

———— . *Minutes of the Akron Baptist Association.* N.p., 1920.

———— . *Minutes of the Ohio Baptist Association.* N.p., 1921.

———— . *Proceedings of the 96th Annual Meeting of the Ohio Baptist Convention.* N.p., 1921.

Ohio, Ku Klux Klan Records, Ohio Historical Society, Columbus, Ohio.

Ohio, *Transcript of Evidence Taken by Military Investigation Board Appointed by General Orders No. 7,* Ohio National Guard, 3 November 1924.

Personal interviews with Anthony Nigro, Jr., Martha Pallante, and twenty-nine former Klan members.

Presbyterian Church of the United States of America. *Minutes of the General Assembly.* Philadelphia: Office of the General Assembly, 1918–25.

———— . *Minutes of the Synod of Ohio.* Cincinnati: Herald and Presbyter, 1918–25.

Protestant Episcopal Church. *Annual Report of the Presiding Bishop and Council.* N.p.: Domestic and Foreign Missionary Society of the Protestant Episcopal Church in the USA, 1918–25.

———— . *Journal of the Annual Convention of the Protestant Episcopal Church in the Diocese of Ohio.* Cleveland: Doan Publishing Company, 1918–25.

Steubenville Herald Star, 1923.

The Fiery Cross, 1923–25.

The Kourier, 1924–25.

The Truth about the Niles Riot. Niles, 1924.

Trumbull County Courthouse, *Criminal Docket and Warrants,* 1921–27.

United Lutheran Church of America. *Minutes of the Synod of Ohio.* Columbus: F. J. Heer Publishing Company, 1918–25.

United Presbyterian Church of North America. *Minutes of the General Assembly.* Pittsburgh: United Presbyterian Board of Publication, 1918–25.

———— . *Minutes of the First Synod of the West.* N.p., 1918–25.

U.S. Bureau of the Census. *Fourteenth Census of the United States Taken in the Year 1920.* Washington, D.C.: Government Printing Office, 1921–23.

U.S. Bureau of the Census, *Fifteenth Census of the United States Taken in the Year 1930.* Washington, D.C.: Government Printing Office, 1932.

U.S. Bureau of the Census, *Religious Bodies: 1926.* Washington, D.C.: Government Printing Office, 1926.

Warren Tribune Chronicle, 1923–25.

Youngstown Board of Education, *Minutes,* 1922–26.

Youngstown *Citizen,* 1915–25.

Youngstown City Council, *Minutes,* 1922–31.

Youngstown City Directory. Akron: Burch Directory Company, 1922–27.

Youngstown Protestant Churches Membership Records.

Youngstown State University. *Joseph L. Heffernan Papers.*

Youngstown State University Oral History Department. Transcripts of interviews with Nicola Criscone, John C. Crow, Joseph Jennings, Jr., Rita Jen-

nings Gregory, Karl Kistler, Frank McDermott, Catherine Ritter, and Pasquale Ruberto.
Youngstown Telegram, 1921–31.
Youngstown Vindicator, 1921–31.

SECONDARY SOURCES

Books

Adorno, T. W., et al. *The Authoritarian Personality*. New York: Harper & Row, 1950.

Allbeck, Willard D. *A Century of Lutherans in Ohio*. Yellow Springs, Ohio: Antioch Press, 1966.

Alexander, Charles C. *Crusade for Conformity: The Ku Klux Klan in Texas, 1920–1930*. Houston: Texas Gulf Historical Association, 1962.

————. *The Ku Klux Klan in the Southwest*. Lexington: University of Kentucky Press, 1966.

Aley, Howard C. *A Heritage to Share: The Bicentennial History of Youngstown and Mahoning County, Ohio*. Youngstown: Bicentennial Commission of Youngstown & Mahoning County, Ohio, 1975.

Allen, Frederick L. *Only Yesterday: An Informal History of the Nineteen Twenties*. New York: Harper & Bros., 1931.

Allport, Gordon W. *The Nature of Prejudice*. Reading, Mass.: Addison-Wesley, 1954.

Anderson, C. Glen. *One Hundred Years of Church History: The Story of First Baptist Church*. Youngstown: First Baptist Church, n.d.

Angle, Paul M. *Bloody Williamson: A Chapter in American Lawlessness*. New York: Alfred A. Knopf, 1952.

Arkin, Herbert, and Raymond R. Colton, comps. *Tables for Statisticians*. New York: Barnes & Noble, 1963.

Asbury, Herbert. *The Great Illusion: An Informal History of Prohibition*. Garden City, N.Y.: Doubleday, 1950.

Bailey, Kenneth K. *Southern White Protestantism in the Twentieth Century*. New York: Harper & Row, 1964.

Banner, Lois W. *Women in Modern America: A Brief History*. 2d ed. New York: Harcourt Brace Jovanovich, 1984.

Banfield, Edward, and James Q. Wilson. *City Politics*. Cambridge: Harvard University Press, 1967.

Barzini, Luigi. *The Italians*. New York: Bantam Press, 1964.

Bell, Daniel, ed. *The Radical Right*. Garden City, N.Y.: Anchor Books, 1963.

Bell, Edward Price. *Creed of the Klansmen*. Chicago: Daily News, 1924.

Blake, Aldrich. *The Ku Klux Kraze*. Oklahoma City: n.p., 1924.

Blau, Peter, and Otis Dudley Duncan. *The American Occupational Structure*. New York: Wiley, 1967.

Blocker, Jack S., Jr. *Retreat from Reform: The Prohibition Movement in the United States, 1890–1913.* Westport, Conn.: Greenwood Press, 1976.

Booth, Edgar Allen. *The Mad Mullah of America.* Columbus, Ohio: Boyd Ellison, 1927.

Boyer, Paul. *Urban Masses and Moral Order, 1820–1920.* Cambridge: Harvard University Press, 1978.

Braeman, John, Robert H. Bremner, and David Brody, eds. *Change and Continuity in Twentieth Century America: The 1920s.* Columbus: Ohio State University Press, 1968.

Brody, David. *Labor in Crisis: The Steel Strike of 1919.* Philadelphia: Lippincott, 1965.

——— . *Steelworkers in America: The Nonunion Era.* Cambridge: Harvard University Press, 1960.

Brown, George Alfred. *Harold the Klansman.* Kansas City, Mo.: Western Baptist Publishing Co., 1923.

Buenker, John. *Urban Liberalism and Progressive Reform.* New York: Scribner's, 1973.

- Burner, David. *Politics of Provincialism: The Democratic Party in Transition, 1918–1932.* New York: Alfred A. Knopf, 1968.

Butler, Joseph G., Jr. *History of Youngstown and the Mahoning Valley, Ohio.* 3 vols. Chicago: American Historical Society, 1921.

Cameron, William Bruce. *Modern Social Movements: A Sociological Outline.* New York: Random House, 1966.

Campbell, Sam H. *The Jewish Problem in the United States.* Atlanta: Ku Klux Klan, 1923.

Cantril, Hadley. *The Psychology of Social Movements.* New York: J. Wiley & Sons, 1941.

Carter, Paul A. *The Decline and Revival of the Social Gospel: Social and Political Liberalism in American Protestant Churches, 1920–1940.* Ithaca, N.Y.: Cornell University Press, 1954.

Cash, William J. *The Mind of the South.* New York: Alfred A. Knopf, 1941.

Chafe, William H. *The American Woman: Her Changing Social, Economic, and Political Roles.* New York: Oxford University Press, 1972.

Chalmers, David M. *Hooded Americanism: The History of the Ku Klux Klan.* 2d ed. New York: F. Watts, 1981.

Chudacoff, Howard P. *Mobile Americans: Residential and Social Mobility in Omaha, 1880–1920.* New York: Oxford University Press, 1972.

Clarke, Norman H. *Deliver Us from Evil: An Interpretation of American Prohibition.* New York: Norton, 1976.

Clason, George. *Catholic, Jew, Ku Klux Klan: What They Believe—Where They Conflict.* Chicago: Nutshell Publishing Co., 1924.

Cole, Stewart G. *The History of Fundamentalism.* Westport, Conn.: Greenwood Press, 1971.

Cook, Ezra A. *Ku Klux Klan: Secrets Exposed.* Chicago: E. A. Cook, 1922.

Cook, Fred J. *The Ku Klux Klan: America's Recurring Nightmare.* New York: Julian Messner, 1980.

Coser, Lewis. *The Functions of Social Conflict.* New York: Free Press, 1958.

Curry, LeRoy A. *The Ku Klux Klan under the Searchlight.* Kansas City: Western Baptist Publishing Co., 1924.

Dau, W. H. T. *Weighted, and Found Wanting: An Inquiry into the Aims and Methods of the Ku Klux Klan.* Fort Wayne, Ind.: n.p., n.d.

Desmond, Humphrey J. *The A.P.A. Movement.* Washington, D.C.: New Century Press, 1912.

————. *Curious Chapters in American History.* St. Louis: B. Herder Book Co., 1924.

Edwards, Alba M. *A Social-Economic Grouping of the Gainful Workers of the United States: 1930.* Washington, D.C.: Government Printing Office, 1938.

Ferguson, Charles. *Fifty Million Brothers: A Panorama of American Lodges and Clubs.* New York: Farrar & Rinehart, 1937.

Ferguson, Charles W. *Organizing to Beat the Devil: Methodists and the Making of America.* Garden City, N.Y.: Doubleday, 1971.

Fleming, John Stephen. *What Is Ku Kluxism?* Birmingham, Ala.: Masonic Weekly Recorder, 1923.

Fogelson, Robert M. *Big City Police.* Cambridge: Harvard University Press, 1977.

Forster, Arnold, and Benjamin R. Epstein. *Report on the Ku Klux Klan.* New York: Anti-Defamation League of B'nai B'rith, 1965.

Foster, William Z. *The Great Steel Strike.* New York: B. W. Huebsch, 1920.

Frost, Stanley. *The Challenge of the Klan.* Indianapolis: Bobbs-Merrill, 1924.

Fuller, Edgar I. *The Maelstrom: The Visible of the Invisible Empire.* Denver: Maelstrom Publishing Co., 1925.

————. *The Nigger in the Woodpile.* Washington: Lacey, 1967.

Furniss, Norman F. *The Fundamentalist Controversy, 1918–1931.* New Haven, Conn.: Yale University Press, 1954.

Gamson, William A. *Power and Discontent.* Homewood, Ill.: Dorsey Press, 1968.

————. *The Strategy of Social Protest.* Homewood, Ill.: Dorsey Press, 1975.

Garrison, Winfred E., and Alfred T. DeGroot. *The Disciples of Christ: A History.* St. Louis: Bethany Press, 1948.

Gatewood, Willard B., Jr., ed. *Controversy in the Twenties: Fundamentalism, Modernism, Evolution.* Nashville, Tenn.: Vanderbilt University Press, 1969.

Gerlach, Larry R. *Blazing Crosses in Zion: The Ku Klux Klan in Utah.* Logan, Utah: Utah State University Press, 1982.

Gillette, Paul J., and Eugene Tillinger. *Inside the Ku Klux Klan.* New York: Pyramid Books, 1965.

Gist, Noel P. *Secret Societies: A Cultural Study of Fraternalism in the United States.* Columbia, Mo.: University of Missouri, 1940.

Glaab, Charles N., and Theodore Brown. *A History of Urban America.* New York: MacMillan, 1967.

Glock, Charles Y., and Rodney Stark. *Christian Beliefs and Anti-Semitism.* New York: Harper & Row, 1966.

Goldberg, Robert Alan. *Hooded Empire: The Ku Klux Klan in Colorado.* Urbana, Ill.: University of Illinois Press, 1981.

Gordon, John J. *Unmasked.* New York: J. J. Gordon, 1924.

Graham, Hugh Davis, and Ted Robert Gurr, eds. *The History of Violence in America: Historical and Comparative Perspectives.* New York: F. A. Praeger, 1969.

Grant, Madison. *The Passing of the Great Race, or, the Racial Bias of European History.* New York: Scribner's, 1916.

Greer, Thomas H. *American Social Reform Movements: Their Pattern since 1865.* Port Washington, N.Y.: Prentice-Hall, 1949.

Griffin, Clifford S. *Their Brothers' Keepers: Moral Stewardship in the United States, 1800–1865.* New Brunswick, N.J.: Rutgers University Press, 1960.

Gurr, Ted Robert. *Why Men Rebel.* Princeton, N.J.: Princeton University Press, 1970.

Gusfield, Joseph R. *Protest, Reform and Revolt: A Reader in Social Movements.* New York: Wiley, 1970.

——— . *Symbolic Crusade: Status Politics and the American Temperance Movement.* Urbana: University of Illinois Press, 1966.

Haas, Ben. *K.K.K.* San Diego, Calif.: Regency Books, 1963.

Hamilton, Richard F. *Class and Politics in the United States.* New York: Wiley, 1972.

Hausknecht, Murray. *The Joiners: A Sociological Description of Voluntary Association Membership in the United States.* New York: Bedminster Press, 1962.

Heberle, Rudolf. *Social Movements: An Introduction to Political Sociology.* New York: Appleton, Century, Crofts, 1951.

Hicks, John D. *Republican Ascendancy, 1921–1933.* New York: Harper & Row, 1960.

Higham, John. *Strangers in the Land: Patterns of American Nativism, 1860–1925.* New York: Atheneum, 1970.

Hofstadter, Richard. *The Age of Reform.* New York: Alfred A. Knopf, 1955.

Horn, Stanley F. *Invisible Empire: The Story of the Ku Klux Klan, 1866–1871.* Boston: Houghton-Mifflin, 1939.

Hughes, Llewellyn. *In Defense of the Klan.* New York: n.p., 1924.

Interchurch World Movement. *Public Opinion and the Steel Strike.* New York: DaCapo Press, 1921.

Iorizzo, Lucianno J., and Salvatore Mondello. *The Italian Americans.* New York: Twayne Publishers, 1971.

Jackson, Kenneth T. *The Ku Klux Klan in the City, 1915–1930.* New York: Oxford University Press, 1967.

Jefferson, Charles Edward. *Roman Catholicism and the Ku Klux Klan.* New York: Fleming H. Revell, 1924.

Jensen, Richard. *The Winning of the Midwest: Social and Political Conflict, 1888–1896.* Chicago: University of Chicago Press, 1971.

Jones, Maldwyn Allen. *American Immigration*. Chicago: University of Chicago Press, 1960.

Jones, Winfield. *Story of the Ku Klux Klan*. Washington, D.C.: American Newspaper Syndicate, 1921.

———. *Knights of the Ku Klux Klan*. New York: Tocsin Press, 1941.

Kerr, K. Austin. *Organized for Prohibition: A New History of the Anti-Saloon League*. New Haven, Conn.: Yale University Press, 1985.

King, C. Wendell. *Social Movements in the United States*. New York: Random House, 1956.

Kinzer, Donald L. *An Episode in Anti-Catholicism: The American Protective Association*. Seattle: University of Washington Press, 1964.

Kirschner, Don S. *City and Country: Rural Responses to Urbanization in the 1920s*. Westport, Conn.: Greenwood Press, 1970.

Kleppner, Paul. *The Cross of Culture: A Social Analysis of Midwestern Politics, 1850–1900*. New York: Free Press, 1970.

———. *The Third Electoral System, 1853–1892: Parties, Voters, and Political Cultures*. Chapel Hill: University of North Carolina Press, 1979.

Kornhauser, William. *The Politics of Mass Society*. Glencoe, Ill.: Free Press, 1959.

Kraditor, Aileen. *The Ideas of the Woman Suffrage Movement, 1890–1920*. New York: Columbia University Press, 1965.

Lang, Kurt, and Gladys Engel. *Collective Dynamics*. New York: T. Y. Crowell, 1961.

Lay, Shawn. *War, Revolution, and the Ku Klux Klan: A Study of Intolerance in a Border City*. El Paso: Texas Western Press, 1985.

Lemons, J. Stanley. *The Woman Citizen: Social Feminism in the 1920s*. Urbana: University of Illinois Press, 1975.

Leighton, Isabel, ed. *The Aspirin Age, 1919–1941*. New York: Simon & Schuster, 1949.

Leuchtenburg, William. *The Perils of Prosperity, 1914–1932*. Chicago: University of Chicago Press, 1958.

Likins, William M. *The Trail of the Serpent*. Uniontown, Pa.: Watchman Publishing Co., 1928.

Lipset, Seymour Martin. *Political Man: The Social Bases of Politics*. New York: Doubleday, 1959.

Lipset, Seymour Martin, and Earl Raab. *The Politics of Unreason: Right-Wing Extremism in America, 1790–1970*. New York: Harper & Row, 1970.

Loucks, Emerson H. *The Ku Klux Klan in Pennsylvania: A Study in Nativism*. Harrisburg, Pa.: Telegraph Press, 1936.

Lowe, David. *Ku Klux Klan: the Invisible Empire*. New York: Norton, 1967.

Lynd, Robert S. and Helen M. *Middletown: A Study in American Culture*. New York: Harcourt, Brace, 1929.

McAllister, Lester G., and William E. Tucker. *Journey in Faith: A History of the Christian Church (Disciples of Christ)*. St. Louis: Bethany Press, 1975.

McBee, William D. *The Oklahoma Revolution.* Oklahoma City: Modern Publishers, 1956.

McCaffrey, Lawrence J. *The Irish Diaspora in America.* Bloomington: Indiana University Press, 1976.

McCarthy, John, and Mayer Zald. *The Trend of Social Movements in America: Professionalization and Resource Mobilization.* Morristown, N.J.: General Learning, 1973.

McWilliams, Carey. *A Mask for Privilege: Anti-Semitism in America.* Boston: Little, Brown, 1948.

Marsden, George M. *Fundamentalism and American Culture: The Shaping of Twentieth Century Evangelism, 1870–1925.* New York: Oxford University Press, 1980.

Marty, Martin. *Pilgrims in Their Own Land: 500 Years of Religion in America.* New York: Penguin Books, 1984.

———. *Righteous Empire: The Protestant Experience in America.* New York: Dial Press, 1970.

Marx, Gary T., ed. *Racial Conflict: Tension and Change in American Society.* Boston: Little, Brown, 1971.

Mast, Blaine. *K.K.K. Friend or Foe: Which?* Kittanning, Pa.: Herbick & Held Printing Co., 1924.

Mecklin, John Moffatt. *The Ku Klux Klan: A Study of the American Mind.* New York: Harcourt, Brace, 1924.

Merz, Charles. *The Dry Decade.* Garden City, N.Y.: Doubleday, Doran, 1931.

Miller, Robert Moats. *American Protestantism and Social Issues, 1919–1939.* Chapel Hill: University of North Carolina Press, 1958.

Monteval, Marion [Edgar Fuller]. *The Klan Inside Out.* Claremont, Okla.: n.p., 1924.

Murray, Robert K. *Red Scare: A Study of National Hysteria, 1919–1920.* Minneapolis: University of Minnesota Press, 1955.

Myers, Gustavus. *History of Bigotry in the United States.* New York: Random House, 1943.

Nash, Gary B., and Richard Weiss, eds. *The Great Fear: Race in the Minds of America.* New York: Holt, Rinehart & Winston, 1970.

Nelli, Humbert S. *From Immigrants to Ethnics: The Italian Americans.* New York: Oxford University Press, 1983.

Nelson, E. Clifford, ed. *The Lutherans in North America.* Philadelphia: Fortress Press, 1975.

Noggle, Burl. *Into the Twenties: The United States from Armistice to Normalcy.* Urbana: University of Illinois Press, 1974.

Norwood, Frederick A. *The Story of American Methodism.* Nashville, Tenn.: Abingdon Press, 1974.

Oberschall, Anthony. *Social Conflict and Social Movements.* Englewood Cliffs, N.J.: Prentice-Hall, 1973.

Odegaard, Peter H. *Pressure Politics: The Story of the Anti-Saloon League.* New York: Octagon Books, 1928.

Pavalko, Ronald M. *Sociology of Occupations and Professions.* Itasca, Ill.: F. E. Peacock, 1971.

Pessen, Edward, ed. *Three Centuries of Social Mobility in America.* Lexington, Mass.: Heath, 1974.

Preston, William, Jr. *Aliens and Dissenters: Federal Suppression of Radicals, 1903–1933.* Cambridge: Harvard University Press, 1963.

Randel, William Pierce. *The Ku Klux Klan: A Century of Infamy.* Philadelphia: Chilton Books, 1965.

Reimers, David M. *White Protestantism and the Negro.* New York: Oxford University Press, 1965.

Reiss, Albert J., Jr. *Occupations and Social Status.* New York: Free Press, 1961.

Rice, Arnold S. *The Ku Klux Klan in American Politics.* Washington, D.C.: Public Affairs Press, 1962.

Roy, Ralph L. *Apostles of Discord: A Study of Organized Bigotry and Disruption on the Fringes of Protestantism.* Boston: Beacon Press, 1953.

Rogoff, Natalie. *Recent Trends in Occupational Mobility.* Glencoe, Ill.: Free Press, 1953.

Ryan, Mary P. *Womanhood in America: From Colonial Times to the Present.* New York: New Viewpoints, 1975.

Rubin, Jay. *The Ku Klux Klan in Binghamton, New York, 1923–1928.* Binghamton, N.Y.: Broome County Historical Society, 1973.

Saenger, Gerhart. *The Social Psychology of Prejudice.* New York: Harper & Row, 1953.

Sandeen, Ernest R. *The Roots of Fundamentalism: British and American Millenarianism, 1800–1930.* Chicago: University of Chicago Press, 1970.

Sawyer, Reuben H. *The Truth about the Invisible Empire, Knights of the Ku Klux Klan.* Portland, Ore.: Northwest Domain, 1922.

Schlesinger, Arthur. *The Crisis of the Old Order, 1919–1933.* Boston: Houghton Mifflin, 1957.

Schneider, Herbert W. *Religion in Twentieth Century America.* Cambridge: Harvard University Press, 1952.

Schriftgiesser, Karl. *This Was Normalcy: An Account of Party Politics during Twelve Republican Years, 1920–1932.* Boston: Little, Brown, 1948.

Selznick, Gertrude J., and Stephen Steinberg. *The Tenacity of Prejudice: Anti-Semitism in Contemporary America.* New York: Harper & Row, 1969.

Shaw, Henry K. *Buckeye Disciples: A History of the Disciples of Christ in Ohio.* St. Louis: Christian Board of Publication, 1957.

Simpson, George Eaton, and J. Milton Yinger. *Racial and Cultural Minorities: An Analysis of Prejudice and Discrimination.* New York: Harper & Row, 1972.

Sinclair, Andrew. *Prohibition: The Era of Excess.* Boston: Little, Brown, 1962.

Sletterdahl, Peter J. *The Nightshirt in Politics.* Minneapolis: Ajax Publishing Co., 1926.

Slosson, Preston W. *The Great Crusade and After, 1914–1928.* New York: MacMillan, 1930.

Smelser, Neil J. *Theory of Collective Behavior.* New York: Free Press, 1963.

Smelser, Neil J., and Seymour Martin Lipset, eds. *Social Structure and Economic Development.* Chicago: Aldine Publishing Co., 1966.

Smith, The Rev. Arthur H., ed. *A History of the East Ohio Synod of the General Synod of the Evangelical Lutheran Church: 1836–1920.* Columbus, Ohio: Lutheran Book Concern, 1924.

Sochen, June. *Herstory: A Record of the American Woman's Past.* 2d ed. Sherman Oaks, Calif.: Alfred Publishing Co., 1981.

Solomon, Barbara Miller. *Ancestors and Immigrants: A Changing New England Tradition.* Cambridge: Harvard University Press, 1965.

Soule, George. *Prosperity Decade: A Chapter from American Economic History, 1917–1929.* New York: Rinehart, 1947.

Stevenson, Elizabeth. *Babbitts and Bohemians.* New York: MacMillan, 1967.

Stewart, John Struthers. *A History of Northeast Ohio.* Indianapolis: Indiana Historical Publishing Co., 1935.

Stoddard, Lothrop. *The Rising Tide of Color against White World Supremacy.* New York: Scribner's, 1920.

Sullivan, Mark. *Our Times: The United States, 1900–1925.* New York: Scribner's, 1935.

Tenenbaum, Samuel. *Why Men Hate.* New York: Beechhurst Press, 1947.

Timberlake, James H. *Prohibition and the Progressive Movement, 1900–1920.* Cambridge: Harvard University Press, 1963.

Tucker, Howard A. *History of Governor Walton's War on the Ku Klux Klan.* Oklahoma City: Southwest Publishing Co., 1923.

Turner, Ralph H., and Lewis M. Killian, eds. *Collective Behavior.* Englewood Cliffs, N.J.: Prentice-Hall, 1957.

Warner, Hoyt L. *Progressivism in Ohio, 1890–1917.* Columbus: Ohio State University Press, 1964.

Welsh, E. B. *Buckeye Presbyterian.* N.p.: Committee of the United Presbyterian Synod of Ohio, 1968.

Wentz, Abdel R. *A Basic History of Lutheranism in America.* Philadelphia: Muhlenberg Press, 1955.

Wiebe, Robert H. *Search for Order, 1877–1920.* New York: Hill and Wang, 1967.

White, Bishop Alma. *The Ku Klux Klan in Prophecy.* Zarephath, N.J.: Good Citizen, 1925.

——— . *Klansmen: Guardians of Liberty.* Zarephath, N.J.: Good Citizen, 1926.

——— . *Heroes of the Fiery Cross.* Zarephath, N.J.: Good Citizen, 1928.

Wilson, James Q. *Political Organizations.* New York: Basic Books, 1973.

Woofter, Thomas Jackson, Jr. *Negro Problems in Cities.* Garden City, N.Y.: Negro Universities Press, 1928.

Articles

Abbey, Sue Wilson. "The Ku Klux Klan in Arizona, 1921–1925." *Journal of Arizona History* 14 (Spring 1973): 10–30.
Alexander, Charles C. "Kleagles and Cash: The Ku Klux Klan as a Business Organization, 1915–1930." *Business History Review* 34 (Autumn 1965): 348–67.
Bettin, Neil. "Nativism and the Klan in Town and City: Valparaiso and Gary, Indiana." *Studies in History and Society* 4 (1973): 3–16.
Bohn, Frank. "The Ku Klux Klan Interpreted." *American Journal of Sociology* 30 (January 1925): 385–407.
Brownell, Blaine A. "Birmingham, Alabama: New South City in the 1920s." *Journal of Southern History* 38 (February 1972): 20–48.
Buccino, Gina. "Niles Remembers Bagnoli." *Warren Sunday Tribune Magazine*, 14 December 1980, pp. 12–16.
Carter, Everett. "Cultural History Written with Lightning: The Significance of the Birth of a Nation." *American Quarterly* 12 (Fall 1960): 347–57.
Chalmers, David. "The Ku Klux Klan in the Sunshine State: The 1920's." *Florida Historical Quarterly* 42 (January 1964): 209–15.
Clark, Malcolm, Jr. "The Bigot Disclosed: 90 Years of Nativism," *Oregon Historical Quarterly* 75 (June 1974): 109–90.
Cook, Philip L. "Red Scare in Denver." *Colorado Magazine* 43 (Fall 1966): 309–26.
Cook, Raymond A. "The Man behind the Birth of a Nation." *North Carolina Historical Review* 34 (Autumn 1962): 519–40.
Coughlan, Robert. "Konklave in Kokomo." In *The Aspirin Age 1919–1941*, pp. 105–29. Ed. Isabel Leighton. New York, 1949.
Cumberland, William H. "Wallace M. Short and the Sioux City Klan." *Midwest Review* 4 (Spring 1982): 27–34.
Daugherty, Robert L. "Problems in Peacekeeping: The 1924 Niles Riot." *Ohio History* 85 (Autumn 1976): 280–92.
Davis, James H. "Colorado under the Klan." *Colorado Magazine* 42 (Spring 1965): 93–108.
Degler, Carl N. "A Century of the Klans: A Review Article." *Journal of Southern History* 31 (November 1965): 435–43.
Duffus, Robert L. "Ancestry and End of the Ku Klux Klan." *World's Work* 46 (September 1923): 527–36.
———. "Counter-Mining the Ku Klux Klan." *World's Work* 46 (July 1923): 275–84.
———. "How the Ku Klux Klan Sells Hate." *World's Work* 46 (June 1923): 174–83.
———. "The Ku Klux Klan in the Middle West." *World's Work* 46 (August 1923): 363–73.
———. "Salesmen of Hate: The Ku Klux Klan." *World's Work* 46 (May 1923): 31–38.

Duncan, Otis Dudley. "Social Stratification and Mobility: Problems in the Measurement of Trend." In *Indicators of Social Change: Concepts and Measurements*, ed. Eleanor Bennett Sheldon and Wilbert E. Moore. New York: Russell Sage Foundation, 1968.

Filene, Peter. "An Obituary for the 'Progressive Movement.' " *American Quarterly* 22 (Spring 1970): 20–34.

Friedman, Norman L. "Nativism." *Phylon* 27 (Winter 1967): 408–15.

Frost, Stanley. "When the Klan Rules." *Outlook* 135–36 (December 1923-February 1924): 674–76, 716–18, 20–24, 64–66, 100–103, 144–47, 183–86, 217–19, 261–64, 308–11, 350–53.

Goldberg, Robert A. "Beneath the Hood and Robe: A Socioeconomic Analysis of Ku Klux Klan Membership in Denver, Colorado, 1921–1925." *Western Historical Quarterly* 11 (April 1980): 181–98.

———. "The Ku Klux Klan in Madison, 1922–27." *Wisconsin Magazine of History* 63 (Autumn 1974): 31–44.

Granger, Frank. "Reaction to Change: The Ku Klux Klan in Shreveport, 1920–1929." *North Louisiana Historical Association Journal* 9, 4 (1978): 219–27.

Greene, Ward. "Notes for a History of the Klan." *American Mercury* 5 (June 1925), 240–43.

Hallberg, Carl V. " 'For God and Home': The Ku Klux Klan in Pekin, 1923–1925." *Journal of the Illinois State Historical Society* 77 (Summer 1984): 82–93.

Handy, Robert T. "The American Religious Depression, 1925–1935." *Church History* 29 (March 1960): 3–16.

Hapgood, Norman. "The New Threat of the Ku Klux Klan." *Hearst's International* 43 (January, February 1923): 8–12; 58–61; 110.

Higham, John. "Another Look at Nativism." *Catholic Historical Review* 44 (July 1958): 147–58.

———. "Social Discrimination against Jews in America, 1830–1930." *American Jewish Historical Society Publications* 47 (September 1957): 1–33.

Hodge, Robert W., Paul M. Siegal, and Peter H. Rossi. "Occupational Prestige in the United States: 1925–1963." In *Class, Status, and Power: Social Stratification in Comparative Perspective*. Ed. Reinhard Bendix and Seymour Martin Lipset. New York: Free Press, 1966.

Holsinger, M. Paul. "The Oregon School Bill Controversy, 1922–1925." *Pacific Historical Review* 37 (August 1968): 327–41.

Hornbein, Marjorie. "The Story of Judge Ben Lindsey." *Southern California Quarterly* 55 (Winter 1973): 469–82.

Hux, Roger K. "The Ku Klux Klan in Macon, 1919–25." *Georgia Historical Quarterly* 62 (Summer 1978): 155–68.

Jackson, Charles O. "William J. Simmons: A Career in Ku Kluxism." *Georgia Historical Quarterly* 50 (December 1966): 351–65.

Jenkins, William D. "Moral Reform after the Klan: Joseph Heffernan as

Mayor of Youngstown, 1928–31." *Old Northwest: A Journal of Regional Life and Letters* 9 (Summer 1983): 143–56.

————. "The Ku Klux Klan in Youngstown, Ohio: Moral Reform in the Twenties." *Historian* 41 (November 1978): 76–93.

Johnson, Guy B. "A Sociological Interpretation of the New Ku Klux Klan Movement." *Journal of Social Forces* 1 (May 1923): 440–45.

Marriner, Gerald Lynn. "Klan Politics in Colorado." *Journal of the West* 15 (January 1976): 76–101.

May, Henry F. "Shifting Perspectives on the 1920s." *Mississippi Valley Historical Review* 43 (December 1956): 405–27.

Mead, Sidney E. "American Protestantism since the Civil War: From Denominationalism to Americanism." *Journal of Religion* 36 (January 1956): 1–16.

Melching, Richard. "The Activities of the Ku Klux Klan in Anaheim, California, 1923–1925." *Southern California Quarterly* 56 (Summer 1974): 175–96.

Merz, Charles. "Sweet Land of Secrecy: The Strange Spectacle of American Fraternalism." *Harper's Magazine* 154 (February 1927): 329–34.

Miller, Robert Moats. "The Ku Klux Klan." In *Change and Continuity in Twentieth Century America: The 1920s*, pp. 215–55. Ed. John Braeman, Robert H. Bremner, and David Brody. Columbus, Ohio, 1968.

————. "A Note on the Relationship between the Protestant Churches and the Revived Ku Klux Klan." *Journal of Southern History* 22 (August 1956): 355–68.

Moseley, Clement Charlton. "The Political Influence of the Ku Klux Klan in Georgia, 1915–1925." *Georgia Historical Quarterly* 57 (Summer 1973): 235–55.

Murphy, Paul L. "Sources and Nature of Intolerance in the 1920's." *Journal of American History* 51 (June 1964): 60–76.

Neuringer, Sheldon. "Governor Walton's War on the Ku Klux Klan: An Episode in Oklahoma History." *Chronicles of Oklahoma* 45 (Summer 1967): 153–79.

O'Brien, Kenneth B., Jr. "Education, Americanization, and the Supreme Court: The 1920's." *American Quarterly* 13 (Summer 1961), 161–71.

Racine, Philip M. "The Klux Klan, Anti-Catholicism, and Atlanta's Board of Education, 1916–29." *Georgia Historical Quarterly* 57 (Spring 1973): 63–75.

Rambow, Charles. "The Ku Klux Klan in the 1920's: A Concentration on the Black Hills." *South Dakota History* 4 (Winter 1973): 63–81.

"The Riot at Niles." *Outlook* 138 (12 November 1924): 396.

Schaefer, Richard T. "The Ku Klux Klan: Continuity and Change." *Phylon* 32 (Summer 1971): 143–57.

Schuyler, Michael W. "The Ku Klux Klan in Nebraska, 1920–1930." *Nebraska History* 66 (Fall 1985): 239–56.

Shepherd, William G. "How I Put Over the Klan." *Collier's* 82 (14 July 1928): 5–7, 32, 34–35.

————. "Ku Klux Klan." *Collier's* 82 (21 July 1928): 8–9, 38–39.
Simmel, George. "The Sociology of Secrecy and of Secret Societies." *American Journal of Sociology* 2 (January 1906): 441–98.
Skinner, R. Dana. "Is the Ku Klux Klan Katholik?" *Independent* 3 (24 November 1923): 242–43.
Sloan, Charles William, Jr. "Kansas Battles the Invisible Empire: The Legal Ouster of the KKK from Kansas, 1922–1927." *Kansas Historical Quarterly* 40 (Autumn 1974): 393–409.
Smith, Norman. "The Ku Klux Klan in Rhode Island." *Rhode Island History* 37 (May 1978): 35–45.
Snell, William R. "Fiery Crosses in the Roaring Twenties: Activities of the Revived Klan in Alabama, 1915–1930." *Alabama Review* 23 (October 1970): 256–76.
Swart, Stanley L. "A Memo on Cross Burning—and Its Implications." *Northwest Ohio Quarterly* 43 (Fall 1971): 70–74.
Swallow, Craig A. "The Ku Klux Klan in Nevada During the 1920s." *Nevada Historical Society Quarterly* 24, 3 (1981): 202–20.
Thornbrough, Emma Lou. "Segregation in Indiana during the Klan Era of the 1920's." *Mississippi Valley Historical Review* 47 (March 1961): 594–617.
Toll, William. "Progress and Piety: The Ku Klux Klan and Social Change in Tillamook, Oregon." *Pacific Northwest Quarterly* 69 (April 1978): 75–85.
Toy, Eckard V., Jr. "The Ku Klux Klan in Tillamook, Oregon." *Pacific Northwest Quarterly* 53 (April 1962): 60–64.
West, William Elliott. "Cleansing the Queen City: Prohibition and Urban Reform in Denver." *Arizona and the West* 14 (Winter 1972): 331–46.
White, Walter F. "Reviving the Ku Klux Klan." *Forum* 65 (April 1921): 426–34.

Unpublished

Atchison, Carla Joan. "Nativism in Colorado Politics: The American Protective Association and the Ku Klux Klan." Master's thesis, University of Colorado, 1972.
Avin, Benjamin Herzl. "The Ku Klux Klan, 1915–1925: A Study in Religious Intolerance," Ph.D. diss., Georgetown University, 1952.
Bradley, Laura Lipsey. "Protestant Churches and the Ku Klux Klan in Mississippi during the 1930s: Study of an Unsuccessful Courtship." Master's thesis, University of Mississippi, 1962.
Cates, F. Mark. "The Ku Klux Klan in Indiana Politics: 1920–1925." Ph.D. diss., Indiana University, 1970.
Cocoltchos, Christopher Nickolas. "The Invisible Empire and the Viable Community: The Ku Klux Klan in Orange County, California during the 1920s." Ph.D. diss., University of California, Los Angeles, 1979.
Davis, James H. "The Rise of the Ku Klux Klan in Colorado, 1921–1925." Master's thesis, University of Denver, 1963.

Davis, John Augustus. "The Ku Klux Klan in Indiana, 1920–1930: An Historical Study." Ph.D. diss., Northwestern University, 1966.

Dunwoody, Doris L. "Building a City." Master's thesis, Youngstown State University, 1971.

Harrell, Kenneth Earl. "The Ku Klux Klan in Louisiana, 1920–1930." Ph.D. diss., Louisiana State University, 1966.

Hart, Nelson Hodges. " 'The True and the False: The Worlds of an Emerging Evangelical Protestant Fundamentalism in America, 1890–1920." Ph.D. diss., Michigan State University, 1976.

Howson, Embrey Bernard. "The Ku Klux Klan in Ohio after World War I." Master's thesis, Ohio State University, 1951.

Jackson, Charles Oliver. "The Ku Klux Klan, 1915–1924: A Study in Leadership." Master's thesis, Emory University, 1962.

Marec, Ronald E. "The Fiery Cross: A History of the Ku Klux Klan in Ohio, 1920–30." Master's thesis, Kent State University, 1967.

Moore, Leonard Joseph. "White Protestant Nationalism in the 1920s: The Ku Klux Klan in Indiana." Ph.D. diss., University of California, Los Angeles, 1985.

Moseley, Clement Charlton. "Invisible Empire: A History of the Ku Klux Klan in Twentieth Century Georgia." Ph.D. diss., University of Georgia, 1968.

Steers, Nina A. "The Ku Klux Klan in Oklahoma in the 1920's." Master's thesis, Columbia University, 1965.

Torrence, Lois E. "The Ku Klux Klan in Dallas, 1915–1928: An American Paradox." Master's thesis, Southern Methodist University, 1948.

Toy, Eckard V., Jr. "The Ku Klux Klan in Oregon: Its Character and Program." Master's thesis, University of Oregon, 1959.

Walrod, Stephen T. "The Ku Klux Klan in Colorado, 1921–1926." B.A. thesis, Princeton University, 1970.

Weaver, Norman Frederic. "The Knights of the Ku Klux Klan in Wisconsin, Indiana, Ohio, and Michigan." Ph.D. diss., University of Wisconsin, 1954.

Zimmerman, Paul E. "The Ku Klux Klan in Trumbull County, Ohio, 1923–1925." Master's thesis, Youngstown State University, 1977.

Index

Elyria, Ohio, Klan in, 103
Episcopalians, ix, 13
Epworth Methodist Episcopal Church, 48
Evangelistic campaign, 29–30
Evans, Hiram Wesley, vii, 6–9, 10, 63,
    104, 107, 114, 115
Ewry, Ralph, 78

Farrell, John, 156–57
Farrell, Thomas, 156
Federated Council of Churches, 25, 29–30,
    34, 35, 36, 48, 111
Federation of Women's Clubs, 26, 28, 35,
    36, 101, 165
Filkins, Byron, 132
First Baptist Church (Girard), 39, 46–47, 73
First Baptist Church (Youngstown), 30–31,
    32, 54
Flask, Marty, 134, 149, 150
Ford, Rev. George, 34
Fordyce, George, 44
Foster, William Z., 21
Frost, Stanley, 78
Fry, Henry, 5, 78; quoted, 77
Fundamentalism, 90–92, 164
Fusco, Patrick, 121, 122, 124
Fye, John S., 106
Fye, Sam, 106

Games, Ralph, 134, 147–48
Garfield, James A., 57
Gary Plan, 110
Gas stations, Sunday closing and, 98–99
General Electric Glass Works. See Glass
    Works field
Gerlach, Larry, 161, 162
Germans: in Niles, 65; in Youngstown, 19–
    20, 89–90
Gessner, George, 98
Gibson, Rev. George, 34–35, 40, 49, 81,
    90, 104
Gilbert, Lt. Charles A., 122–23
Gillen, B. J., 58, 62
Girard, Ohio, 37, 72–73
Glass Works field, anti-Klan forces at, 130,
    132, 134, 135, 137; photo, 136
Gledhill, J. M., 69, 71

Glossner, Doyle, 33, 55, 59, 104
Goldberg, Robert A., vii, 9, 79–80, 162, 163
Gordon, T. Lee, 75
Greco, Peter, 130, 147
Greek American Club, 58
Griffith, Rev. A. E., 49
Grimmesey, O. R., 57
Gunder, Col. C. A., 44–45, 52, 80, 104,
    124, 125, 145

Hall, Tom, 71
Hamilton, David C., 35, 81
Hammaker, Rev. W. E., 98
Harmon, O. P., 160–61
Hare, Rev. C. M., 58
Harper, Rev. W. O., 42
Hart, Dr. B. A., 59, 121, 125, 137, 141, 152
Hartenstein, Fred, 19, 40
Harold, C. L., 10
Harwood, Brown, 115
Hawkins, Rev. W. O., 98
Hays, Will, 37
Heaton, James, 65
Heffernan, Joseph, 106–7, 127, 155–58;
    photo, 107
Henderson, Fred, 146
Heslip, Rev. John, 49–50, 97, 98
Hewitt, O. O., 71, 118
Hickory Club, 156
Hillman, W. E., 133
Hoffman, Mary, 134
Home ownership, Klan membership and, 83
Hosack, John, 127
Hough, Maj. Gen. Benson, 139, 141
Hudnut, Rev. William H., 50; quoted, 16
Huffman, Cal, 35

Immigrants: Archibald's view of, 31; But-
    ler's view of, 22; diversity of, in Youngs-
    town, 18–20; as mission field, 22–23;
    Morris's view of, 154; in Niles, 65–66;
    pietists question morality of, x; as un-
    skilled peasants, in Warren, 57
Indiana, Klan in, ix, 10, 153
Industrial Workers of the World (IWW),
    20–21
Interchurch World Movement, 92

Mahoning County Klan, 104–5; Idora Park
rally, 124; membership roster, xi, 80–81;
in parade, 55. See also Youngstown Klan
Mahoning Valley Klan, viii, 10, 90, 152–
53, 160–61, 165. See also Mahoning
County Klan; Trumbull County Klan
Mango, Sam, 149
Marion County, Ohio, 163
Marital status of Youngstown Klan mem-
bers, 81, 83 (Table 3)
Marshall, John H., 60–62, 64, 99, 103, 109
Martin, Steve, 123, 124
Martin Luther Church, 89
Massillon, Ohio, delegation from, 55
Mears, Father Edward, 48
Mears, Joseph, 119
Membership lists, Klan, xi, 77, 80–81, 114
Metcalfe, Wallace T., 78
Methodist Episcopal Church, 23, 92
Methodists, ix, 11, 15, 23, 88, 92, 93,
118, 162, 164
Miller, Robert Moats, 90
Mineral Ridge disturbance, 123
Ministerial Associations: Baptist, 95; Col-
ored, 42; Niles, 122; Youngstown, 99, 102
Ministers, Protestant: depicted as comic
figures, 32; as Klan supporters, 49, 90;
made honorary Klan members, 11
Mohan, Joseph, 133
Mohr, George, 74
Montague, Mr. (a.k.a. Col. Watkins), 144
Moore, Edmund H., 19, 26, 114–15, 156
Morris, Paul, 35–36, 88, 112–13, 153–55, 161
Morrison, Rev. Charles Clayton, 29–30
Motivation for Klan membership, 87–94
passim. See also Social class, Klan mem-
bership and
Mount Carmel Church, 66, 130, 151
Movies: moral concerns about, 11, 12, 23,
24, 37, 59; on Sunday, 58, 96, 99
Muldoon, Thomas, 40–45, 47, 50–53, 114
Mullen, William, 119, 148
Murphy, Dennis ("Dude"), 121, 129, 135,
146, 149, 150
Myers, Rev. Leroy, 74, 152

Naples, Michael ("Brea"), 119
Nativism, 2, 11, 154, 160, 163

New York World, 5, 6, 78
Nickols, Dorothy, 48
Nicolay, H. J., 62
Nigro, Tony, 119, 122, 124, 129, 149, 150
Niles, Ohio, 65–72, 99; Klan appears in,
71; rioting in, 117–39 passim; riot probe,
142–43; riot trials, 146–50; street
map, 131
Niles Daily News, 67–68
Niles Evening Register, 69, 70
Niles Firebrick Company, 65, 66
Niles Ministerial Association, 122
Nondiscrimination: promised by police
chief, 108–9; promised in Youngstown
mayoral campaign, 41, 47

Oaks, the, 27
Oberholtzer, Madge, 153
Oberlin, Ohio, 14
Occupations of Youngstown Klan members,
81–83, 84 (Table 4)
O'Donnell, Patrick H., 77
Ohio Anti-Saloon League. See Anti-Saloon
League
Ohio Citizen, 152. See also Citizen
Ohio Federation of Churches, Council of, 59
Ohio National Guard, 75, 134, 137, 139
Ohio State Police (OSP) (Klan police), 143–
44, 146; members sworn in by Kistler, in
riot, 117, 132–35 passim, 140, 141, 148;
members ruled illegal, 148, 150; some
arrested, 134; two attacked, 135
Oles, George, 26–28, 29, 37, 45
Osborne, Clyde: background, 97; Klan
roles, 81, 87–88, 102, 105–6, 114–16,
125–27, 132, 140, 142, 143–44, 149,
152, 153; as law director, 97, 100, 102,
109–10; speeches by, 46, 47, 112

Pallante, Joseph, 66, 127
Parker, Don V., 68, 69
Payne, Harry, 53, 109
Peebles, Edward, 42
Pennsylvania Klan, 161
Perone, Dominic, 133, 147
Philo, Dr. Isidor, 154
Pierson, Wick W., 142, 146, 148